President Gore …

… and other things that never happened

PRESIDENT GORE ...

... AND OTHER THINGS THAT NEVER HAPPENED

edited by

DUNCAN BRACK

POLITICO'S

First published in Great Britain in 2006 by
Politico's Publishing, an imprint of Methuen Publishing Limited
11–12 Buckingham Gate
London SW1E 6LB
www.methuen.co.uk/politicos

10 9 8 7 6 5 4 3 2 1

A CIP catalogue record for this book is available from the British
Library.

ISBN10:   1 84275 172 7
ISBN13:   978 1 84275 172 5

Printed and bound in Great Britain by Cromwell Press, Trowbridge,
Wiltshire.
Designed and typeset in Bembo by Duncan Brack.

Contents

Introduction

Duncan Brack

People make their own history but they do not make it just as they please; they do not make it under circumstances chosen by themselves, but under circumstances directly encountered, given, and transmitted from the past.

Karl Marx

Here in this book you will find nineteen examinations of things that never happened, from the Great Reform Bill being defeated in the Commons in 1831, to Gavrilo Princip failing to assassinate Franz Ferdinand in 1914, to Britain entering the Common Market in 1957, to Al Gore becoming President of the United States in 2000.

In 2003 Iain Dale and I co-edited this book's predecessor, *Prime Minister Portillo … and other things that never happened.* That volume contained a similar collection of political 'what ifs', or counterfactuals, including Michael Portillo becoming Prime Minister, J. F. Kennedy dodging the assassin's bullet, Margaret Thatcher being unceremoniously removed as Conservative leader after losing the 1978 election, and Lenin's sealed train never reaching Petrograd in 1917. The book proved popular, both with reviewers and the public. I am grateful to everyone who wrote in to suggest additional topics, some of which make their appearance in this book.

As Iain and I observed in *Prime Minister Portillo*, historians have tended to look down on the study of counterfactuals; E. H. Carr, for example, dismissed them as a 'parlour game', while Tristram Hunt, writing in *The Guardian* in 2004, claimed to detect in them a right-wing conspiracy, glorifying the role of individual choices at the expense of an understanding of social structures and economic conditions. Hunt rather undermined his own argument, however, by using the quote from Karl Marx at the head of this introduction to illustrate his contention that it is the interaction between individual choices and historical context which governs the events of the past.

I agree with that conclusion, and have used it to govern my choice of topics for inclusion in *President Gore*. For I believe that counterfactual history does have its uses. It can reinforce the analysis of what actually happened by identifying the points at which things could have happened differently, and the relevance at each of these key points both of individual choices and of broader socioeconomic forces. It can help in analysing the causes underlying particular events; arguably, as Robert Fogel pointed out, in making claims for causes of any kind, historians are always implicitly considering and discarding potential counterfactuals.

But to achieve in these aims, the counterfactuals must be plausible. Start to change one decision or happening or event in history, and it can be difficult to justify not changing others. There have to be boundaries, and the more rigorously these are policed the more convincing – and the more analytically useful – the results become. So the chapters in this book are limited to occasions where very little needed to have happened differently for the ultimate outcome to have been transformed – and, mostly, to changed individual choices or actions set against unchanged economic and social backgrounds.

Two of the chapters, for example, deal with assassinations: of Franz Ferdinand in 1914 and Yitkhak Rabin in 1995. Assassinations are always a chancy business, and there are plenty of failed attempts in history; there is no guarantee that weapons will fire or assassins will hit their mark. However – and again demonstrating a value of counterfactuals – the Rabin chapter shows how quite probably the ultimate outcome might not have been very different. The Franz Ferdinand chapter does not assume that the Great War did not break out, just that it might not have broken out in 1914. Two other chapters also deal with the – possibly highly significant – consequences of deaths avoided: of Sir Robert Peel in 1850 and Gustav Stresemann in 1929.

Other chapters maintain the focus on individual choices by considering the consequences of decisions taken differently by key personalities: of a failure to negotiate the Gladstone–MacDonald Pact in 1903 (the absence of which would have made the rise of the Labour Party more difficult), of a decision by the Liberal leader Asquith not to support a minority Labour government in 1924 (he almost didn't), of a meeting between Mao and Roosevelt in the 1940s (Mao made the request, in 1945), and of a decision by President Mitterrand in 1986 not to introduce proportional representation for parliamentary elections. Perhaps most intriguingly, the consequences of a wedding that never happened, but could have – between Joseph Chamberlain and Beatrice Webb – are followed through, with significant consequences for twentieth-century British politics and society.

My own chapter, on the disastrous row between the Liberal Party and the SDP over nuclear weapons policy in 1986, considers not so much *what* might have happened differently, but why it *should* have done, charting the calamitous series of mistakes and misjudgements made by almost everyone involved in the episode. And two further chapters look at the outcomes of different decisions made by governments: by the Czechoslovaks, to fight to defend their country in 1938, and by the British, to enter the Common Market in 1957.

Since this is a book of *political* counterfactuals, several chapters consider different possible outcomes of parliamentary or public votes: of the debates on the Great Reform Bill in 1831 (where, in reality, one division was won by just one vote), the Irish Home Rule Bill of 1886, the Labour leadership election of 1922 (where Ramsay MacDonald's winning margin was lower than the number of Labour MPs absent from the meeting), the Scottish devolution referendum of 1979, the general election of 1992 (as a consequence, in the chapter, of John Major being appointed Chief Whip rather than Chief Secretary to the Treasury in 1987 and Margaret Thatcher then surviving the leadership election in 1990), the Conservative leadership election of 1997 and the US Presidential election of 2000 (where, as everyone knows, Al Gore won half a million votes more than George W. Bush).

As in *Prime Minister Portillo*, the authors have adopted a variety of approaches, including scholarly analyses of the possibilities and causalities of different outcomes and fictional accounts of alternate political histories – and sometimes both. Many of them are written with wit and humour: you will read, for example, of Asquith and Lloyd George striking a deal over the Prime Ministership in an obscure restaurant in Islington, of former European Commissioner Margaret Thatcher publishing her memoirs, *A Housewife in Brussels*, of an insular and cash-strapped Scottish Assembly abolishing the Edinburgh Festival, of Ann Widdecombe's memorable reference to 'something of the knight', and of Politico's Publishing bringing out an audacious book of political counterfactuals entitled *Prime Minister Blair ... and other things that never happened.*

If any reader has ideas for topics, or authors, for a potential third volume, I would be very pleased to hear them; send me an email at duncan@dbrack.org.uk. In the meantime, I hope you are stimulated and entertained by *President Gore ... and other things that never happened* ... but could have.

Acknowledgements

My warmest thanks go to Jonathan Wadman, of Politico's, for his constant encouragement and support; to Siobhan Vitelli, for painstaking proofreading; to Richard Briand, Matt Cole, Richard Grayson, Tony Little, Mark Pack, Jaime Reynolds, Ben Rich and Helen Szamuely for helping me review draft chapters; and, above all, to all the chapter authors, for producing high-quality work to a demanding timetable.

Chapter 1

What if the Great Reform Bill had been defeated on its second reading in 1831?

Mark Pack

The general election of July and August 1830 took place in an atmosphere of intense political crisis. The 1829 harvest had been very poor and food prices rose sharply. Widespread agricultural riots and organised protests spread, triggered not only by the state of the economy but also by the make-up of the political system. Demands for electoral reform – in particular an extension of the franchise to give more people the vote, and the granting of seats to the new industrial towns – were common. Revolutions overseas, notably in France, added to the sense that the political system was flirting with collapse.

The election itself saw clear gains for those campaigning for reform, but failed to remove immediately the Conservative government led by the Duke of Wellington, victor of Waterloo. Its demise was only postponed until November, however, when Wellington's misjudged – and unpopular – comment that the British constitution was perfect and needed no change was swiftly followed by defeat in a key vote in the House of Commons.

A largely Whig government took its place, under the leadership of probably the country's most reluctant Prime Minister, Lord Grey. He had no great appetite for holding office – he called being Prime Minister 'a damn inconvenience' – but in the midst of economic and political crises he formed a Cabinet which believed it essential to introduce radical constitutional reform to save the country from revolution.

The electoral system of the House of Commons had come under increasing criticism because of its limited electorate and an allocation of seats that had not been updated despite the Industrial Revolution bringing dramatic population changes across the country. As a result, many MPs sat for constituencies with tiny electorates, whilst large new areas of population, such as the new and growing industrial towns, had no MPs directly representing them.

Plans for reforming the electoral system were hatched in secret by a small government committee over the winter. When unveiled in the spring they caused astonishment, including as they did the abolition of 168 Commons seats, 106 of which were to be reallocated primarily to those growing urban areas lacking their own parliamentary representation.

There had already been seven long, intense days of debate on the first reading of the Reform Bill a fortnight before the second reading debate in the Commons. As the vote on the second reading approached, its outcome was widely believed to rest on a knife-edge. The government's earlier defeat on timber duties – by a majority of forty-six, no less – strained nerves. Heavy betting took place on the vote, with the odds suggesting a very close result.

The dramatic vote, on a Tory proposal to defer further consideration of the bill for six months (in effect, its rejection), came in the early hours of 23 March 1831. Debate continued until just before 3 A.M. While the Tory Chief Whip (Holmes) and the unofficial counter-in for the reformers (Hume) exchanged pleasantries and predictions, they both foresaw a very close result. As was then traditional, one side (in this case the Tories and those supporting them) filed out into the lobbies to vote in favour of the motion, whilst those against stayed in the Commons chamber itself to be counted. As MP after MP trooped out to vote against reform, the hopes of those left in the chamber sank. Members anxiously looked around – were there more MPs still sitting than had walked out?

The tellers in the chamber got to work; as the numbers mounted towards 300, victory seemed more likely. Given how common it was for MPs to be absent from parliamentary votes in those days (and today's pairing system did not exist), surely 300 would be enough to win? It would have to be the largest turnout in the Commons' history for 300 votes *not* to bring victory.

But as the Tories flooded back into the chamber, all sorts of rumours circulated as to their numbers – 303, 307, 309 or even 310. The tellers for both sides pushed through the crowd to stand before the Speaker. As they made their way through the melee the result became clear: it was the government tellers who lined up on the right, the position taken by the tellers of the winning side. By a margin of just one vote – 302 to 301 – the bill made it through.

~

It took another fifteen months, including a general election and the resignation of the government, before the final legislation was passed, but what if the bill had instead been defeated at this early stage? Amongst the many last-minute shifts that determined the result were those of John Calcraft and Charles Wynn. Calcraft had supported Wellington's government and spoken against the bill whilst Wynn had resigned from the Whig government and also opposed the bill – yet both voted in favour of it. Sir Andrew Agnew also switched at the last moment. Had just one of them not changed their minds the bill would have been defeated. And then what ...?

~

As the Tories flooded back into the chamber, all sorts of rumours circulated as to their numbers – 303, 307, 309 or even 310. The tellers for both sides pushed through the crowd to stand before the Speaker. As they made their way through the melee the result became clear: it was the Tory tellers who lined up on the right, the position taken by the tellers of the winning side. By a margin of just one vote – 302 to 301 – the bill had been defeated.

The Whig historian Macaulay, who was present himself, described what happened next:

> Shouts broke out and many of us shed tears. We went out cursing, cry-ing and shouting anguish into the lobby. And no sooner were the outer doors opened then another shout answered that within the House. All the passages, and the stairs into the waiting rooms, were thronged with people who had waited until four in the morning to know the issue. We passed through a narrow lane between two thick masses of them; all the way down they were cursing and talking – what is to be done? what will happen? is reform dead? I called a cabriolet, and the first thing the driver asked was, 'Is the Bill defeated?' 'Yes, by one.' 'D—n. May God forgive us, Sir.'

In the early hours of the morning, riots started in London. As news spread around the country, so did the disturbances. When Grey and his Cabinet met later that day it was in a gloomy mood of gathering crisis. As one Cabinet member, Graham, put it to another, Stanley (later to become the Earl of Derby), it had been 'a dreadful race, lost by an accident at the last'.

Grey showed little enthusiasm for remaining in office. Not only had the Reform Bill been rejected at the earliest stage possible – for even if it had scraped through, how could it possibly have survived the committee stage and the inevitable plethora of amendments? – but the earlier defeat over timber duties had revealed how pre-carious general support was for his ministry in the Commons. With the defeat of the bill the central purpose of his ministry was gone and it was only a matter of when, not whether, it would fall. With little dissent, the Cabinet agreed to tender their resignations to the King forthwith, hoping at least that prompt action would minimise the rioting and unrest.

The King was faced with a difficult choice as to who to ask to be Prime Minister in succession to Grey. Turning back to the Tories, for example by asking Peel, would put in place a weak and minority government at a time of great public unrest. Moreover, many Tories still viewed Peel with suspicion after his volte-face over Catholic emancipation only a few years previously. Could he really lead a united government? A heavy exertion of royal influence might swing many MPs behind supporting a Peel administration, but only at the risk of inflaming popular passions even further and possibly triggering violent opposition to the monarchy itself.

The most senior members of Grey's Cabinet were also ruled out as possible Prime Ministers: they had all backed widespread parliamentary reform, which the Commons had just rejected. Nor was the King willing to break with tradition and call a general election, given the risk of inflaming unrest around the country. 'I consider dissolution tantamount to revolution', he commented.

Amidst the wreckage of the Whig government, therefore, the King turned to the group of conservative Whigs led by Stanley, a member of Grey's Cabinet but as Chief Secretary for Ireland and thereby removed, to a degree, from complicity in the defeated Reform Bill. From his Irish standpoint, Stanley readily accepted the King's desire to restore stability as his first priority. He also, wisely, let it be known that he was willing to be generous in the financial settlements voted for the King's sons – winning favour with the monarch and ensuring that at least discreet support would come his way from the King.

Stanley's Cabinet was shorn of the most eager proponents of the Reform Bill, excluding not just Grey but Russell, Althorp, Melbourne and Palmerston too. It was not a strong Cabinet, but it only needed to manage one issue in the short term – deciding what to do over parliamentary reform. Stanley's answer was a watered-down measure of the initial bill, designed this time to appeal especially to Tories. Gone was the proposal to cut the number of English MPs, a particular anathema to the Tories. Radically cut back were the proposals to axe MPs from certain seats. But in a move designed to ensure popular support, the proposals to establish MPs for the big towns were retained.

The boldest move was a return to an original pair of proposals put forward by the committee that had drawn up Grey's Reform Bill — a careful compromise which had been rejected by Grey's Cabinet. The electorate was still to be increased, but only to a more limited extent. The qualification for the franchise for those living in boroughs was to be set at ownership of property with a rental value of at least £20 a year, rather than the £10 proposed in Grey's bill. This higher level was balanced by the introduction of the secret ballot, replacing the then-current practice of voting in public.

This mix of proposals left critics on both sides divided and unsure, allowing Stanley to make progress with getting the legislation through. For many Tories the proposals were still too much — but on the other hand the franchise extension had been restricted, England was to keep its MPs and even the secret ballot — a standard demand of radicals — had its attractions in protecting voters from mob rule and public pressure. For radicals the loss of many of the measures in the Reform Bill was deprecated, but at least they could welcome the secret ballot, ensuring that radical votes could be cast free of interference and pressure from the aristocratic orders.

In both camps, views were split on whether the new plans were better or worse than the original ones. This was exactly as Stanley wanted it. As *The Times* commented, when a vessel comes to rescue you from a desert island, you are not overly concerned with its design being perfect. With all sides split, and the debate frequently descending into arcane detail over the franchise rights in county boroughs and the like, radical protestors outside Parliament found little on which to focus their anger. They called for 'nothing but the Great Reform Bill', but without its revival ever being a serious proposition in Parliament, their impact was muted. Even the fiercest riots, in Bristol and Nottingham, eventually came to an end, and with no clear focus for the protestors' claims the political establishment was unmoved.

The more moderate Tories, led by Peel, recognised that they had been backed into a corner. Faced with a Whig administration, the weakness of their own numbers in the Commons and the King's refusal to agree to an early general election, there was clearly no alternative but to let Stanley govern. Whilst many moderate Tories spoke fiercely against the reform proposals as they made their way through Parliament in April and May 1831, they knew better than to force any of the key measures to a vote, either in the Commons or the Lords. Serious defeat would just bring deadlock and further unrest, together with the risk that it might trigger the return of the more drastic reform proposals which had, after all, only be seen off by one slender vote.

By June Stanley's 'Lesser Reform Bill', as radical critics mocked it, was law. It was a blessed relief for the Prime Minister, as on nearly all other measures his government was regularly defeated. Missing Grey, Althorp, Russell, Palmerston, Melbourne and others, Stanley's government was never a strong one and there was little enthusiasm for supporting it beyond the minimal necessity of letting it limp on until the Lesser Reform Bill was passed.

Once it was, the King was willing to call an election. Now it was no longer a matter of an early contest bringing the risk of unrest, or of being seen as an attempt to abuse his powers to force through particular legislation; rather, the introduction of a new electoral system provided a dignified reason for calling an election to implement it.

Stanley's government went down to a modest defeat, not so much because its keenest supporters lost out at the polls – they did not – but rather because the highly fractured nature of the make-up of the Commons was maintained. Shorn of the main reason for his ministry – to carry some measure of electoral reform – Stanley was still not in a strong enough position to ensure support for his government.

In many of the new urban seats, radicals and Whigs polled well, but continuing Tory strength in the countryside saw them make modest gains. As John Wilson Croker, one of the key Tory election organisers, wrote afterwards:

> An election held in the midst of tumult for reform would have seen us
> go down and reformers elected north, south, east and west. Thank the
> King for refusing an election until Parliament had settled the reform
> question. With the bill passed the rioting crowds could do no more than
> shout their futility.

The Tories' position was also buttressed by the much more minor
changes in Scotland introduced by the Lesser Reform Bill, compared to those proposed originally by Grey. Instead of gaining the
scores of Scottish seats the Great Reform Bill would have given
them, the Whig numbers were little changed.

Although many Radicals had hoped for an outburst of popular
support for reform and a landslide election victory, the reality
was that the very limited extension of the franchise continued to
deprive most of their supporters of the vote, whilst the weakness
of Stanley's government had encouraged Tories to contest far more
seats than they would have if a radical reform measure been brought
in by a popular and successful government.

The new parliament was therefore fundamentally split between
radicals, the Great Reformers (the group of Whigs who had backed
Grey and then fallen out of favour with Stanley), the Lesser Reformers (Stanley's supporters), the moderate Tories led by Peel and the
Ultra-Tories (some of whom had backed reform out of horror at the
way in which Peel and Wellington had been able to override popular sentiment and introduce Catholic emancipation in the 1820s).
It was no surprise that it was Peel who was summoned to form a
ministry, for he could hope at least for the acquiescence of both
Ultra-Tories and Lesser Reformers. On taking office, Peel pleased
his more conservative supporters by pledging that the matter of
parliamentary reform was now settled and closed. Radicals might
fulminate, but as Peel's ministry got on with slowly introducing
moderate reform in other areas of public life he secured broad support, as it became clear that his measures were helping to secure the
existing political system rather than radically changing it.

It was local government, in the form of the Municipal Corporations Act, which proved the most troublesome. The previously highly restricted electoral franchise benefited the Tories considerably, yet was increasingly difficult to justify when compared with the Lesser Reform Act's changes to parliamentary elections. Peel concentrated on administrative reforms, such as the introduction of a paid town clerk and treasurer for every corporation, along with a requirement to produce audited accounts. Over the electorate, the government proposed the same franchise as for parliamentary elections – more generous than many Tories had wished yet less than the Whigs had demanded. A series of concessions became necessary to keep the government's supporters happy, including exempting both Ireland and the City of London from the provisions of the bill and ensuring that elections would not take place more than once every four years. They were sufficient to ease the measure through Parliament.

Typical of other modest reforms that Peel was willing to introduce was the extension, in 1835, of the rule that driving should be on the left from London Bridge to the whole country. The most radical reform of his period in office, the abolition of slavery, in 1833, came through a private bill promoted by the Society for the Mitigation and Gradual Abolition of Slavery rather than through a government measure.

Amongst the rising stars in Peel's government was William Gladstone, elected as Conservative MP for Newark in 1832. Although his talent would surely have resulted in a successful political career under any circumstances, Gladstone benefited from filling one of Peel's political needs. Given the Prime Minister's support for Catholic emancipation, many of the Ultra-Tories continued to be suspicious of him and his motives. Peel needed to reassure them, and including staunch defenders of the Church of England in his ministry fitted the bill.

Gladstone was one such person. He forged his ministerial career in Ireland, where his presence reassured the Ultra-Tories that

Catholic emancipation would not prove to be the first in a series of concessions from Peel that would undermine the established church or threaten the union. Gladstone vigorously campaigned for the protection of the Anglican Church and opposed the provision of any monetary support to other religious institutions. He never felt on strong enough grounds to cut the aid given since before the 1830s to the Catholic Maynooth Seminary in Ireland, but he was successful at blocking any discussion of extending greater financial support to it.

The firm line of Gladstone and others in thus protecting the established Church brought political benefits for Peel's government, in the shape of the continued strong support of William IV. The King's backing proved vital in enabling Peel to hold together the shaky coalition of factions that had first put him in government.

Peel also benefited, as his ministry continued into the mid-1830s, from the fractured nature of the opposition. Grey, never keen on becoming Prime Minister in the first place in 1830, retired from active politics. Rivalries between Melbourne, Palmerston and Russell stopped any of them establishing themselves as the undisputed alternative to Stanley. The support for the disestablishment of the Church of Ireland felt by many Whigs and Radicals was vigorously disputed by Stanley; but, out of power, these arguments were largely academic. It was clear that Peel's government – particularly with Gladstone in Ireland – would never support such a proposal. As Gladstone explained, 'I was brought up to distrust and dislike liberty'. Revolutions abroad were seen as a stark warning of what could happen in Ireland if a firm line was not taken over religious and nationalist demands.

Gladstone's hard line in Ireland, however, made the Irish nationalists, led by Daniel O'Connor, keen to support any possible alternative to Peel's government. In 1835 an abortive series of meetings at Lichfield House saw O'Connor try to secure promises of moderate reforms in Ireland in return for supporting the Whigs in Parliament. Stanley's conservative Whigs were not willing to countenance such concessions and in the end no agreement could be reached. This further reinforced Peel's position, as the O'Connor's followers increasingly dropped out of Commons proceedings, seeing both sides as being as bad as each other. Despite the best attempts of Althorp as a conciliator – 'the tortoise on whose back the world reposes' – the Opposition remained fractured and unable to present a united front against the government.

Not only were the Irish and Radicals pushing for policies which Stanley and his followers could not support, but even the other Whigs were split. Some, led primarily by Russell, still hankered after more widespread electoral reform and also wished to see greater tolerance in Ireland and religious reform. The Whigs' disunity over purpose and policy was very similar to that in the fifty-year period running up to 1830, when they so rarely held power or even stayed united. Grey's brief premiership had turned into a false dawn, destroyed on the rock of excessive enthusiasm for parliamentary reform and returning the Whigs to their previously factionalised state.

During the 1830s a new generation of opposition MPs came to prominence, including the unsuccessful Radical candidate for High Wycombe in 1832. Benjamin Disraeli lost that election, but his instinctive rebelliousness and contrariness – a combination familiar to many liberals – combined with a desire to make a name for himself, kept him as an Opposition gadfly. Victory in a by-election in 1834 gave him the House of Commons as a stage on which to declaim. He frequently spoke up in support of the poorest in society, arguing that it was not only morally correct but in their own self-interest for the rich to make greater efforts to care for the poor. It was their Christian duty – and also the best way of ensuring that revolution and unrest was kept at bay.

In 1837, the death of the King brought Queen Victoria to the throne. It also, under the rules of the time, meant a general election. Peel went into the contest confident of triumphing again over the divided Opposition and planning – as Lord Liverpool had done so successfully earlier in the century – to bring in an infusion of new blood to senior Cabinet posts. Top of his list was promoting Gladstone to Chancellor. Stanley was still the de facto leader of the Opposition, though MPs such as Disraeli were by far the most active in speaking and pamphleteering against the government's record. Faced with such a divided Opposition, Peel's government was safely re-elected, with his own position strengthened by the increased stature derived from another election victory. So began the long Victorian ascendancy of moderate Toryism, with its record of modest political reform, increasingly radical administrative improvements and – under Gladstone's guidance – an increasingly strong attachment to free trade.

~

Note for those unfamiliar with the actual course of events: Gladstone was initially a High Tory, and a supporter of Peel, prior to becoming a Liberal Prime Minister, Stanley (Derby) was a Whig and Cabinet member in the early 1830s, prior to becoming a Tory Prime Minister, and Disraeli was a Radical candidate before joining the Conservatives and becoming a Conservative Prime Minister.

Chapter 2

What if Sir Robert Peel had not gone out riding on 29 June 1850?

Matt Cole

The second Sir Robert Peel was a man whose life reflected his times more fully than the lives of most men do. During his political career across the first half of the nineteenth century he tackled the controversies of British rule in Ireland, penal reform and the establishment of the Metropolitan Police, trade union rights, Chartism and the extension of the franchise. At the culmination of these controversies, his abandonment of the Corn Laws saw him wrestle with the issues of taxation and trade.

In party politics, Peel is widely regarded as the founder of the modern Conservative Party for his authorship of the 'Tamworth Manifesto' and his reorganisation of the party and the revival of its fortunes thereafter. Yet at the end of this process he was rejected by his Tory colleagues and inspired a group of MPs who later went on to help found the Liberal Party. His personal biography and family background mirror the social changes of emerging industrial Britain: son of a millionaire manufacturer, grandson of a Lancashire calico printer, his struggle to break into the aristocratic leadership of the Tories demonstrated both his prodigious talents and contemporary tensions between the landed establishment and the urban arrivistes. Yet this life which so richly illustrated and significantly shaped its times was cut unnaturally short by a random riding accident. What developments of the second half of the nineteenth century would Peel's influence have prevented, altered, delayed or caused, had he survived?

~

Robert Peel died on 5 July 1850. Six days earlier he had ridden into London, taking a bay mare only recently acquired through a friend. Other potential purchasers had refused the horse because of its bucking and kicking, and Peel's own coachman had warned him against riding it. Returning from meetings in central London, he was approaching Hyde Park Corner, up Constitution Hill, when the animal threw him as he halted to address a friend; the fatal aspect of the fall was that the horse then collapsed upon its rider. The former Prime Minister was taken in great pain to his house and rested under medical observation, but died of a broken rib which had punctured and infected his lung.

At sixty-two Sir Robert Peel was not a young man, but in 1850 he had reasonable expectation of at least another decade of active politics. His father had lived to eighty, his younger brother to sixty-nine, and his son Robert (like the first Sir Robert, also an MP) lived to seventy-three. Peel was generally regarded as a man of robust health, and it is plausible for the purposes of the speculations which follow to assume that his natural life would have extended to the date of the formation of the Palmerston administration in 1859, and possibly to the foundations of the Conservative and Liberal Parties as national organisations in 1867 and 1870. By the later of these dates he would have been eighty-two. Although by modern standards this would have been long beyond the retirement point of any statesman, it should be remembered that at this age Peel's protégé Gladstone had yet to begin his fourth stint as Prime Minister. Palmerston continued in that position into his eighties, and Aberdeen, Russell, Salisbury and Disraeli all occupied 10 Downing Street in their seventies.

Peel had a reputation unmatched by that of any of his contemporaries: educated at Harrow and Christ Church, he became the first student to win a double first degree (in Classics and Maths) under the new Oxford regulations. He entered the Commons at the age of twenty-one, and within three years he was the Chief Secretary for Ireland. He held the post of Home Secretary throughout most of the 1820s, in which position he controversially supported a volte-face in Tory policy to grant certain civil rights to Catholics. In 1834, when King William IV dismissed the Whigs, Peel agreed to lead a Tory administration supported by little more than a quarter of the MPs; his government survived less than six months. He remained Conservative leader, however, and has been credited with refashioning the party's identity, and building up its organisation in the country, so that it was in a position to win the 1841 general election outright, making him Prime Minister for the next five years. It was from this position that Peel made his most dramatic gesture – of scrapping the Corn Laws, which had raised bread prices by guaranteeing markets for British grain producers unless prices reached excessively high levels.

The repeal of the Corn Laws reflected not only the impact of a successful campaign by urban interests but also important aspects of Peel's character: his determination to do what he thought to be his duty, and his willingness to abandon party commitments and allegiances to do it. In a Commons debate on the Corn Laws, he was at one point so struck by the force of the argument of his Whig opposite number, Lord John Russell, that he handed his notes to his Home Secretary, Sir James Graham, informing him that he could no longer answer for the government. He was noted also, both by critics and supporters, for his remoteness, which some took to be the result of an outsider's nervousness, others the haughtiness of a talented egoist.

The majority of Tory MPs were horrified by Peel's reversal in policy, attacking (as they saw it) the stability of British agriculture and landed interests, and in 1846 they removed him as Prime Minister. His supporters, the 'Peelites', up to 130 Conservative MPs, including important figures such as Sir James Graham and future

Prime Minister William Gladstone, operated as a loose parliamentary grouping distinct from the two main parties until they joined
the Whigs and Radicals in the formation the Liberal Party from
1859 onwards. Following this serious split, the Tories held office for
less than a decade in the years from 1846 until 1885; and only in the
general election of the year after that did the Conservative Party
again reach the share of the popular vote they had gained in Peel's
victory of 1841.

Peel and the coalition government of 1852

The first episode in which Sir Robert Peel would certainly have
made a difference is the formation and conduct of the Aberdeen
administration. The politics of mid-nineteenth century parliaments
were unpredictable in the extreme, 'as unstable as water', as Lord
John Russell put it,[1] and in many ways this environment would have
invited the talents of a respected loner such as Peel. In December
1852, the Conservative government of Lord Derby, which had taken
office only ten months earlier after the failure of Russell's Whigs,
fell on the issue of protectionism following Disraeli's Budget. Leading Peelite William Gladstone had played a key role in the attack
on Derby's economic policies, and, following a general election,
the Peelites effectively held the balance of power in the Commons.
They joined forces with the Whigs, whose policy of free trade was
the raison d'être of Peelite politics, and a coalition Cabinet was
formed in which the Peelite Earl of Aberdeen was Prime Minister,
Gladstone was his Chancellor, and the leading Whigs Russell and
Palmerston were Foreign and Home Secretaries respectively.

What might have been Peel's role in this? After his resignation in
June 1846, Peel remained active in public life. He supported awards
for achievement in the fields of science and the arts, and continued
to contribute to Parliamentary debate. Indeed on the night before
his fatal journey, he had made a notable speech in the debate on the
Don Pacifico affair; the following morning, he had been returning
from a meeting working on the plans for the construction of the

Crystal Palace. He remained in regular correspondence with lead-ing Peelites such as Aberdeen, and the guidance he gave them, and his general support for Russell's Whig government, were received with respectful, even eager, gratitude. He advised Russell's inex-perienced Chancellor, Sir Charles Wood, and was regarded, in one historian's account, as being 'in danger of becoming a prisoner of the government.'[2] Cartoonists for publications such as *Punch* con-tinued to depict him as a leading figure in Parliament.[3] None of this suggests that Peel had become a political recluse, a course of action easier then than today, without the intrusive curiosity of the media. In fact, by comparison with recent former Prime Ministers such as John Major and Jim Callaghan, Peel evinced a comparatively strong desire to engage with contemporary issues.

Peel would certainly have commented on the Aberdeen govern-ment. Might he have joined it, or even led it? There would have been no shortage of encouragement to do so: Peel's biographer, Norman Gash, accepted that the Peelites found it 'a source of pride to count themselves as the followers of a man who had stood supreme amongst contemporary politicians, and whom Greville more than once observed would be swept back into power on any popular vote.'[4] When the Peelites did take office in 1852, the private references to Peel's legacy had a tone of understated messianic rev-erence momentarily reminiscent of Soviet wistfulness about Lenin. Aberdeen insisted to Victoria that his must be 'a liberal Conserva-tive Government in the sense of Sir Robert Peel', and the following year the Prime Minister praised Gladstone to Leopold of Belgium as a minister who had 'placed himself on the level of Sir Robert Peel'.[5] The door would have been open to Peel, but would he have walked through?

At first glance the evidence looks rather less strong. Peel very definitely did not wish to lead a party, and following his resignation he repeatedly gave the most emphatic statements of his distaste for the idea of a return to office. On offering his resignation to Queen Victoria, Peel told Greville that he had made only one request of the monarch – that she never ask him to serve in office again. Of the Peelites, 'as they are called', he wrote dismissively to Aberdeen in 1847, 'I do not know whether they are sixty or six, and rather hope they may be the latter in preference to the former or a larger number'.[6] Peel was certainly a proud, perhaps even a vain, personality, and there was more than an element of Heathesque pique in his reaction to the loss of office. He did not anticipate another such bruising experience with anything other than antipathy, and had at one point even contemplated leaving the Commons altogether. 'Peel', wrote Gash, 'made it excessively clear to his friends that he had no intention of returning to office or leading a party again'.[7]

On the other hand, there may have been good reasons for the excessive nature of his clarity – namely the fact that he was disbelieved, something which became a source of irritation to him. Even Queen Victoria had to be reminded by Aberdeen in September 1847 of Peel's reluctance to take office, at which she expressed surprise. Nor was this a reading of his mood to which Peel's actions had failed to give nourishment; he had, after all, not left the Commons, a fact that led Greville to doubt the permanence of his decision. 'That Peel meant this as he said it I have no doubt, but his remaining in the House of Commons is rather inconsistent if such is his determination'. Greville believed that going to the Lords would have given greater credence to Peel's claims of retirement; he also thought it significant that although Peel had told him of his last request to Queen Victoria as premier, he had not said what was her reply.[8]

Though Peel made efforts to deny ambition, in fact he had always done so, devotion to duty being the hallmark of his reputation. This, however, had not prevented him from changing his mind (over the Corn Laws in the 1840s, franchise reform in the 1830s, or Catholic emancipation in the 1820s) or taking office even with minority support when he felt that duty required it. His protestations, like those of Michael Heseltine about seeking the Conservative leadership, or Ken Livingstone about his Independent candidature for Mayor of

London, could be regarded as anything from sincere but conditional (and therefore temporary) to pure political coquettishness.

In the manner of his departure and in his conduct afterwards, Peel had, like a well-scripted soap-opera character, left open the possibility of an unexpected return, to rapturous applause. The circumstances would have to be right, as they proved to be for his Peelite protégé Gladstone forty years later; but, as Gash wrote some years after his biographical study, 'while Peel was still alive, there was always the hope for his followers that sooner or later he would return to power'.[9] If the fluid circumstances of the Aberdeen coalition's formation did not offer the right circumstances, the issues of its term of office surely would have.

The coalition was always vulnerable to division, being populated with strong, talented personalities, and led by the experienced but somewhat detached Aberdeen (Aberdeen's reservedness was curiously reflected even in his burial, the location of which remained unknown from his death in 1860 until the chance discovery of his crypt in 1991).[10] The leadership of the Whig element was disputed between Palmerston and Russell, particularly after the latter's attempt to extend the franchise with the Reform Bills of 1852 and 1854. Palmerston was also at the centre of arguments about foreign policy, taking a more robust and less diplomatic approach than many of his colleagues, and being willing to act without consultation with them. This had been reflected in the Don Pacifico affair of 1850, and had caused his dismissal as Foreign Secretary the following year after he unilaterally recognised a Bonapartist coup in France. In 1853 the coalition faced Russian claims to rights of protection over Christians in the Turkish Empire, and became embroiled at length in the Crimean War, against Aberdeen's better judgement and at the encouragement of Palmerston. The poor conduct of the war – blamed largely, if unfairly, upon Aberdeen's lack of leadership – eventually brought the coalition down in January 1855 after it was defeated in the Commons on a motion for a select committee to enquire into the conduct of the war.

It is difficult to speculate in detail about what Peel's attitude to, and impact upon, these events might have been, but we know from his critical speech over the Don Pacifico affair that he favoured a much more diplomatic approach than Palmerston. On the other hand, he did not share Russell's enthusiasm for further reform. He had in 1834 conceded, in the Tamworth Manifesto, that the Conservatives would have to accept the extension of the franchise which the Whigs had already undertaken, but this was as the price for guaranteeing that there would be no more. Guizot wrote after Peel's death that the latter's 'constant and passionate preoccupation' in conversations during his last days was 'the state of the working classes in England' whom Peel regarded as 'a disgrace as well as a danger to our civilisation'.[11]

The Crimean crisis might well have been the opportunity to call Peel back into public service; and once there – or even if only coaching from the sidelines – he could have strengthened diplomatic resolve before the war started, or its administration once it was under way. Most importantly, he would have given political heart to the Peelite element of the coalition, and perhaps even settled disputes amongst Whigs. The coalition might have survived, but as a rather different political beast: a more genuinely equal partnership between Peelites and Whigs. The implications of this for the development of the main political parties are substantial.

Peel and the political parties

Let us imagine, then, that Peel's intervention had, perhaps by his membership or even leadership of the government, turned the Crimean episode into a triumph rather than a source of embarrassment for the coalition. Depending upon the exact point of his return to office, Peel was able either to avert war by skilful and assertive diplomatic measures, or to galvanise and discipline the military leadership which under Aberdeen was so divided and ineffective. As a result, Palmerston was unable to claim the mantle of the imperial patriot which he in reality assumed; domestic politics, notably economic reform, remained at the top of the agenda, and the dynamic Chancellor Gladstone was increasingly seen as the natural successor to Peel. Most importantly, rather than there being a change of government in 1855 as the discredited Aberdeen gave way to the apparently vindicated Palmerston, the crisis administration formed when Peel returned to office in 1853 or 1854 was consolidated, with Aberdeen making way for the man who had been de facto leader of the government since his return to its ranks (and who was in fact four years his junior), and Russell remaining in office rather than resigning, as he did in reality.

Peel, now sixty-seven, had laid the ghost of his previous ejection from Downing Street, and, like Lloyd George sixty years later, wanted to set the seal on his achievement with a general election victory – in this case probably his last. The election of 1857 would in these circumstances prove to be a personal endorsement not of Palmerston (as it in reality was) but of Peel and, by implication, of his now self-confident parliamentary grouping – albeit he refused (like Aberdeen before Peel's return) to acknowledge any formal position as its 'leader', and the group itself remained indeterminate in size and inconsistent in discipline.

Following a convincing victory at the polls, the coalition of Whigs and Peelites resumed office. Upon his seventieth birthday, on 5 February 1858, Peel accepted a peerage – the Earldom of Drayton – as a mark of Victoria's appreciation for his services, and shortly afterwards announced his retirement from the premiership and from government altogether. This time Peel was determined to stick to his word, and he did stay out of office – though the vacuum left by his departure made it impossible for him to stay out of politics.

At this point in historical reality there began the emergence of the two main British political parties as modern parliamentary and campaigning organisations. The 'Willis's Rooms' meeting of 6 June 1859 brought together 274 of the 356 MPs amongst the disparate elements willing to be recognised as in some sense 'Liberals', to agree to support a government headed by Palmerston, but including contrasting Whigs such as Russell, together with Peelites and a small Radical element. The following year saw the establishment of the Liberal Registration Association, and with these and already-existing local Radical Associations, the Liberal Party appeared, at least in embryonic form.

If Peel had survived, the balance and relationship between these elements would have been substantially different. Both Palmerston and Peel opposed extension of the franchise and reforms such as the secret ballot: Peel rejected the Chartist petitions up to and including 1848, and Palmerston successfully resisted reform bills until his death in 1865. This might have deterred Radicals such as John Stuart Mill or John Bright from supporting the Liberal project. Palmerston, on the other hand, would have had his claim to leadership reduced if he had not led the government while Peel remained in office; Russell might have been unwilling to serve under him, and Gladstone, now entering his fifties and emboldened by the strength of Peelite achievement and representation, might have felt entitled to make a claim. It is rightly assumed, however, that the prospect of Palmerston's leadership was what brought many of the Whigs to Willis's Rooms. Peel himself might not have attended (as, in fact, Gladstone did not), but his presence would have been felt. Having left a tense atmosphere amongst his erstwhile allies, his disdain for party politics would have led him to eschew the whole project, and his opinion would doubtless have reached his followers.

Suppose that a smaller and more divided Liberal Party was formed in support of Palmerston, after a bruising contest for the leadership with the more stable Gladstone and the experienced Russell, and without the support of most Radicals. This coalition – similar to Aberdeen's, but very differently led – might have ruled in the 1860s, but it would have been far less able to deal with the challenges of parliamentary reform which dominated the second half of that decade.

After Palmerston's death in 1865, Gladstone and Russell brought forward reform proposals which were the starting point of the 1867 Reform Act eventually passed by Disraeli's Conservative government. This measure faced resistance from 'Adullamite' critics in the Liberal Party like Robert Lowe, and was only carried into effect in its fuller form under Disraeli because of the pressure from Radicals who formed a bridge between Westminster and the trade unions, the Working Men's Associations, the Reform Union and the Reform League: what Maurice Cowling called 'a link between the excluded classes and the inner sanctum of power'.[12]

The so-called 'Hyde Park railings' incident of 23 July 1866, in which a mass rally of reformers was confronted by police refusing them access to the Park, was only defused with the mediation of Radical MP John Stuart Mill. Together with other huge open-air demonstrations in Birmingham, Glasgow and elsewhere, this would have been just the type of occasion to stir Peel's memories of the crisis of 1830–32. Some of the leaders of the reform movement, such as George Odger, were Chartist veterans, and had little trust for Peel. If the Radicals had been warned off by the shadow of Peel in 1859, they would not have been in a position to play their mediating role.

If Peel – by this time, in his late seventies, only an occasional contributor in the Lords – had still have been willing to bring the weight of his prestige into play, then the job of progressives would have been harder still. The former Prime Minister, who had granted Catholic emancipation, repealed the Corn Laws and settled the Eastern Question, would in a final gesture – a halting, brief but impassioned address to a packed upper house over the second reading of the 1866 Reform Bill – stand, as he had in 1832, against the extension of the suffrage and the threat of mob rule. Peel had personal anxieties on this score; shortly before his birth his grandfather had been driven out of Blackburn by rioting handloom weavers, and by 1846 Peel had already fortified his home against attack more times than any other nineteenth-century Prime

Minister. He would have looked back to the legacy of Palmerston, and to his own prophecy of a third of a century earlier when he had argued against the Great Reform Act because 'I was unwilling to open a door I saw no prospect of being able to close'.[13] The resolve of the Whig doubters would have been strengthened; the link between the Liberals and Radicals would have been weakened; and the birth of an independent party of labour might have come forty years earlier than it eventually did.

Of course, the Reform Bill of 1866 did in fact fail, and was revived by the Conservatives; but how would they have reacted to the new set of circumstances described here? The survival of Peel would have made any reunion of his followers even less likely than it proved to be when attempted in the 1850s after his death. The greater robustness of the Peelite group as an independent force might have attracted some of those who later went to the Conservatives, such as W. H. Smith, in response to their willingness to broaden their class appeal to the nouveaux riches and to adapt to a policy of free trade under Salisbury. Some have argued that Peel represented that free-trade part of Conservatism to which Margaret Thatcher appealed so successfully.

The Tories might then have remained a smaller and less modernised force — and not one that saw any need to respond to isolated extra-parliamentary demands for reform. Peel's last address to the Lords would have pricked the consciences of the Tories longest in the tooth, as a last hurrah of pre-modern politics. Ironically, Peel — in his day the most modern of Prime Ministers — had become the most reactionary of former holders of that office. Like Gladstone a generation later, he staggered into history teetering along the thin line between Grand Old Man and grumpy old man. Yet in seeking to preserve the eighteenth century, he had hastened on the twentieth, with a new left-wing force campaigning at the polls, on the streets and in industry.

The possibility of an earlier breach between socialist and Liberal forces opens up any number of other outcomes in party politics. It makes less likely, for example, the development of the tradition of Lib-Lab MPs from the 1870s onwards, and suggests that Gladstone's resistance to Chamberlain's 'Unauthorised' Liberal programme of 1885, and the Newcastle Programme of 1891, would have been more successful, and might have stifled the emergence of the New Liberalism in the Liberal Party of the twentieth century. It would certainly have made less likely the Gladstone–MacDonald Pact of 1903 and the subsequent 'progressive alliance' between Liberals and Labour, from the 1906 Liberal election victory to the First World War. Whether the Labour Party or the Conservative Party would have benefited most from this – especially under a restricted franchise – is a question which opens up a very extended debate about short- and long-term outcomes, some aspects of which are addressed in other chapters of this book.

Conclusion
Our imaginary Peel never returned to the red benches of the Lords. He died, like his father, aged eighty, at his estate at Drayton in 1868. Instead of the popular emotional response to his death which actually occurred in 1850 – when spontaneous demonstrations of workers and almost endless eulogies in print mourned his untimely passing – the imaginary Peel was given a respectful but very retrospective farewell by certain elements of the political community, and a private, quiet one by former supporters amongst the public, rather as with Lloyd George.

As he had done repeatedly in his career, Peel had answered some key questions, but left far more unresolved. National leadership was wanting: Aberdeen and Palmerston were gone, Russell was in his last decade of life, Gladstone had been discredited by the failure of reform and the fracturing of the Liberals, and Disraeli led a rump of Tories not big enough to govern alone, and not flexible enough to find allies. Beyond the confines of the Palace of Westminster the labour movement growled its resentment at the continued exclusion of working men and women from politics. This future would have looked very different from the one which actually transpired.

It is, needless to say, possible that even if Peel had not gone out on the horse which threw him on 29 June 1850, the events of his remaining years would have been less touched by his impact than the speculation above suggests. He might have stayed on the sidelines keeping his counsel, or been increasingly disregarded by his former allies, as time wore on. In a sense, though accidental and tragic, Peel's death was for political purposes timely, coinciding with or coming shortly before the inevitable rise of mass parties and more popular politics to which he was so opposed. Perhaps Peel's life reflected its times so closely partly because it was unnaturally curtailed. Even Gladstone was eventually forced to concede that Peel's awkward position in the last four years of his life was 'thoroughly false' because of his unwillingness to take up the leadership role so naturally his in the Commons.[14]

However, it would be a rare Prime Minister who at Peel's age stayed out of the fray. Most holders of the office, like the current occupant, are reluctant to relinquish it, and having done so, they can find it difficult, like Margaret Thatcher, to resist the temptation to comment upon their successors. They can even hope for a return from retirement in a 'once-and-future-king' role, even when age and changed circumstances make it implausible, as Thatcher claimed Macmillan thought he might in the 1970s,[15] Churchill effectively did in 1951, and Gladstone actually did. Moreover, modern politics has not been without its dynamic and influential figures who rejected or switched parties. The generation after Peel saw Joe Chamberlain hold Cabinet office in both major parties, and wreck the election chances of both from that position. Lloyd George fashioned a position for himself virtually independent of party allegiances at the highest point of his career, and Churchill took pride in 're-ratting' on his party, and told his grandson and namesake that he regarded parties like chargers, and that a politician should take 'the best hack in the stable'.[16] The impact of these personalities could be destructive of interests around them, and arguably of the national interest; but few would argue that they were without importance because they rejected their party. It is always possible that Peel – given his record of abandoning important policies when he thought it fit – could have turned to support wider enfranchisement and even mass party politics, rather than pursuing the line to which his existing record points.

The account of Peel's imaginary life sketched here is perhaps unlikely. It may be that his influence would have been merely to delay a little the development of the party system and the careers of certain politicians, without altering permanently the driving forces of British politics. But for the time that the delay lasts, it is absolute in its effect: at any given moment, there is no such thing as the long term; and for mid-Victorian politics, even if only as an *éminence grise*, it is inconceivable that a man such as Peel could have made no difference at all. In the long term, Peel could not have set aside altogether the developments of economics, education, technology and society which made mass parties the building blocks of modern politics, but he could have altered forever the shape and character of those parties that emerged from the Victorian era, and thereby he might have altered government and public life long after his own demise – whenever it occurred.

Notes

1 Russell to Lord Minto, 22 July 1855.
2 M. E. Chamberlain, *Lord Aberdeen* (London, 1983), p. 414. Chamberlain acknowledges that this is also the conclusion arrived at by Gash.
3 A well-known example was the 1847 *Punch* cartoon, 'The Rising Generation – in Parliament', which depicted a self-assured Peel patronising a juvenile Disraeli.
4 N. Gash, *Sir Robert Peel: The life of Sir Robert Peel after 1830* (Longman, 1972), p. 618.
5 Aberdeen to Victoria, 19 December 1852; Aberdeen to Leopold, 4 May 1853.
6 Peel to Aberdeen, 19 August 1847.
7 Gash, *Sir Robert Peel,* p. 617.
8 Greville's diary entry, 12 December 1846.
9 N. Gash, 'The Peelites after Peel', *Modern History Review*, Vol. 5 No. 3 (1994), p. 2.

10 The discovery of Aberdeen's body at Stanmore in north-west London was reported in *The Times* of 20 December 1991. The edition of 26 December published correspondence commenting upon Aberdeen's reputation.

11 M. Guizot, *Sir Robert Peel* (Paris, 1856), p. 78.

12 M. Cowling, *Disraeli, Gladstone and Revolution* (Cambridge University Press, 1967).

13 Robert Peel speaking in the House of Commons, 6 July 1831.

14 Cited in R. Foster, 'Peel and his Party: the "Age of Peel" reassessed', *Modern History Review*, Vol. 5 No. 1 (1993), p. 4.

15 M. Thatcher, *The Path to Power* (Harper Collins, 1995), p. 319.

16 The younger Winston Churchill (b.1940) retold this anecdote in the first episode of Martin Gilbert's television biography of the Prime Minister of the same name, *Churchill: Renegade and Turncoat* (BBC, 1992).

Chapter 3

What if Joseph Chamberlain had married Beatrice Webb?

David Boyle

B eatrice Potter, handsome, clever, and rich, seemed to unite some of the best blessings of existence. How was it that fate reserved a place for her – not, I should stress, her only slightly less influential contemporary, Beatrix Potter – as one of the architects of dour state socialism, Beatrice Webb?

That is the question at the heart of this chapter: was it inevitable? And if not, would British social history have been different had it not been for an awkward romantic encounter in her back garden?

~

There were other differences from Beatrix Potter. While the future creator of Peter Rabbit and Mrs Tiggywinkle was shy and reclusive, Beatrice was one of nine sisters, brought up by an exuberant speculator father and an imperious mother, and surrounded during her childhood by the brightest utilitarian minds of her parents' generation. In and out of her childhood homes in Gloucestershire, Westmoreland and London wandered the philosopher and pioneer sociologist Herbert Spencer and other evolutionists like T. H. Huxley and Francis Galton.

It was Spencer's belief, inculcated in his young friend on their walks together, that human civilisation had an inevitable path. It could not have developed otherwise than the way it did.

Maybe he was right, maybe he was wrong. It was two generations at least before philosophical positivists dubbed statements of that kind 'meaningless'. But was it true of Beatrice? Was it inevitable that the brilliant and beautiful Beatrice Potter, steeped in the Liberal utilitarian tradition of John Stuart Mill, should have become the fearsome Fabian mainstay Beatrice Webb, the architect of the dullest and most technocratic form of socialism?

Did the structure of the universe decree that someone who promised so much, who had two Liberal MPs as brothers-in-law, should enter knowingly into marriage to a man she did not love and found physically repulsive, and end her life a devotee of Stalin, claiming that – as other old ladies fall in love with taxi drivers – she had 'fallen in love with Soviet communism'?

Could evolution have turned out differently, and turned – as it so nearly did – the potential Stalinist Beatrice Webb into the brilliant Liberal organiser and philosopher Beatrice Chamberlain?

It is worth asking the question because it could provide at least one answer to the questions of why, of the various competing strands of the left at the turn of the century, it was miserable technocratic Fabianism – rather than co-operative socialism or mutualism or local liberalism – that won through to dominate the century ahead in the UK.

The question of whatever happened to mutualism – who killed the idea a century or so before? – is now much discussed in the current movement to mutualise public services and housing. And it is an important question, because as Fabian centralisation came to dominate the left in Britain, it also tainted the emerging solutions to welfare in other countries too.

Yet the critical parting of the ways between these two potential futures has remained elusive to most writers on the co-operative movement. Why did class-based confrontation come to dominate, rather than the politics of co-operative welfare? Why did the co-operative and voluntary sector, which promised so much at the end of the nineteenth century, unravel so fatally at the beginning of the twentieth, so that it had to be reinvented three generations later?

Luckily, I am now in a position to reveal the answer. The vital moment of decision came after lunch in the garden of the Potters' London home on 12 January 1884.

~

It was here that the leading radical Liberal of his generation, Joseph Chamberlain, led Beatrice out for a quiet conversation to ratchet up the momentum of their courtship. And it was here that she decided both that she was deeply in love with him and that she could not quite bring herself to marry him and keep her self-respect and independence of mind.

Beatrice was then twenty-five, and an active member of the Charity Organisation Society, visiting the poor in Soho. She had just signed a petition condemning the idea of women's suffrage. Chamberlain was forty-seven, though he looked younger, and was at the height of his powers as an orator and political operator. He had been married twice before, but both wives had died in child-birth. He was then President of the Board of Trade in Gladstone's Cabinet.

They had met at a dinner party some months before. Chamberlain's boast that it was his intention to confiscate the land of the peer sitting next to Beatrice had both thrilled and fascinated her.

He had reason to believe, as the leader of the Radical wing of the Liberal Party, that he might succeed Gladstone shortly as party leader, promising to do for the country what he had done as mayor of Birmingham – 'parked, paved, assized, marketed, gas-and-watered and improved.'[1] He had advanced ideas on land nationalisation and old age pensions and he wanted a wife he could rely on for emotional and political support in the turbulent years to come. It was this issue on which the budding relationship with Beatrice foundered.

They disagreed about education over lunch – as her silent family wondered why such an eminent man had arrived at their house – and in the garden, he set out to her some of the principles which governed his politics. She stayed silent and the conversation veered dangerously on to the subject of gender and marriage.

Chamberlain said he hoped for 'intelligent sympathy' from women in his family. 'Servility, Mr Chamberlain, think I,' said Beatrice, unwisely, but in a flash of inspiration about her future life. 'Not sympathy, but intelligent servility.'[2]

Later that night, she confided in her diary: 'I shall be absorbed into the life of a man ... who will refuse me all freedom of thought in my intercourse with him, to whose career I shall have to subordinate all my life, mental and physical.'[3]

The conversation might have ended awkwardly, but the relationship was not over quite yet. There were other encounters, culminating in the exchange in Chamberlain's own greenhouse where he proudly showed her the orchids which he wore in his buttonhole – so distinctively, along with his monocle – every day. She said, with great emphasis, and some regret, that she preferred her flowers wild.

Nevertheless, although they saw each other with increasing infrequency over the next four years, despite her fears, Chamberlain consistently asked her advice on economic and welfare issues. Beatrice agonised over the unconsummated affair, using pages in her diary to obsess over Chamberlain, writing him the occasional impassioned letter. As she did so, she became involved in the most formative experience of her life, working as an assistant to the Liberal ship-owner Charles Booth as he began his monumental survey of poverty in London.

The 1870s had been a period of shocking agricultural depression, and former farm-workers had flooded into the cities. By 1886, when the survey began – launched with a suggestion by Chamberlain himself that they should start by interviewing school board visitors, and then check their evidence with door-to-door interviews

– the farm-workers' poverty had transferred to the city slums. Over seventeen years, Booth's surveys established just how widespread poverty was in the capital, and how unrelated it was to personal failure or deliberate debauchery. Often it affected those most whose folly was merely age or ill health.

Even so, the study was originally undertaken to counteract the propaganda of the socialist leader H. M. Hyndman who, Booth believed – mistakenly – had overestimated the spread of poverty in London. Neither Beatrice nor Booth were socialists at this stage, but their relationship of mutual support did provide a glimpse for Beatrice of a way out of her obsessive love for Chamberlain.

'We are very fond of each other,' Beatrice confided in her diary in 1887, well into the first year of working side by side with Booth. 'A close intimate relationship between a man and a woman without sentiment (perhaps not without sentiment, but without passion or the dawning of passion). We are fellow workers both inspired by the same intellectual desire.'[4]

In the early years of their courtship that never was, Chamberlain had been setting out the details of what became known as his 'Unauthorised Programme', which – although it was considered dangerously radical at the time – was actually designed to undermine socialism. It was formulated to provide ordinary people with a measure of economic independence by distributing small plots of land, as well as setting out a programme of education, democratic reform and decentralisation. It was a new kind of populist Liberalism.

'If you go back to the early history of our social system,' he said in his speech on the Reform Bill of 1885, 'you will find that … every man was born into the world with natural rights, with a right to share in the great inheritance of the community, with a right to a part of the land of his birth.'[5] This was not exactly Gladstonian Liberalism.

When, two years after this speech, Beatrice heard the news that he was engaged to marry instead the daughter of the American

Secretary of State for War, she gasped in horror and hurried to St Paul's Cathedral to pray. 'He must become a Tory,' she confided to her diary, with great perception and some horror.[6] At the moment that he was making his vows in America, she was spending the evening prostrate in Westminster Abbey.

She met Sidney Webb, with his pince-nez and goatee beard, at the beginning of 1890. He had 'a huge head and a tiny body', she told her diary.[7] The experience of passionless productivity with Booth opened her eyes to a similar possible relationship with Webb, but the discovery of her secret engagement to him horrified Booth and his wife Mary, Beatrice's cousin, and her relationship with them never really recovered.

Beatrice described the decision to marry the Fabian workhorse as a deliberate mortification of the flesh, compared to the self-gratification of her alternative marriage to Chamberlain.[8] 'On the face of it, it seems an extraordinary end to the once brilliant Beatice Potter,' she told her diary, '… to marry an ugly little man with no social position and less means'.[9]

The wedding was an unpleasant surprise for Beatrice's increasingly Liberal family. It was also the start of her conversion to Fabian socialism. Before Webb, she had given evidence to the House of Lords just after the Great Dock Strike that there was no case for legislation to control the sweating system. Before Webb, also, she had looked to the leaders of the co-operative movement as a potential solution to the evils she was uncovering. After Webb, having agreed rather reluctantly to eschew children and to devote her life to study and socialist polemic – and putting the growing co-operative movement under the microscope – she was beginning to wonder 'whether profit is not on the whole a demoralising force'.[10]

In fact, she had set her face against Chamberlain's Liberal populism with all the disdain of the English upper middle class. 'How inexpressibly ugly are the manners and ways of a typical middle-class man', she told her diary, 'brought up in the atmosphere of small profit-making'.[11]

Even so, the Fabian Society, only just renamed from the rather heavy-handed 'Fellowship of the New Life', was then an uneasy collection of intellectual misfits like George Bernard Shaw, the serial adulterer Hubert Bland, his wife Edith Nesbit, the future suffragette leader Emmeline Pankhurst, the future Theosophist leader Annie Besant, and others, and very unsure of its strategy. Apart from a commitment to 'ameliorism' which was shared equally by Booth and Chamberlain, they were still concentrating efforts on influencing the Liberals well into the 1890s.

But all that was about to change. In 1893, only two years after the adoption of the Newcastle Programme of 'Fabian' Liberalism, Shaw and Sidney Webb urged the working classes to abandon the Liberals and form their own party. It split the society and led directly to the formation of the Labour Party.

The years after meeting Beatrice were destined also to turn Chamberlain's career inside out. He had been the leading figure in the disastrous split over Irish Home Rule that had sent the Liberal Unionists – an uneasy alliance of Whigs and radicals loyal to Chamberlain – into a new party organisation and an increasingly close relationship with the Conservative Party.

Chamberlain had been convinced that Home Rule would lead to war, and was furious that Gladstone had overlooked his own devolution blueprint for 'national councils' in Edinburgh and Dublin. Gladstone distrusted him and was glad to have engineered his departure. There were efforts to bring him back, and for many years, Chamberlain seems to have been unsure quite which way to go. But he had glimpsed possibilities in enacting his Unauthorised Programme in alliance with the Conservatives. He had also noticed that his brand of Liberal imperialism won him by far the biggest cheers during the 1886 election hustings.

Nearly a decade later, after Gladstone finally stood down, there was one last effort to reunite the Liberal Party – a dinner between Chamberlain and the new leader and Home Rule sceptic, Lord

Rosebery. 'If it had not been for Gladstone,' Rosebery told him over the dinner table, 'our differences might have been arranged'.[12]

But whatever deal there was fell through, and Chamberlain's populist programme – the allotments and smallholdings, county councils, free elementary education and the rest – were enacted in tepid form by the Conservatives. For eight turbulent years, Chamberlain would also become the most formidable Colonial Secretary in the history of the British Empire – and in a Conservative Cabinet. Beatrice had been right.

Those areas of the Unauthorised Programme that he could not swing past Conservative legislators – land reform, progressive income tax on the amount of land held, council housing, universal manhood suffrage – withered on the vine. His commitment to parish councils remained, though his measure was emasculated by the Lords, as was his plan for old age pensions, to which Chamberlain, like Beatrice Webb, remained passionately committed. He proposed pensions in detail in 1891, but to no effect.

The burgeoning co-operative movement, with its commitment to voluntaryism and self-help, had also been rocked by Beatrice Webb's 1891 investigation and her incisive analysis of the basic difference in interests between co-operators and trade unionists. She claimed, also, that the 10 per cent of co-op members who regularly turned out for meetings was a sign of apathy.[13]

The Fabian world view, a vision of government by central technocrats, was carving out a different and impoverished approach. Shaw was in the forefront, ridiculing any brand of politics which suggested – as other radicals did – that money was not all that was required to tackle poverty and alienation. 'The universal regard for money is the one hopeful fact in our civilisation, the one sound spot in our social conscience', claimed Shaw in his preface to *Major Barbara*. 'It represents health, strength, honour, generosity and beauty as conspicuously and undeniably as the want of it represents illness, weakness, disgrace, meanness and ugliness.'[14]

Yet despite Shaw and the Fabians and their obsession with money as the only solution, the early years of the twentieth century appeared to be the dawn of a new kind of welfare based on self-help and mutuality. Backed by Liberal politicians like Henry Vansittart Neale and Henry Vivian, the co-partnership societies for which records survive built over 8,600 homes between 1901 and 1912, and there were thirty-five other societies whose records have been lost. Six are still in existence.[15]

Vivian was MP for Birkenhead, an ally of the Liberal reformers, such as George Cadbury and Joseph Rowntree, who were determined to unleash a new kind of working-class mutualism that could provide for people's needs and fight the causes of poverty. The co-partnership societies had their own direct works departments, playing-fields, clubhouses and garden parties – and lectures; this was the great age of the lantern slide. Letchworth Garden City included a host of Liberal supporters.

The co-operative movement was just the tip of a looming iceberg, and the engine of much else besides. Within weeks of the start of the First World War, the Co-operative Wholesale Society was turning out 10,000 tunics a day for the army and its ships were rescuing the survivors of torpedoed vessels.[16] But it was too late. In the years since Chamberlain's abortive courtship of Beatrice Potter, politics had ossified around the classes. The alliances between Liberal business leaders and working-class institutions like consumer co-ops, which had been the route by which people like Vivian – a carpenter by profession – had reached Parliament, now looked naïve.

Meanwhile, the co-operative movement was about to be bludgeoned out of existence by the new totalitarians across Europe. Fascists in Italy burned out co-operative stores. In Vienna, where half the population was supplied by consumer co-ops, the leaders were arrested within weeks of the Anschluss. In Russia, where the co-operative movement ran its own university and central bank, all co-op property was confiscated by the Bolsheviks. Only in Iceland and Scandinavia did mutualism survive on any scale. By the 1930s, even George Orwell was parroting the Shavian ridicule of any radicalism that was not Fabian: 'If only the sandals and pistachio-coloured shirts could be put in a pile and burnt,' he wrote in 1937, 'and every vegetarian, teetotaller and creeping Jesus sent home to Welwyn Garden City to do his yoga exercises quietly'.[17]

By then, the Webbs had graduated to some political ideals that remain an embarrassment to Fabians. Their admiration for Stalin, despite numerous visits to the Soviet Union at the time of the famines and the purges, lasted for the rest of their lives. They were deeply disapproving of the Beveridge Report: 'It will either be rejected, which I think is the most probable result, or if accepted and applied will be catastrophic in its results,' wrote Beatrice. 'And in both cases it will divide the country into two political parties, those who insist on maintaining our present capitalist civilisation and those who would substitute the new civilisation of Soviet communism.'[18]

This did not prevent Sidney and Beatrice becoming the first and only husband-and-wife team to be buried in Westminster Abbey.

Their attack on Beveridge was influential. When the new National Health Service arrived, the existing structures of health provision – built up so laboriously by volunteer effort – were swept away, along with Beveridge's own blueprint. 'It would be disastrous if the spirit that has gone to building up these associations should now be lost,' he warned in 1948, urging new powers for friendly societies and state-supported institutions for self-help and voluntary action rather than centralised technocracy.[19]

But centralised technocracy is what we got, leading to other costly disasters like the destruction of working-class neighbourhoods and the deliberate unravelling of informal social networks that had played such a key role in keeping people healthy. And leading, in turn, to the present crisis in welfare of overburdened professionals, disempowered clients and vastly expensive centralised giantism.

Was it inevitable? Well, for those who took Herbert Spencer's dictum too literally, and believed that nothing could have happened differently, I have some news. It so nearly went another way altogether.

~

So enter with me, if you will, the parallel universe in which Chamberlain's conversation in the garden with Beatrice Potter on 12 January 1884 ended just a little differently. But only just – there was the same look of mutual embarrassment and silence, the same flash of misunderstanding and hint of entreaty. In both universes, Beatrice settled into her bed at the end of the day, reached for her diary, and explained the spell that Radical Joe held over her mind:

> The commonplaces of love have always bored me. But Joseph Chamberlain, with his gloom and seriousness, with the absence of any gallantry or faculty for saying pretty nothings, the simple way in which he assumes, almost asserts, that you stand on a level far beneath him and that all that concerns you is trivial, that you yourself are without importance in the world except in so far as you might be related to him: this sort of courtship (if it is to be called a courtship) fascinated, at least, my imagination.[20]

Beatrice realised it was far from over. But this time, Chamberlain also saw that he had been misunderstood – as he claimed later in letters to her – and when they met again in his greenhouse, he was ready.

'I may have given you the wrong impression when he last met, Miss Potter', he says, plucking an orchid and handing it to her. 'I believe any man would be improved by having, as a companion, a woman who can broaden his mind.'

'Not servility, then?'

'Servility? Certainly not. Partnership, I would say. Partnership and inspiration.'

Their wedding took place the following year, coinciding with the greatest political crisis of Chamberlain's life – the first skirmishes in what would become the rift over Home Rule. But through the two exhausting elections of 1885 and 1886, Beatrice Chamberlain was loyally at her husband's side. After the defection of the Liberal Unionists, it was only too clear to Chamberlain that, if it wasn't for Home Rule, the Liberals would still have a natural majority, potentially under his leadership, and could dominate British politics throughout the 1890s.

Rosebery's repudiation of Home Rule may have been temporary, but it made the dinner of reconciliation possible. Sir William Harcourt's 1894 Budget, with its introduction of graduated death duties – backed by Chamberlain, to the fury of the Conservative whips – had finally broken the old Gladstonian economic mould and opened the way to old age pensions. He knew this, and Beatrice knew it too.

It was this issue, above all, that bound Chamberlain together with his new bride. There was little prospect for pensions under the Conservatives; Chamberlain had to reunite the Liberals and claim the leadership to force his proposal through. Married to Beatrice, pensions had become the central goal of his life, as it was of hers.[21]

And so it was that the Chamberlains' radical programme came to be enacted on a much larger scale by a Liberal Party reunited with its Liberal Unionist colleagues. It was a brand of populist Liberalism that reinforced their natural majority – devolution, education, land reform and smallholdings. It put Chamberlain's slogan of 'three acres and a cow' into widespread effect and it shifted the political boundaries in a whole new way. It devolved major power to Dublin and Edinburgh. Not only were the Liberals again the majority party, but they had repossessed their radical populist tradition and prevented it falling into the hands of the Conservatives.

It was inevitable, given that he had delivered the Liberal majority, that Chamberlain should claim his crown as leader of the party and take office as Prime Minister at the head of a reforming government.[22] And at the heart of the legislation was Joseph and Beatrice's Old Age Pensions Bill, attacking head on the idea that poverty in old age was somehow uniquely the result of debauchery or drunkenness.

While Chamberlain delivered the oratory, Beatrice delivered the figures: half the population would inevitably live to sixty-five, and 40 per cent of those could expect to be forced to throw themselves on the mercy of the Poor Laws.[23] Their bill was introduced repeatedly in the final years of the century, only to be thrown out by the Conservative majority in the House of Lords.

There were divisions within the grand Liberal coalition, of course, over public spending, free trade and the Empire. There were many in the party who doubted whether free trade was compatible with imperial preference.[24] Chamberlain's meddling in colonial affairs led to war in South Africa in 1899, with initially humiliating results for the British forces. The peace wing of the Liberals, under a young radical lawyer called David Lloyd George, came close to splitting the party on the issue – but the so-called 'Khaki election' returned Chamberlain and the Liberals with a thumping majority.

There were divisions on the left of politics too. The Labour Representation Committee was set up in 1900 by a narrow group of disaffected trade unionists, who believed that pensions were a middle-class irrelevance because few of their members managed to reach retirement age.[25] The Fabians backed the government, both on pensions and the war.

State socialism, advocated by Sidney Webb – a dusty bachelor from the now muddled Fabian Society – was a fringe issue, an irritating irrelevance for the mainstream left, who were advocating the same advanced voluntaryism linked to low-interest state loans that the Chamberlain government had been rolling out. The British political divide developed along the lines that it did in the US, a non-socialist left and a state-socialist fringe that barely succeeded in attracting parliamentary representation.

Chamberlain used his 1901 landslide majority to force the pensions issue. Torpedoed by the Lords again, he was forced to ask the new king for help. Edward VII agreed to create 600 new Liberal peers to force the legislation through, if Chamberlain could win a general election on the issue in 1902.[26] The revelation of this agreement to the Conservative opposition finally forced through the legislation and the first pensions were paid in 1903.

Even so, this second election and the bitter infighting with the Liberal peaceniks whittled away Chamberlain's majority, until his devastating stroke in 1906 was followed by the Conservative victory of that year. He was succeeded as Liberal leader by Sir Henry Campbell-Bannerman, and as the first few months unfolded of twelve dark years out of office, Beatrice tended her stricken husband at his bedside and struggled to speed his exhaustingly partial recovery.

Together they had transformed the nation, providing small loans for mutual homes for tens of thousands, and low-cost interest to help working people buy their own leases, wresting control of millions of acres from the big landowners by means of punitive taxation. They had redistributed these as tens of thousands of smallholdings in rural areas and allotments in towns, to provide some measure of independence for the struggling poor. They had launched the necessary infrastructure for a whole national network of consumer co-ops providing affordable food and other services at low prices for the poor, and set up the basis for a system of mutuals providing unemployment and health insurance. They had also founded a new dispensation of local self-government, from county councils down to powerful parishes, in town and countryside, that managed most of the details of local life.

Although these were measures that earned the undying opposition of the unreformed Tories and landowners, they found it hard to unravel the new local leviathan once it was in place. They also split the tiny socialist movement, which bitterly and uncomfortably condemned the Liberal programme as a complication in the class war.

Tory attempts to turn back the tide were set aside as they plunged with enthusiasm into the First World War, with the Liberals in opposition. Lloyd George's brilliant forensic talents, brought to bear on their conduct of the war in 1916, played a major role in reuniting the Liberal Party while opening bitter political divisions in the country. The Liberals refused to enter a coalition government that backed conscription, so there was no national government of unity to conduct the war, and the 1918 election saw a resurgent Liberal Party capturing the spirit of reconstruction by a new generation, as well as benefiting from the nation's rage at the hideous waste of life. The Conservatives were identified with the slaughter of the Somme for two generations.

The new Liberal government had a great deal to do. There was expansion of the housing mutuals to every corner of the country. There was further extension of land reform and unemployment insurance, as well as a renewed decentralisation of power to claw back the local influence lost during the war years.

They were difficult years to be in power. The Liberal Chancellor, Winston Churchill, presided over a disastrous return to the gold standard. But Prime Minister Lloyd George was quick to adopt not just a Keynesian new deal, but sweeping control of the banks and a rapid expansion of public credit – not through borrowing, but by money issued debt-free by the Treasury into the economy for infrastructure.[27] Britain was, as a result, among the first countries to drag itself out of the Great Depression.

By the late 1930s, it was increasingly clear that the League of Nations – on which the Liberal government had lavished so much attention – was not the bastion against fascism they had imagined. Once more the party split between factions supporting war and those supporting peace, or – as they put it at the time – rearmament and appeasement. Churchill, now out of office, rampaged across the newspaper columns urging the nation to stand up against Hitler's expansionism. The new Liberal Prime Minister, Joseph's son Neville, forged instead a policy of appeasement that unravelled disastrously after the Munich crisis of 1938.

As the Nazi blitzkrieg was unleashed in western Europe, and the Liberal-led coalition government tottered in London, Winston Churchill found himself Prime Minister – and, as they say, the rest is history.

Except that this parallel universe sees a Britain that is not quite as we know it.

This is now a decentralised nation, where a great deal of local power is wielded by powerful parish, town and city councils, and where the nations – Ireland, Scotland and Wales – are governed by national assemblies in their capital cities. There is no Republic of Ireland.

The welfare state is locally managed, mutually based, and financed by systems of local insurance. It is the creature of Beveridge and not the centralising Bevan, and is much as Beveridge actually designed it. It has succeeded in reducing the level of ill health and in evening out disparities in standards of health between the classes.

The financial system is more like it is in Scandinavia, with intricate networks of local banks supporting mutual organisations that manage local housing, healthcare, schools and much else besides, and providing low-cost loans for enterprise and innovation. District councils are responsible for energy but not for council housing.

The Labour Party lost its last MP in 1950. Britain has been a member of the European Union since its inception. David Cameron is a backbench Liberal MP.

Notes

1   R. Harrison, *The Life and Times of Sidney and Beatrice Webb 1858–1905: The Formative Years* (Basingstoke, 2000).

2   Ibid.

3   N. and J. MacKenzie (eds.), *The Diaries of Beatrice Webb* (London, 1979), p. xxvii.

4   D. Boyle, *The Tyranny of Numbers* (London, 2001).

5   J. Garvin, *The Life of Joseph Chamberlain* (London, 1932), p. 549.

6   P. Marsh, *Joseph Chamberlain: Entrepreneur in Politics* (New Haven, 1994), p. 312.

7   Boyle, *The Tyranny of Numbers.*

8   B. Caine, *Destined to be Wives: The Sisters of Beatrice Webb* (1986), p. 91.

9   MacKenzie, *The Diaries of Beatrice Webb*, p. xxxix.

10 Harrison, *The Life and Times of Sidney and Beatrice Webb*, p. 155.

11 Ibid., pp. 154–55.

12 Marsh, *Joseph Chamberlain*, p. 354.

13 B. Potter, *The Co-operative Movement in Great Britain* (London, 1899).

14 G. B. Shaw, *Major Barbara* (London, 1904).

15 J. Birchall, *The Hidden History of Co-operative Housing in Britain* (Uxbridge, 1991), pp. 5–6.

16 J. Birchall, *Co-op: The People's Business* (Manchester, 1994), p. 110.

17 G. Orwell, *The Road to Wigan Pier* (London, 1937).

18 MacKenzie, *The Diaries of Beatrice Webb*, pp. 602–03.

19 W. Beveridge, *Voluntary Action* (London, 1948) p. 292.

20 Marsh, *Joseph Chamberlain*, p. 230.

21 In reality, pensions remained the central concern of Beatrice Webb's career, even after her marriage, and she joined Booth as a member of the Royal Commission on the Poor Laws to push for them in 1903.

22 His fellow Liberal radical leader, Sir Charles Dilke, had lost his seat and his reputation following the 'three in a bed' scandal and the allegations of Mrs Crawford – a particularly mysterious affair, not least because Mrs Crawford had visited Chamberlain secretly before going public.

23 This was, in fact, the conclusion of his article on old age pensions in January 1892.

24 But since Liberals two generations later convinced themselves that it was compatible with EEC preference, I imagine they would have swallowed some of their doubts.

25 This was, actually, the position of many trade unionists. The Fabians supported the Boer War.

26 This was what Edward agreed with Asquith just before he died in 1910, so it is not stretching credulity too much that he might have agreed the same thing nine years earlier.

27 This may sound far-fetched, but it is the policy Lloyd George adopted as Chancellor in 1914 to prevent a collapse of the banks.

Chapter 4

What if the Home Rule Bill had passed in 1886?

Tony Little

One of the golden moments of our history.

W. E. Gladstone[1]

Ireland, Ireland. That cloud in the west, that coming storm.

W. E. Gladstone[2]

How often did twentieth-century British Prime Ministers echo the words of the Victorian Liberal premier William Ewart Gladstone as they contemplated their continued inability to solve the Irish problem, whether through parliamentary or military means? Yet there was an opportunity, one golden moment, in 1886, when a peaceful resolution of the Irish Question was possible. How might Gladstone have carried out his plan for devolving government to Dublin, a plan acceptable to the outstanding Ireland Nationalist leader of his generation, Charles Stewart Parnell, and with the potential to advance the reforms that Liberals proposed for the rest of Great Britain?

My mission is to pacify Ireland

On 8 June 1885, Gladstone's second government was defeated on a Budget proposal, brought down, like his first, by the dissatisfaction of its Liberal supporters. Lord Salisbury formed a minority Conservative administration. Among the late Liberal Cabinet there was, undoubtedly, relief on laying down the burdens of office.

Gladstone's second government had been a frustrating experience. The Grand Old Man, seventy-one when he resumed the premiership in 1880, had found it harder than anticipated to escape the legacy of Beaconsfieldism, so magnificently denounced in his Midlothian campaigns. The costly colonial wars and the imperial expansion embraced so romantically by Lord Beaconsfield's[3] government of 1874–80, were less lightly laid aside than Gladstone wished and, at the beginning of 1885, the government's reputation was deeply damaged by its failure to rescue 'Chinese' Gordon from Khartoum. Parliamentary business was regularly disrupted by the atheist Charles Bradlaugh's attempts to take his seat without taking the oath and by the obstructionist tactics of Irish Nationalist MPs. Liberal efforts to solve the Irish 'Question' by coercion and by land reform had been unavailing. Within the Cabinet, Gladstone's inclination to retire, always postponed, increased the tensions between the Whigs, led by the solid patrician Lord Hartington[4], heir to the Duke of Devonshire, and the Radicals, whose self-appointed champion was Joseph Chamberlain.

Nevertheless the government had its achievements, foremost among them the Third Reform Act, which equalised the franchise across the boroughs and counties, giving equal treatment to all parts of the United Kingdom, and converted most constituencies to single-member seats. To cater for the enlarged, more rural and more working-class, electorate, Chamberlain had produced his Radical, or 'Unauthorised' Programme, which the resignation of the Liberal government left him able to promote free from collective Cabinet responsibility.

The government's resignation also left Gladstone at liberty to contemplate his future. At his age, he felt that continuation as leader came with two preconditions: he needed to be endorsed by his colleagues as a necessary unifying force, and he needed a significant political question which could be resolved through his unique combination of legislative and administrative abilities. Gladstone spent the summer mulling over the issues and consulting his former Cabinet colleagues.

Ahead of an unpredictable election, neither Hartington nor Chamberlain was ready for a leadership challenge and so Gladstone's first condition was easily met. But what of the second? For Gladstone, the answer was obvious. In 1868, when assuming the premiership for the first time, he declared, 'My mission is to pacify Ireland'.[5] Despite all his efforts Ireland remained unpacified. But convincing the party of the need to resolve the Irish Question once and for all was not so easy.

The Irish people had been notably ungrateful for past Liberal efforts,[6] electing Nationalist or Home Rule MPs in place of the Irish Liberals. The behaviour of the Nationalist MPs in the Commons disturbed mainland MPs of all parties and the violent Irish campaigns against landlords outraged the British public. Hartington's younger brother, Lord Frederick Cavendish, had been assassinated in 1882. Parnell, the leader of the Irish Nationalist MPs, was tainted, in British eyes, by his association with rural violence and had been jailed for the provocative speeches that had formed part of those agrarian campaigns.

Events also militated against Gladstone. Earlier in 1885, Chamberlain had proposed a central board, based in Dublin, to take over local government in Ireland, a scheme for which Chamberlain believed he had Parnell's agreement but for which he failed to secure consent from the Cabinet. The unprecedented Conservative attacks on Lord Spencer's administration of Ireland and Salisbury's refusal to renew coercion clearly showed that the Tories were cynically bidding for Irish support in the Commons and the country for their minority administration. Unknown to the Liberal leadership at the time, in July 1885 Parnell had held discussions with Lord Carnarvon, Salisbury's Lord Lieutenant of Ireland, which had led him to believe that Home Rule might be obtained from the Conservatives.[7] Any new Liberal policy for Ireland would therefore need to be an advance on the central board scheme before Parnell would begin to entertain it.

On 16 June, Gladstone circulated a memo on Ireland to colleagues, which was followed by a series of bilateral meetings. At Hartington's insistence, a reluctant Gladstone agreed to a meeting of the Shadow Cabinet. While proposing no new policy, Gladstone was able to convince the other Liberal leaders that, whatever happened in England, the forthcoming election could see a sharp increase in the number of Irish Nationalist MPs and that the combination of policies employed over the previous five years had not resolved the Irish Question. He urged his colleagues not to make any commitments that would inhibit future flexibility.

In this he was not wholly successful. Provoked by a speech of Parnell's which suggested that Home Rule was inevitable, and the only question was how much independence the Irish would be cheated of, Hartington responded on 29 August, describing the Irish demands as 'fatal' and 'mischievous'. 'I am confident there exists no political party', he added, 'which will consent either to acquire or to retain office by conceding the terms by which alone Mr. Parnell says that his alliance can be purchased'.[8] This appeared to rule out his ever accepting Home Rule.

Returning from holiday at the beginning of September, Gladstone sat down to draft his longest-ever election address. Conscious of the risk to his throat, he had planned to rely less on barnstorming speeches in his Midlothian constituency and more on his manifesto. Its references to Ireland were suitably bland and left him plenty of room for manoeuvre:

> ... the wants of Ireland have to be considered as well as her grievances. Down to this hour Ireland has continued greatly in arrear both of England and of Scotland with respect of those powers of local self-government which associate the people in act and feeling with the law, and which lie at the root, as I believe, of political stability, of the harmony of the classes, and of national strength ...

In my opinion, not now for the first time delivered, the limit is clear within which any desires of Ireland, constitutionally ascertained, may, and beyond which they cannot, receive the assent of Parliament. To maintain the supremacy of the Crown, the unity of the Empire, and all the authority of Parliament necessary for the conservation of that unity, is the first duty of every representative of the people. Subject to this governing principle, every grant to portions of the country of enlarged powers for the management of their own affairs is, in my view, not a source of danger, but a means of averting it, and is in the nature of a new guarantee of increased cohesion, happiness, and strength.[9]

However, after receiving a letter from Hugh Childers, Gladstone's recent Chancellor of the Exchequer, stating that he intended to set out his ideas for a Home Rule scheme to his Pontefract constituents, Gladstone decided to set aside his hopes that the Conservatives would take Home Rule out of politics and accept the risk that Parnell would use the election to create a bidding war between the English parties.[10] He needed to prepare the Liberal Party for the challenge ahead. In accordance with his normal working habits, Gladstone conducted substantial research into the history of the union with Ireland and read the best constitutional authorities. Through Mrs O'Shea,[11] he passed a message to Parnell to try and gather a sense of his concrete demands. Although Parnell's perennial elusiveness delayed a response, when it came, at the beginning of November,[12] Gladstone was able to convince himself that Parnell's intentions were practical and constitutional.

He sketched the outline of a measure for a devolved parliament in Dublin which made clear its subordination to the imperial parliament at Westminster and provided safeguards for Ireland's Protestant minority, but otherwise authorised all the functions of a domestic legislature, including responsibility for taxation, the police and the judiciary. In a memorandum sharing his thoughts with a select group of colleagues, he drew heavily on comparisons between Ireland and the self-governing settler colonies such as Canada and Australia.

Their sceptical reaction emphasised the problems he would face when the plan became public. How would it appeal to the new rural English electors? How could he reconcile the fears of British sceptics, some of whom entertained a visceral anti-Irish prejudice and saw Home Rule as a first step to Irish independence, with convincing Parnell's party that the proposals met his ambitions and represented a full settlement of the Irish question? The solution he hit upon was to combine the new Dublin parliament with proposals for elected county government across all parts of the British Isles in a 'Better Government of the United Kingdom Bill'. Separately, he devised a two-part land bill which would give the new counties the power to acquire land for smallholdings and would allow Irish tenants to acquire property from their landlords with the assistance of a government mortgage.

Gladstone began his election campaign with a speech in Edinburgh on 9 November 1885, keeping to the precise but obscure language of which he was a master – later described by his official biographer as 'culpably vague, blind and elusive'.[13] On 22 November, two days before polling began and still relying on his conversations with Carnarvon, Parnell urged Irish voters in English constituencies to vote Conservative. In response, Gladstone's son, Herbert, briefed the London newspapers on his father's true views about Ireland, an episode known as the 'Hawarden Kite'. Gladstone's final speech on 24 November attempted to deny the details of the newspaper reports but in language that only emphasised the truth of their substance.

Three acres and a cow

The result of the elections surprised all the parties. Chamberlain's Radical Programme helped to ensure a favourable outcome for the Liberals in the counties but, in the urban areas, a new psephological phenomenon, the 'Villa Conservative', was discovered. The big winners were Parnell's party, which won 85 out of 103 Irish seats, including a majority in Ulster, and one seat on the mainland. The

Conservatives increased their representation to 250, 40 more than Liberal expectations, while the Liberals were down to 334, just short of a majority and with no remaining representation at all in Ireland.[14]

Herbert Gladstone's Kite had come too late to have much impact on the outcome of the voting, but had a significant impact on what followed. He had furthered his father's aim of limiting the number of Liberals who had taken up an anti-Home Rule position and he had made clear that Gladstone's conversion to Home Rule was in advance of the election, not in response to the outcome. But Herbert had fatally undermined his father's hope that the Conservatives would still introduce a bi-partisan measure for local government in Ireland. While they waited for Parliament to meet, the Liberal leaders anxiously debated Gladstone's paper on local government, with Lord Granville working his usual magic as conciliator and explainer of Gladstone's prose. Gladstone kept himself aloof from these debates but chose this time to show Chamberlain his paper on land reform, as a measure of his intentions to conciliate Radical demands.

Ireland caused divisions in both the main parties. For the Tories, the issue was brought to a head while drafting the Queen's Speech with which their minority government intended to test support in the new parliament. Since Gladstone looked likely to embrace Home Rule, they opposed it, but disagreed about alternative legislative plans to suppress the Parnellite grassroots National League, thereby triggering the resignation of Carnarvon. Salisbury hoped that these new coercion plans would be the focus of the parliamentary debate, associating Liberals with Irish violence. Still seeking to preserve his freedom of action and to avoid confronting Hartington's supporters head on, Gladstone chose instead to defeat the government on an amendment to the Address, asking for Chamberlain's 'three acres and a cow'.[15] This fooled no one at Westminster as to what truly divided the parties and the Liberal forces were depleted by eighteen MPs who voted with the Conservatives, including Hartington and

Goschen. A number of others were missing. The Conservatives resigned immediately and Gladstone set about forming his third government.

Here his preparations paid dividends. Although Hartington, Goschen and some of the Whig lords could not be enticed into the government they were prepared to advise their friends to give the policy a fair trial and to seek to amend the inevitable Better Government bill in committee rather than reject it. Gladstone prevailed upon Hartington to issue a statement on refusing office in which he declared that: 'I am fully convinced that the alternative policy of governing Ireland without large concessions to the national sentiment presents difficulties of a tremendous character'.[16] Radical imperialists such as Chamberlain, while unhappy at the extent of the powers to be conceded to Dublin, accepted that a further round of coercion was intolerable to Liberals and were reluctant to lose the significant reform of county government on the mainland. Gladstone went to considerable trouble to conciliate Chamberlain and secure his left wing if he could not retain the right.

Once confirmed in office, the new Cabinet congregated to settle the details of its proposed Better Government of Great Britain Bill. Gladstone delegated John Morley, his Irish Secretary, to ascertain the points of greatest concern to Irish members. Morley later described Parnell as 'a party chief, not a maker of constitutions'.[17] Parnell had 'given no thought' to the various proposals to protect minority (i.e. Protestant) interests, though a Protestant himself, and Gladstone settled on a group elected by a narrower, property, qualification to perform a role analogous to aldermen in local government. Since the majority of these larger landowners were Protestant rather than Catholic, this increased Protestant representation in the Dublin parliament above what might be expected from the Ulster enclave alone and forced landowners to take a continuing role in politics.

Where Parnell did have strong views was on the proportion of Irish tax revenue to be paid to London for the defence and foreign affairs functions retained by Westminster. This provoked the strongest arguments with Gladstone, whose reputation had been made as Chancellor of the Exchequer. Surprisingly, Parnell requested the presence of both Catholic and Protestant bishops in the 'aldermanic' section of the parliament but sought the prohibition of clergymen standing as members of the Dublin parliament.

Within the Cabinet, the greatest arguments concerned the continued presence of Irish MPs at Westminster, and the choice between delegating specific powers to Dublin or giving the Irish full powers with some reservations. For many, particularly the Whigs, the exclusion of the uncouth and obstructive Irish MPs was the strongest selling point of the bill, but the Irish themselves were anxious to participate in decisions that related to the UK as a whole. For Chamberlain, this was crucial for the preservation of imperial supremacy at Westminster. In the end, the Bill went to the House with a clause which excluded Irish MPs but was open to amendment. The Cabinet also resolved to allow the Irish parliament full authority to legislate on domestic issues, with the exclusion of customs duties (to guard against tariffs on British imports) and any power to create an established religion (to guard against accusations of 'Rome Rule'). Astonishingly little attention was given to the peculiar position of Ulster.

Were these men fit to appoint judges?

Gladstone's speech introducing the legislation in April 1886 is regarded as one of his finest, but the sensation of the debate was created by Parnell.[18] Provoked by Conservative damnation of the whole principle of an Irish legislature in the vituperative speeches of Lord Randolph Churchill and Sir Michael Hicks-Beach, Parnell was roused to reveal the substance of his secret discussions with Carnarvon. Carnarvon was forced to respond in a personal statement in the Lords, and his evident discomfort and the revelation of Salisbury's duplicity was instrumental in resolving the doubts of many of the Whigs.

During the bill's committee stage, Chamberlain's backbench allies proposed amendments to restore Irish representation in the imperial parliament, reduced to reflect the proportion of the Irish electorate to the whole UK. Although the reduction in Irish seats to 85 in a revised House of 652 seats did not go far enough for the most bigoted, it helped consolidate Liberal support for the bill and suited Parnell, who wanted the best qualified Irish MPs to spend their time in Dublin. Gladstone firmly rebuffed Conservative efforts, stirred up by Churchill, to play the Orange card, culpably failing to recognise the significance of the Ulster Protestant enclave and its embattled culture.

The debate on the administration of justice was the focal point of anti-Irish prejudice and reflected the violent agrarian campaigns of the early 1880s. Were the Nationalists fit to appoint judges and protect from revenge the magistrates who had served on the bench during those campaigns? Once again, however, Conservative intransigence turned the debate into a party issue, leading Liberal dissidents to abstain rather than join the Tories in the no lobby. The climax to the committee debates came over the financial clauses, where the Irish threatened to bring the Bill down but where the Tories much preferred Gladstone's insistence on Ireland meeting its full share of imperial expenses. By contrast, the clauses establishing elected county government throughout the country enjoyed cross-party support and went almost undebated.

For the third reading, at the beginning of June 1886, both sides rallied their forces. The scale of any Liberal rebellion would be critical to the passage of the bill through the Lords. Some of the younger Hartingtonian Whigs wished to consolidate a revolt around the issue of Irish representation, but they were unable to gain any support from the other wing of the party. This division minimised the scale of the revolt, and Gladstone's rousing peroration –

> This, if I understand it, is one of the golden moments of our history – one of those opportunities which may come and may go, but which rarely return, or, if they return, return at long intervals, and under

circumstances which no man can forecast ... Ireland stands at your bar expectant, hopeful, almost suppliant. Her words are the words of truth and soberness. (*'Oh, oh' from the Opposition benches.*) She asks for a blessed oblivion of the past, and in that oblivion our interest is deeper than even hers ... She asks also a boon for the future; and that boon for the future, unless we are much mistaken, will be a boon to us in respect of honour no less than a boon to her in respect of happiness, prosperity, and peace. (*Loud and prolonged cheers.*)[19]

— may have changed no minds but it sent the vast majority of Liberals into the lobbies in good heart. The bill was carried by 365 to 260. The minority included 20 Liberals and it is estimated that a further 20 Liberals among the abstainers represented opponents of the bill.

Aristocratic landlords of both sides grabbed the opportunity

The passage of the bill through the Lords was inevitably more difficult, not only because of the inbuilt Tory majority but also because of Whig hostility. Salisbury's opening arguments that such a fundamental constitutional change had not been sufficiently discussed at the election for the result to have reflected the views of the English electorate was supplemented by arguments over protection for the non-Catholic minority and for landlords in particular. After the Carnarvon scandal, Salisbury was unwilling to reject the bill outright but, repeating the tactics he had used with the 1884 Reform Bill, he held up the Better Government Bill until the government brought forward a Land Bill, assuming that the time needed to prepare it would ensure that the bill would be lost when the session expired.

Again, Gladstone's foresight paid off and the Cabinet quickly assembled a bill from the scheme of land reform that Gladstone had discussed with Chamberlain the previous winter. Although the Land Purchase and Small Holdings Bill went against the laissez-faire principles of private property, the proposal to buy out Irish landlords at a 'fair' price in order to release land for peasant farmers was built on legislation introduced by Salisbury's minority administration. Salisbury's bluff had been called. Aristocratic land-lords of both sides grabbed the opportunity to escape from their troubled relationships with their Irish tenants and with some show of discontent the two bills were passed in time to allow an escape from the London summer.

Loosening the tie

The first elections to the new Home Rule Dublin parliament in 1887 confirmed the dominance of Parnell, who won sixty-five of the eighty-five seats up for election. But the campaign was notable for the inter-communal violence that attended Belfast hustings meetings, requiring military intervention. Protestant Ulster opinion divided between those who wished to boycott the new assembly and those who wished to inflict on the Parnellites the obstructionism they had seen in the Commons. However the rules of the Dublin parliament were more tightly drawn than those of the Commons and in due course the Ulster Protestant bloc, adopting the title Unionist, settled for arguing for a return to a better yester-day, in collusion with the Conservative Party on the mainland.

Parnell, unfortunately, bore out John Morley's description of him as a leader rather than an administrator, and while he managed to maintain discipline over his followers, he was less able to give them a sense of direction. He found combining the role of premier in Ire-land with leadership of the Irish party at Westminster particularly stressful. The situation was only resolved when Parnell was named as the co-respondent in the O'Shea divorce case at the end of 1890. Parnell refused to recognise that his position as the Protestant leader of a party which drew its support from a predominantly Catholic electorate was untenable, and his party split acrimoniously into two factions. The larger was led by Justin McCarthy and the smaller by Parnell himself, until his death in 1891 when he was succeeded by John Redmond.

Although the initial split was entirely due to personal differ-ences, in time the two factions came to be aligned with ideological divisions: McCarthy's faction came to be identified with the rural tenant vote while Redmond's faction gained its support mainly from the commercial classes in the towns. This division in the nationalist or Catholic ranks gave opportunities for influence to the Unionists, who found that they frequently held the balance of power.

After Parnell's death, the politics of the Dublin parliament settled into a mundane reality, disappointing the hopes of the hotheads who had seen this local institution as a step towards independence. The success of the land legislation which had accompanied the 1886 Better Government Act created a countryside dominated by small but independent farmers of a conservative bent, who proved a perennial disappointment to republican agitators. Furthermore, the cost of servicing the loans needed to purchase the land from the former English landlords severely restricted the ambitions of the Irish parliament to introduce constructive legislation to solve the problems of the Dublin or Belfast poor.

Nationalist sentiment, however, celebrating the new parliament, also provided the inspiration for a new wave of Irish literature and theatre. This, in turn, inspired a new generation of activists for full freedom for Ireland. Their agitations were supplemented by those of the more extreme socialists, frustrated by the lack of attention given to trade-union ambitions.

Although the police intelligence apparatus of Dublin Castle was reduced after Home Rule and more concentrated on the sporadic unrest in Belfast, it proved more than equal to deal with the activities of the Fenian rebels during the First World War. A rebellion promoted by the Germans among the British prisoners of war of Irish extraction was inevitably betrayed to the Irish authorities. A more serious attempt was made, under the leadership of Pearse, Connolly and De Valera, to seize control of the principal strategic points of Dublin during the Easter holiday weekend of 1916. But the scale of the rebellion was inadequate for the task in hand and it went unsupported by the countryside; the rebel leaders were quickly captured and their men disarmed. Since the rebellion had occurred in the midst of war and its leaders had been clearly financed and armed by the Germans, the Dublin government came under considerable pressure for them to be tried for treason in London. Prime Minister Redmond resisted, however, and the men were held in Kilmainham gaol until the end of the war. In the calmer atmosphere that followed victory, they were sentenced to life imprisonment, with the exception of De Valera who was deported to America. The others were freed at varying times in the 1930s in response to campaigns from expatriate Irishmen living in the US.

The Easter uprising was the last armed attempt to overthrow the Home Rule settlement and Ireland took its place as a modest-growth agricultural economy, until its transformation under the impact of the European Common Agricultural Policy. The two world wars provided a stimulus to the heavy engineering activity centred around Belfast, but this growth of prosperity in Ulster was never enough completely to undermine the rancorous inter-communal rivalry between those of Catholic and Protestant origin. Nevertheless, the most visible sign of it, the July marches organised by the Orange Order, had by the 1960s become less of a focus for local protest than in the first twenty years of Home Rule and more an excuse for display and celebration.

Home Rule had disappointed the nationalists looking for an independent republic but it had also confounded the fears of the Conservatives who had seen it as the first step in the break-up of the United Kingdom and the decline of the British Empire. As Gladstone argued in the main Home Rule debate:

Gentlemen speak of tightening the ties between England and Ireland as if tightening the tie were always the means to be adopted. Tightening the tie is frequently the means of making it burst, whilst relaxing the tie is very frequently the way to provide for its durability, and to enable it to stand a stronger strain (*hear, hear*); so that it is true, as was said by the hon. member for Newcastle, that the separation of Legislatures is often the union of countries, and the union of Legislatures is often the severance of countries.[20]

An unexpected resignation

The passing of the 1886 Better Government Act also transformed mainland politics. Most of his colleagues expected Gladstone to step down at the completion of his Irish mission, but the old warhorse still had the scent of battle in his nostrils. Home Rule for Ireland inspired calls for further federation, devolving power to Scotland and Wales. More immediately, there was a sharp upturn in the campaign to disestablish the Church. But Gladstone's mind was engaged elsewhere – on his old principle of retrenchment, and in particular on the proposed military budget, and the rising cost of the navy. The premier pushed hard for cuts but Lord Ripon and Henry Campbell-Bannerman, the War Office ministers, resisted with somewhat quieter but equal vehemence. Backed into a corner, Gladstone escaped on holiday to the south of France from where a series of increasingly querulous memorandums disturbed the Cabinet. Spared the still-powerful voice and penetrating gaze of the Grand Old Man, the Cabinet braced itself to face him down. Gladstone resigned in February 1888, using his age and health as public excuses. The age of retrenchment had ended.

This unexpected resignation, in strained circumstances, meant that no celebration of Gladstone's retirement, after more than fifty years front-bench service, had been contemplated. As he retained his seat in the Commons, there was always a fear among the Liberal leadership that the dormant volcano might once again erupt. It also meant that the choice of his successor lay in the hands of the Queen.

Victoria sought advice from Lords Salisbury and Rosebery, already a favourite, but not from Gladstone. Salisbury, the Tory leader, mischievously suggested that the monarch should send for the still dissident Lord Hartington, but Rosebery persuaded her that Hartington would now be unacceptable to the mass of the Liberal Party and promoted Lord Spencer in his place. Spencer was an experienced minister, known as the Red Earl, not for his politics but for the colour of his luxuriant beard. While no substitute for

Gladstone as an orator in Parliament or on the platform, he was an efficient co-ordinator and conciliator who could possibly draw back into Liberalism the anti-Home Rule Whigs.

His position as a Liberal premier in the Lords, however, was a weakness needing to be offset by strong leadership in the Commons. The choice lay between John Morley, Sir William Harcourt and Joseph Chamberlain, with Chamberlain the best qualified but most divisive. In the end the choice fell upon Chamberlain, who combined the Leadership of the House with the Colonial Secretaryship, in place of Lord Granville who retired with Gladstone. Rosebery remained at the Foreign Office and Harcourt at the Exchequer.

Inevitably the nature of the Liberal Party began to change, with the younger generation of Chamberlain and Rosebery providing the drive and the initiative. Superficially the prickly, energetic, Nonconformist Birmingham businessman and the temperamental, depressive, horse-racing aristocrat had little in common. But both were enthusiastic exponents of Britain's imperial mission and both were willing to give the government a larger and more constructive role in domestic policy. Neither was hidebound by the traditions of Gladstonian financial orthodoxy.

Liberal progress over the remainder of the Home Rule parliament was modest. The difficulty of agreeing the next big question in Gladstone's absence was compounded by a recovery in nerve by the Tories in the Lords. Further devolution for Wales and Scotland was frustrated by the Conservative majorities in the Upper House and the government withdrew its bill to disestablish the Church of England when the lesser measure to disestablish the church in Wales was amended beyond recognition by their lordships. Nevertheless, a start was made in slum clearance through a Housing of the Working Classes Act in 1890 and, in 1891, primary education was made free, though the funding for it was left undetermined.

Despite the undoubted achievements of the government, the blockage by the Lords created a sense of dissatisfaction among the party's activists and among the enlarged rural electorate. With Lord Spencer adhering to the convention that peers played no part in elections, the Liberal campaign in the 1892 election was inevitably dominated by Chamberlain, and his strident tone created as much hostility as support, resulting in a narrow Tory victory. Deprived of its greatest populist by Lord Randolph Churchill's illness, Lord Salisbury's government concentrated its efforts on foreign rather than domestic policy, with Salisbury seeing any reform as a change for the worse, but equally recognising that he could not turn back the clock on Ireland.

For the Liberals, this was a time for consolidation. The withdrawal from active politics of many of the Whig lords over Home Rule had represented a bitter blow to the party's finances. A more broadly based organisation was required, and Chamberlain oversaw the consolidation of his Birmingham-based National Liberal Federation with the Liberal Central Association (the party's electoral headquarters controlled by the Chief Whip), bringing in Francis Schnadhorst to mastermind the new organisation. Spencer regularly addressed the annual meeting of the Federation which came to function as the conference of the whole party.

It was at the annual conference of the Federation in 1895 that Chamberlain articulated the second of his radical manifestos, encapsulating the New Liberalism. While this included elements from the old programme such as disestablishment of the Church, the payment of MPs and reforms to 'end or mend' the House of Lords, it was the new elements that were central. Chamberlain proposed a new role for the state, not as a controlling element preventing interference in the freedom of the individual but as a constructive enabler of the weaker elements in society, allowing them to undertake a fuller life. Principal elements of the new policy included measures to provide an old age pension, to be funded from graduated income tax, a system of labour exchanges to be run by local councils and measures to provide compensation for workers injured in industrial accidents, to be funded by a compulsory insurance scheme. Chamberlain also proposed a vision of closer economic co-operation among Britain's colonies using Rosebery's description of the Empire as a 'Commonwealth of Nations', and for closer co-operation between Britain and Germany. The Liberals had a new ideology fit for the new century.

Reality check

In reality, Gladstone failed to carry Home Rule in 1886, as ninety-three Liberals voted against the second reading of the 1886 Home Rule Bill, the greater part of them identifiable as followers of Hartington but including Chamberlain and around twenty of his supporters. After the 1892 election Gladstone succeeded in piloting another Home Rule Bill through the Commons, but it foundered in the Lords. It was left to the Conservatives to introduce elected county government, in 1888 and 1889.

Although evidence suggests that Gladstone was convinced of the need for Home Rule ahead of the 1885 election, his hope that the Conservatives would rise to the challenge and make it a non-partisan issue meant that he had not prepared the party for what appeared to be a cynical reaction to a hung parliament. Gladstone did not accede to Hartington's request for an early meeting of the Shadow Cabinet, the Hawarden Kite was not flown until after the election and even when forming his government, in January 1886, Gladstone would not admit to any commitment to a Home Rule Bill. My hypothesis has been that earlier education of the party and greater flexibility would have reduced the scale of the rebellion.

The meetings between Carnarvon and Parnell did take place but those generous to Salisbury would argue that Carnarvon went beyond his brief. Salisbury persuaded Carnarvon not to disclose his resignation earlier. Parnell's disclosure of the meeting with Carnarvon, and Carnarvon's statement in the Lords, came too late to have any impact on the voting intentions of MPs. It is implausible that a pure Home Rule Bill would have passed the Lords. My combined Home Rule/county government bill and my land purchase/smallholdings bill are implausible specimens of parliamentary draughtsmanship but are designed to circumvent some of the failings of the real bills, which offered nothing to the mainland voter or MP beyond the prospect of relief from Irish obstruction.

Gladstone did resign in protest against rising military expenditure, though in 1894, not in 1888 – though Randolph Churchill resigned the Exchequer on similar grounds at the end of 1886. Spencer would have been Gladstone's nomination for Prime Minister if the Queen had asked him. She didn't.

Hartington and Chamberlain eventually joined Salisbury's government. Chamberlain became Colonial Secretary and was an early advocate of old age pensions, though he thought pensions could be funded by taxes on imports from which the colonies would be exempted through 'imperial preference'.

When, in 1922, Ireland was given the dominion status that led in due course to full independence, it was partitioned, and Ulster, the part of Ireland that least supported the concept, became the only province to experience Home Rule. The partition of Ireland led to a civil war within the new dominion which shaped Irish politics until the end of the twentieth century, and saw continued bloody efforts by militant nationalists to 'free' Ulster from British rule. Ulster's Protestant leadership still clings to the union with Great Britain with an intransigence that Lord Salisbury and Lord Randolph Churchill would have admired.

Further reading

For those interested in what did happen:

- A. B. Cooke & John Vincent, *The Governing Passion* (Harvester Press, 1974)
- F. S. L. Lyons, *Charles Stewart Parnell* (Gill & Macmillan; paperback edition, 2005)
- Peter Marsh, *Joseph Chamberlain: Entrepreneur in Politics* (Yale University Press, 1994)
- H. C. G. Matthew, *Gladstone 1809–1898* (Oxford University Press; paperback edition, 1997)
- Alan O'Day, *Irish Home Rule 1867–1921* (Manchester University Press, 1998)
- Andrew Roberts, *Salisbury: Victorian Titan* (Phoenix; paperback edition, 2000)

Notes

1   W. E. Gladstone, speech to the House of Commons, 7 June 1886.
2   W. E. Gladstone, letter to his wife, 12 October 1845, quoted in Philip Magnus, *Gladstone* (John Murray, 1963), p. 45.
3   Lord Beaconsfield was the title embraced by Benjamin Disraeli when elevated to the Lords in 1878.
4   Hartington had led the party between 1874 and 1880, jointly with Lord Granville, Liberal leader in the lords, when Gladstone was at least nominally in retirement.
5   John Morley, *The Life of William Ewart Gladstone* (Macmillan, 1903), vol. 2, p. 252.
6   Principally, disestablishment of the Church of Ireland, education reform, land reform.
7   For details of Carnarvon's meeting with Parnell, see Andrew Roberts, *Salisbury: Victorian Titan* (Phoenix, 2000), pp. 348–51.
8   Bernard Holland, *The Life of the Duke of Devonshire* (Longmans Green & Co, 1911), vol. 2, pp. 67–68.
9   From *The Times*, 19 September 1885.
10 Morley, *The Life of William Ewart Gladstone*, vol. 3, p. 235.
11 Mrs O'Shea was of a Whig family and the wife of a Home Rule MP. She was also Parnell's mistress, though it is unclear whether Gladstone was aware of this.
12 Printed in Alan O'Day, *Irish Home Rule 1867–1921* (Manchester University Press, 1998), pp. 317–18.
13 Morley, *The Life of William Ewart Gladstone*, vol. 3, p. 244.
14 C. Cook & B. Keith, *British Historical Facts 1830–1900* (St Martins Press, 1975), p. 141. For Liberal expectations see Morley, *The Life of William Ewart Gladstone* vol. 3, pp. 246, 249–55.
15 A proposal to allow local authorities compulsory powers to acquire land to create smallholdings for agricultural workers.
16 Morley, *The Life of William Ewart Gladstone*, vol. 3, p. 292–93. An unpublished quote from Hartington pressed by Gladstone on the Queen.
17 Ibid., vol. 3, p. 305.
18 The text of Gladstone's speech may be found in A. Tilney Basset, *Gladstone's Speeches* (Methuen, 1916), pp. 601–44.
19 The quotation is from Gladstone's speech, winding up the second reading debate on 7 June 1886; D. Brack & T. Little, *Great Liberal Speeches* (Politico's Publishing, 2001), pp. 194–95.
20 W. E. Gladstone, speech in the House of Commons, 7 June 1886.

Chapter 5

'A serpent in the bosom': What if the 1903 Gladstone–MacDonald Pact had never happened?

Robert Waller

I The 1903 Pact

In 1903 the Liberal Chief Whip Herbert Gladstone (the fourth son of the former Prime Minister William Ewart), and Ramsay MacDonald, the Secretary of the Labour Representation Committee (renamed the Labour Party in 1906) concluded a secret agreement at Leicester Isolation Hospital.[1] The two parties entered into an arrangement whereby in a number of key constituencies each would withdraw candidates in favour of the other in order to avoid splitting the anti-Conservative vote. At the time there were still a number of two-member seats in large towns, and in some of these LRC and Liberal candidates would run effectively in harness, in a form of electoral alliance.

There seemed to be good prima facie reasons for both parties for such cooperation. In 1903 the Liberals had been out of office for all but three years (1892–95) since 1885. The infant LRC had only been in existence since 1900, when it had won just two seats in the general election of that year. There were grounds for thinking that its new strand of 'labourist' appeal, and its working-class candidates, might be able to attract relatively newly enfranchised voters who otherwise might prefer the Conservatives (known as Unionists at the time) or might abstain. There was already evidence

67

that three-cornered contests resulted in a damaging division of the anti-Tory vote which had cost the Liberals seats.

The advantages to a party that had not yet established itself were clear. However, did the Liberals nurture at this crucial point a potential rival, which was to supplant them as the chief alternative to the Conservatives just twenty years later? The prominent northern Liberal, Samuel Storey, Chairman of the Executive of the National Liberal Federation, argued forcefully against such pacts following his resignation on 2 July 1903: 'The effect of surrendering to this new policy will be the destruction of organised liberalism ... nursing into life a serpent which will sting their party to death'.[2]

What would have happened if Gladstone and MacDonald had not semi-formalised the 'Progressive Alliance' in 1903? Would Labour still have survived, progressed, and replaced the Liberals as a governing party and the principal opponents of the Conservatives over the next hundred years? Or might they have been strangled in infancy, leading to an entirely different pattern of political competition and to an alternative chain of events? To some extent this judgment will link to the well-known debate about the reasons for the decline of the Liberal Party in the first quarter of the twentieth century – whether this was predominantly due to the rise of Labour and 'class politics' or to more contingent events, including the split between Asquith and Lloyd George in the First World War. However, as with any 'what if', we may also indulge in more subjective speculation about a very different course of history, one in which the Labour Party did not become a viable separate party and the Liberals prospered, albeit as a 'social democratic' force, for many decades.

~

If we commence with the genesis of the 1903 pact, it will be seen that the foundation of the LRC/Labour Party did present such a serious and fresh challenge to the Liberals that a response was required from their leadership. The Liberal Party had long thought of itself as the party in which working-class voters should feel themselves at home. Not only had this been reflected in the radical Newcastle Programme of 1891, with its acceptance of land reform and disestablishment,[3] but in the adoption of working-class Lib–Lab candidates since 1874, when the miner Thomas Burt was first elected at Morpeth. Between 1885 and 1900 there had been between nine and eleven Lib–Lab MPs.[4] However, there seemed no prospect of these numbers increasing to counter the impression that the Liberals were overwhelmingly led by the middle and upper classes. Local party associations were looking for people who could contribute to the costs of campaigns, and apart from those sponsored by the MFGB miners' union, working-class candidates had no such financial resources. By 1903 there was only one Lib–Lab MP outside the mining areas, Henry Broadhurst in Leicester. There were no Lib–Labs in Scotland, and only one in Wales – the very areas where Labour and socialist candidates made their earliest breakthroughs.

The foundation of the LRC in 1900 was an alarming sign of discontent with the Liberals among the working-class movement. As the historian Bernstein put it, 'a concerted challenge by the LRC could be a disaster for the Liberals. By splitting the working-class vote, it would allow normally safe seats to fall to the Unionists, as the second Leicester seat did in 1900'.[5] The view that Labour had definable interests which were opposed to capital challenged the Liberal belief that both should promote the interests of society as a whole, rather than any one section, thereby precluding the need for a separate working-class party.

However, even at this earliest stage the pressure exerted by the creation of the LRC had its effects. In 1900 the Liberals did not put up a candidate against them in the working-class stronghold of South West Manchester, and Herbert Gladstone persuaded the local association that only one of the parties should stand, leaving a free run at Derby for the LRC's Richard Bell, general secretary of the Amalgamated Society of Railway Servants. In speeches at Leeds in October 1901 and Bristol in May 1902 Gladstone expressed the desire to make an arrangement with the LRC. He was supported by two of the most influential organs of advanced Liberalism, the *Daily News* and the *Manchester Guardian*,[6] and by more senior figures in the party. The party leader, Henry Campbell-Bannerman, was favourably disposed to demands for more working-class representation in Parliament,[7] as he made clear, for example, in a speech on 2 January 1903: 'We are in sympathy with the representation of Labour. We have too few of them in the House of Commons.'[8] The leader may ostensibly have been calling for more working-class Liberal candidates, but he would certainly have known of the intentions of Gladstone and others in the central party organisation to make informal links with the LRC.

In the October 1902 Clitheroe by-election, the local Liberal association very reluctantly made way to allow a victory for David Shackleton. By early 1903, LRC membership had grown to 800,000, nearly double that of June 1901. From February 1903, an LRC parliamentary fund, supported by leading unions, had been created. It was time for a more permanent and more national agreement.

On 6 March 1903 James Herbert, who was responsible for candidates at the Liberal Central Association, first met Ramsay MacDonald to discuss an arrangement for the next general election.[9] The LRC insisted on complete independence for their candidates participating in any pact – this was to be solely an electoral alliance. As an added threat, they raised the spectre of campaigning against Liberals even if there was no labour candidate in the field. The prospect of losing borough seats and county divisions in Lancashire and Yorkshire was a negative stimulus for the Liberal negotiators, but they also believed that a pact might save them £15,000 and would help them to win the next election by siphoning working-class votes from the Conservatives and establishing themselves as the major party more clearly favourable to the interests and issues of working men.

Before the pact was finalised, there were two key by-elections which added more evidence for its desirability. At Woolwich, in east London, later in March, no Liberal candidate stood and several MPs spoke in favour of the LRC's Will Crooks; *The Daily News* even collected £844. Crooks gained the seat from the Unionist and the contest was seen as a model of cooperation. On the other hand, the local Liberals would not withdraw their opposition to Arthur Henderson at Barnard Castle in County Durham in July 1903, and finished a poor third. This was seen as a stark lesson of the dangers of failing to accommodate Labour in its strong locations.[10] On 27 July 1903 the *Leicester Daily Post* demanded 'some sort of understanding in order to prevent a waste of forces', though the divisions within the party were shown by their rival local newspaper, the *Mercury*; 'The Liberals have to show the LRC they cannot be butted out of the way and treated as of no account',[11] However, despite such local objections, on 6 September 1903 Gladstone and MacDonald formalised the arrangements broached in March. There was to be an electoral pact.

~

The implementation of the 'alliance' in the general election of January/February 1906 was patchy. There was still widespread local opposition among Liberal associations. In Scotland the pact did not operate at all. In the north-east of England nineteen out of twenty-three presidents of constituency organisations were opposed.[12] In the West Riding of Yorkshire, where the Liberal Party was still largely in the grip of wealthy industrialists, 'progressivism' was weaker; even in Herbert Gladstone's own city, in East Leeds, a candidate was found to oppose the LRC's James O'Grady. (This was also a result of the LRC's inroads into Liberal wards on the council, having risen from one to seven councillors between 1903 and 1905.[13])

However, overall the 1906 election proved very fruitful, at least for the young LRC. Of their twenty-nine MPs, twenty-four were elected in straight fights with the Unionists or in harness with the Liberals in two-member constituencies. The Liberals too had reason to be pleased with the outcome. Of course they won a landslide victory across the country, but there was evidence that the electoral pact may have helped. In London, for example, the two parties won thirty-nine seats between them (only three of these allotted to the LRC), sixteen of which had not been taken since 1886 and another fifteen not since 1892. In the crucial 'swing' Lancashire and Cheshire section of the North West of England, the LRC took thirteen and the Liberals forty-one of the seventy constituency seats. Moreover, in the areas where there had been no effective pact, in twenty-five Liberal–LRC contests and in thirteen between Liberals and independent socialists, the Unionists won seven and two seats respectively on a minority vote. There were now fifty-five working-class MPs – including thirteen Liberal miners and twelve Lib-Labs who were not miners.[14]

Nevertheless, the question arises as to whether this substantial boost for what became the Labour Party after the 1906 election was in the long-term interests of the Liberal Party. After all, they did not need it to win that election. They won 400 seats altogether, to the Unionists' 157; they would clearly have won a landslide regardless of the pact. Claims that the labour movement controlled one million extra votes were grossly exaggerated.[15]

The pact appeared in 1906 to be of one-sided benefit, giving a helping hand to a potential rival. Many working men would have swung to the Liberals anyway, given the issues which decided the election. These were not so much the radical, or 'New Liberal', social reforms which were to be introduced by the Liberal government after 1908, such as old age pensions and the National Insurance Act of 1911, for these were scarcely mentioned in 1906 – in fact future policy on these issues was confined to a mere two paragraphs of Campbell-Bannerman's election address which served as a manifesto.[16] It was, rather, Joseph Chamberlain's proposals for tariff reform, with its threat of food taxes and the 'little loaf', which swung working-class votes decisively behind the traditional Liberal principle of free trade, and the 1902 Education Act, with its 'church schools on the rates', which had irritated the powerful Nonconformist voting bloc of whatever class.

The continued operation of mutual withdrawal of candidates might have made a more significant apparent difference to the numbers of MPs elected in the two 1910 general elections: in

January, the Liberals won 275 seats, only two more than the Unionists, while in December 1910 the two parties were tied with 272 MPs each. Nevertheless, the outcome of these elections would still have been a hung parliament, with the eighty-strong Irish Nationalist contingent holding the balance of power – which would still have enabled them to use this leverage to press Asquith into introducing the controversial third Irish Home Rule Bill in 1912.

Indeed, one profoundly negative effect of the pact may have been further to discourage the adoption of working-class Liberal candidates, a feature which was identified by the historian G. R. Searle as a crucial mistake contributing to the party's 'disintegration' as a party of government: 'though they were willing to reformulate their programme in order to accommodate the new welfare issues, the Liberals could not bring themselves to make any very great effort to place significant numbers of working-class candidates in winnable seats'.[17] It may have been believed by the party's leaders that the notion of Lib-Labism had been superseded by the sustenance of the Gladstone–MacDonald Pact.

Whatever the short- and medium-term benefits and disadvantages of the pact, though, it is possible that there would have been no profound effect in the long term if it had never taken place. The first of our two explorations of the counterfactual presents this argument, in the context of the inevitable overtaking of the Liberals by Labour, either as a result of the inexorable impact of class politics as the predominant cleavage in voting or as the outcome of the First World War proving to be the runaway 'omnibus' which had unexpectedly crushed the previously healthy party, as suggested in Trevor Wilson's famous metaphor.[18]

II Inevitability: Labour's rise and the fall of the Liberals

Even if Labour had not been granted a smoother path to establishing itself as a parliamentary party through the existence of the 1903 Gladstone–MacDonald pact, its rise may still have take place in any case.

In the latter part of the nineteenth century, the most important single cleavage which determined voting patterns was not that of class but of religion, with Nonconformists such as Methodists, Baptist and Congregationalist chapelgoers forming the bedrock of Liberal support, while Anglican churchgoers were strongly associated with the Conservative Party. However, over the turn of the century, this cleavage was gradually replaced by the divide between the working and middle classes.[19] This was a result of long-term social and economic changes such as industrialisation, urbanisation and secularisation, uniting Britain geographically but exacerbating 'vertical' social divisions.[20] More specifically, Edwardian England saw the rise of 'an acutely developed working-class consciousness',[21] associated with the rapid rise of the industrial wing of the organised labour movement, the trade unions, who rose rapidly to a membership of two and a half million in 1910 and four million in 1914. 'There was a growing feeling that the Liberal Party was no longer the party of the working classes, but in some perceived if undefinable way the Labour Party was'.[22]

Meanwhile, as Edwin Montagu had observed to Asquith after the 1906 election, 'there is no getting away from the fact that ours is a Nonconformist party with Nonconformist susceptibilities and Nonconformist prejudices'.[23] In that election, Stephen Koss calculated that there were 191 Liberal Nonconformist candidates, 157 of whom were elected, compared with just 9 Nonconformists among the Unionists, six of whom became MPs. After December 1910 there were 107 Nonconformists in the parliamentary Liberal Party, 20 among the Labour ranks, and 7 Unionists.[24]

If the basis of voting was changing from religion to class, then the appeal of a party would be based on its class rather than its chapel credentials. Whether the Gladstone–MacDonald pact had been made and sustained or not, this would have left the Liberals in a weaker position. As G. L. Bernstein put it, 'if ... the transition to class politics were to proceed to the point where labour saw capital as its principal enemy, then liberalism would have little to offer the workers. Liberalism was an ideology based on the harmony of capital and labour'.[25] The LRC and then the Labour Party, from 1906, by contrast, was clearly a party 'of and for the working class',[26] a party created by the burgeoning trade union movement, as its very name implied. It is hard to imagine that the Liberals, with their middle-class leadership, would ever have been able to satisfy a demand for a separate working-class organisation, working closely with the industrial wing of the labour movement, still less to encompass the ideological socialism which played an important, though not dominant, role within the Labour Party – despite the Liberals' espousal of relatively socially radical policies after 1908. The last major union to affiliate to the Labour Party was the Miners' Federation of Great Britain, in January 1909.[27] There had only been limited operation of the Gladstone–MacDonald pact on the coalfields, in Durham for example, and the Lib-Lab miners' MPs transferred more or less en bloc to the newer, working-class party.

The Liberal government would still have been embarrassed by the massive industrial unrest of the immediate pre-war years. Without an electoral pact, the Labour Party would have survived and filled a new demand as long as the Liberals remained overwhelmingly middle class themselves: 'it should come as no surprise that the Liberals were out of touch with the class aspirations of workers. Both in Parliament and in the constituencies, the Liberals were a party of the middle class.'[28] Indeed, they were the party of not only the middle class, but in many parts of the country the industrial employers. In 1914 there were 105 businessmen on the Liberal benches in the House of Commons and only eight manual workers.[29]

A survey of Liberal MPs after 1906 reveals that safe seats were often dominated by long-established industrial interests. In Yorkshire, for example, were to be found Sir James Kitson in Colne Valley, Alfred Illingworth in Bradford, and the textile magnate Alfred Hutton in Morley; the industrial dynasty of the Pease family spread across North Yorkshire to County Durham; Charles Palmer MP employed 15,000 men in Jarrow on the Tyne;[30] there were also the Brunner-Monds in Cheshire, where the Northwich constituency was handed from father to son in January 1910.[31] And this is not to mention the non-industrial family networks which crop up so prominently in the higher reaches of the Liberal Party – the Churchills, Harcourts, Aclands, Buxtons, Trevelyans, and the Gladstones themselves.

The roots of left-wing Liberalism were less deep than some suppose. Sir James Joicey of Durham opposed workmen's compensation as 'socialistic' and voted against the miners' eight-hour working day bill in 1901.[32] In Scotland and Wales, there were almost no social radicals or 'New Liberals', committed to a greater role for state intervention in welfare and the economy. As Kenneth O. Morgan concluded in his assessment of the pre-First World War Welsh Liberal Party, 'the new liberalism barely existed'.[33] The Nonconformist churches in Wales were 'conspicuously silent on social issues' up to 1914.[34] 'In fact, Welsh Nonconformist Liberals made few concessions to working-class demands in the period up to 1914, both in terms of programmes and personnel'.[35] There was increasing friction over the adoption of 'labour' candidates in traditional Liberal constituencies. For example, in Mid Glamorgan in March 1910 the local party would not give a free run to Labour's Vernon Hartshorn despite pressure from the Liberal Chief Whip, the Master of Elibank. Hartshorn ascribed this subsequent defeat to 'chapel influence' – and this even in the land of Lloyd George!

For Wales, Morgan's assessment suggests that the future of the Liberal Party in an age of class politics was indeed cloudy; he suggests that local parties were perhaps even narrower in social composition in the 1900s than they had been twenty years earlier, as the power of organised labour had developed.[36] However, if the Liberal Party was not becoming more working class itself, perhaps it might not have needed to, if it had moved to the left to accommodate – or even lead – demands for more social radicalism and state intervention. In short, could the Liberals have become the party of the left, if not of the working class? Stymied by the lesser progress the early LRC and Labour Party would have made if the Gladstone–MacDonald pact had never taken place, might these have fallen away in the face of the New Liberalism?

Within this 'inevitable', or from the Liberal point of view pessimistic, interpretation of the counterfactual, the Liberal Party's commitment to a more radical approach would not have been sufficient to stave off the Labour challenge. New Liberalism was not wholly accepted within the Liberal Party; indeed, it created tensions with more traditional elements. While the move to the left alienated conservatives, the transformation of the Liberal Party did not go far enough to eliminate the need for a working-class/trade-union/socialist political force. In short, the Liberals 'fell between two stools'. They were neither Conservative nor socialist nor – more relevantly, perhaps – working class. All this would have been true even without the Gladstone–MacDonald pact ever having been concluded in 1903 – so it was, ultimately, irrelevant to the decline of the Liberals as a party of government.

As H. V. Emy put it, the strains caused by New Liberalism or social radicalism meant that 'the party was unable to accommodate itself to becoming a party of the left or of the right ... paradoxically, perhaps, what we have is a picture of a party whose political achievements are at least a partial cause of its own long-term decline'.[37] The changes in the party's policy made possible social reforms, from old age pensions in 1909 to the National Insurance unemployment and sickness benefits of 1911, associated with the radicalism of the 'People's Budget' of 1909 followed by the constitutional crisis and the Parliament Act reducing the power of the House of Lords in 1911. However, this broader ethical commitment to government intervention and planned social change 'caused frictions, which had serious consequences for the ability of the party to function as an effective electoral organisation, offended traditional manufacturing interests, and polarised the party's own supporters'.[38]

Nor did radicalism keep Labour at bay. Pelling asserted that the National Insurance Act (itself not the most generous of measures, with its limited application, short periods of relief, and low remuneration rates) was not popular with the workers it was intended to help: 'this hostility derived from working-class attitudes of suspicion or dislike towards existing institutions which were the expressions of national social policy'.[39] Two referendums of electors at Walsall and Rutland in 1911 showed large hostile majorities.[40] Even Lloyd George admitted that National Insurance was unpopular with workers for some time after its enactment.[41]

McKibbin believed that the electoral pact was already breaking down before the war, between 1910 and 1914, with three-cornered contests in by-elections demonstrating that Labour was no longer prepared to be a junior partner in a Progressive Alliance. What is more, hostilities were widespread in municipal politics well before 1914. Local Liberals – always a bugbear to the smooth and full operation of the Gladstone–MacDonald pact, and who would surely have been more combative still if it had never existed – were becoming more hostile to cooperation. Even with a pact it looked likely that there would be a serious challenge to the alliance in the next election, due in 1915. Even with the holding out of the helping hand of 1903, hostilities were about to be joined in more senses than one.

The Liberal Party failed to carry out the delicate balancing trick of satisfying working-class demands by adopting new policies while holding on to their middle-class backing on more traditional issues.[42] By 1914, pact or no pact, 'if class politics were coming, so was the decline of the Liberal Party – not imminently, perhaps, but eventually and inevitably'.[43] Paul Thompson, in *Socialists, Liberals and Labour*, concurred that the Liberals were in a cleft stick: 'Once Labour was separately organised, creating its own loyalties and interests, the ultimate outlook for Liberalism was bleak. The Liberals must either challenge Labour, thus alienating working-class support, or help the growth of Labour as an ally, fostering the cuckoo in the nest. They chose the second course ... in the long run fatal.'[44]

III If the cuckoo had been ejected from the nest ...

However, there are alternative interpretations, and hence a different course of history can be constructed. Perhaps if the Gladstone–MacDonald pact had never been concluded, the infant Labour Party would have been strangled, and the Liberals would have taken advantage of the situation to garner the lion's share of working-class votes – even in an era of class politics, and even given the extension of the franchise to voters of whatever class in the Fourth Reform Act of 1918.

This possibility rests strongly on the arguments of historians such as P. F. Clarke, who believe that 'class had already clearly emerged as the bedrock of voter alignments in the pre-war period, yet at this stage the Liberals had been able to benefit from the process'.[45] By adopting the ideology of social radicalism or 'New Liberalism' after 1906, and particularly after Asquith became Prime Minister, with Lloyd George and Churchill as prominent reformers, in 1908, the Liberal government commenced the construction of a 'social democratic' programme which attracted working-class support and offered a way to survive and prosper in twentieth-century politics. 'The development of a coherent ideology which lay behind the 1910 elections gave the progressives a cutting edge. Insofar as election issues turned increasingly on economic and social questions this was meat and drink to the new Liberals.'[46] This confused old Liberals, surely, but baffled the Conservatives and outflanked Labour. 'At the beginning of the second decade of the twentieth century it looked as though Labour and Liberals would be subsumed in progressivism. It seemed that social democracy in England was bound up with the prospects of the Liberal Party.'[47]

In the 1910 elections it seemed to be the Liberals who were the party cornering working-class support. There was indeed a polarisation on class lines, but they were the chief beneficiaries. Due to the government's veering towards unprecedented 'social democratic' state intervention, Labour candidates now found it hard to carve out a clear role for themselves. The Labour Party failed to develop a distinct and practicable programme of their own, clearly distinguishable from the policies and promises of the Asquith–Lloyd George government. As the historian of the 1910 elections, Neal Blewett, pointed out, Labour literature endeavored to sound as if *they* had been in office for the previous four years.[48]

In January 1910, of the forty Labour MPs elected, thirty won in straight fights against the Unionists when no Liberal was put forward, and the other ten were elected in double-member seats in harness with a Liberal.[49] With the vast majority of Labour's forty and forty-two seats in January and December 1910 won as a result of clear runs under the pact, and given the party's poor performance in by-elections between 1911 and 1914, finishing bottom of the poll with under 30 per cent of the vote in all eleven they contested, and losing four seats, including Hanley (July 1912) and Chesterfield (August 1913) to the Liberals,[50] there was little sign before the First World War that Labour would soon supplant the Liberals as the chief opponents of the Conservatives.

Even after the end of the Gladstone–MacDonald pact in 1911, as Poirier pointed out, 'the mutual dependence of Liberal and Labour facilitated the passage of far-reaching social reform measures prior to 1914 … the foundation of a single Progressive party composed of former Liberals and Labourites was a distinct possibility'.[51] Right up to the outbreak of war, Labour MPs usually voted with the government. The difficulties caused by the Liberals' continuing occupation of the radical ground were recognised at the time. In January 1914 *The Nation* declared that 'the reason why the Labor [sic] party has been able to make so little of a fight against Liberalism has been that Liberalism has gone so far in the direction of a Labor party'.[52] Three months later, in April, Philip Snowden himself adopted a metaphor from chess in *Labour Leader*: 'Labour has been checkmated by Lloyd Georgism'.[53] In Samuel Beer's interpretation, 'so long as Labour's purposes were simply those of trade-union politics, formed in the broad terms of Radical ideology, the independence of the party was still seriously in doubt. Indeed there remained the real possibility that it might become simply a wing of a more socialistic, though not Socialist, Liberal Party'.[54] P. F. Clarke agreed: 'It seemed that social democracy in England was bound up with the prospects of the Liberal Party'.[55]

As Richard Grayson has perceptively observed, the Liberal Party of the twentieth century – and indeed the Liberal Democrats in the present century – owe much to a tradition of social democracy: 'in looking for the roots of party policy, Liberal Democrats should recognise the importance of social democratic thinking'.[56] Grayson traces a tradition of government intervention in the cause of social justice back through time beyond the merger and alliance with the Social Democratic Party in the 1980s, and the political philosophy expounded in Anthony Crosland's perhaps misleadingly titled classic *The Future of Socialism*, published in 1956, to the great reforming governments of Attlee between 1945 and 1951, and of Asquith and Lloyd George from 1908. Collective strategies could be used to enhance individual freedom, happiness and cultural endeavour.[57] The values of liberty, equality and opportunity are 'inextricably linked together'.[58] Keynes and Beveridge, archetypes of the economic and welfare policies associated with subsequent Labour administrations, were both Liberals. It would seem that there is no insuperable theoretical bar to the idea that the Liberals could have developed as a party by building on and developing the elements of social democracy in the 1908–14 government and in the values of New Liberalism, thus incorporating much of the appeal and indeed the support of the Labour Party – if it had not been for the specific and contingent circumstances which altered this potential course of history.

This is strong evidence that it was the events of the First World War and its immediate aftermath that brought down the Liberals. Historians may differ about the prospects of the Liberal Party on the eve of the Great War, but they were in office, and had been for nearly nine years. By the end of 1918 the picture was very different. In December 1916, the two leaders of the radical pre-war government, Asquith and Lloyd George, split over the latter's bid for power in the shape of a compact and powerful 'War Committee' which would form an inner Cabinet dedicated to directing the war under his own leadership.[59] This rift extended from the largely personal divorce between Asquith and Lloyd George to create a schism in the House of Commons in the Maurice debate of July 1918, when Asquith challenged a vital element in the handling of a critical stage in the war, the issue of troop reinforcements in France prior to the German spring offensive. Ninety-eight Liberal MPs, including tellers, voted against Lloyd George on this motion, seventy-one with the government, and eighty-five abstained or were absent. Essentially less than a third of Liberal MPs defended the Liberal Prime Minister against General Maurice's accusation that he had been lying about the disposition of troops on the front line.[60] Two separate Liberal organisations emerged at Westminster, each with their own whips.

Perhaps most damaging of all was the extension of the party split to the constituencies when Lloyd George decided to offer the maintenance of the wartime coalition in the 'coupon' election of December 1918.[61] One hundred and fifty-nine Liberals accepted the endorsement of a 'letter of approval' jointly signed by Lloyd George and Bonar Law, 133 of whom were returned; but 258 Liberal candidates followed Asquith in rejecting the 'coupon', and only 37 of these were elected. Lloyd George achieved his aim of remaining in 10 Downing Street, but in his post-war coalition Liberal MPs were outnumbered by 200 by the Conservatives. This dependence on Conservative support led, after a diplomatic crisis which nearly produced war with Turkey, to the Conservative backbenchers' revolt at the Carlton Club meeting of 19 October 1922, and the final destruction of the last government led by a Liberal (to date). Lloyd George Liberals and 'Squiffites' remained essentially estranged even after the collapse of the coalition.[62]

The events of the First World War and the continuation of the split in the wartime coalition was undoubtedly a crippling blow to the Liberals. Even so, the party might not have declined so dramatically if Lloyd George had backed the report of the Speaker's Conference in 1917 in favour of proportional representation for Westminster elections.[63] Either full proportional representation (PR) or the alternative or preferential vote in single-member constituencies (AV) would have helped the Liberals considerably, and not just in the short term; for under AV Liberal candidates would probably have been the second choice of both Conservative and Labour voters, while full PR would have ensured that the party maintained a solid bloc of MPs which could at the very least have held the balance of power in almost every election after 1918. Only in 1935, in all the elections of the twentieth century, did a single party gain more than 50 per cent of the vote, even under the first-past-the-post system. What is more, a full PR system such as the single transferable vote (STV) would have allowed effective transfers between members of the same party even if split on political, personal or organisational grounds, as the Liberals were in the critical period after 1916.

Moreover, some historians believe that the Liberals might still have been able to recapture the status of a governing party if the leadership had not decided, first to put Labour into office in 1923, and then to remove them under pressure from the right wing of the party, including influential organs of opinion like the *Daily Record* in Scotland, less than a year later.[64] Failures of leadership and continued divisions, allied with the effects of the first-past-the-post system, meant that the Liberal decline was confirmed and accelerated in the 1920s, as Labour established itself as a feasible, if not yet effective, governing party, as well as the chief opposition to the Conservatives.

Under these interpretations, the decline of the Liberals was in no way inevitable. It was not determined by the inevitable rise of class politics and consequently of the Labour Party. Even in the 1923 election, after which Ramsay MacDonald became the first Labour Prime Minister, the Liberals polled a total of 4,311,147 votes to Labour's 4,438,508. As late as 1929, when Labour formed its second government, the Liberals achieved their largest number of votes to that date – over five and a quarter million. This was on the widest franchise yet, confirming that Liberalism was far from dead; and how might it have progressed had it not been for 'Wilson's omnibus', the First World War, and the response of the two main party leaders to the challenges posed therein and thereafter?

Indeed, it is possible that had history taken a different course at an even earlier date, had it not been for the 1903 pact, Labour would never have risen to pose the challenge that it did – though what follows must of course be regarded as speculative and subjective.

IV A fantasy: a 'social democratic' counterfactual

If Herbert Gladstone and Ramsay MacDonald had not met at the isolation hospital, if the predominantly local diehards opposed to cooperation in both the Liberal Party and the LRC had had their way, the course of British political history could have changed dramatically. Let us construct an alternative history – which perforce becomes more wildly divorced from the reality of events as it proceeds through the twentieth century.

In the 1906 general election, for a start, the LRC's progress was severely restricted, as most of their candidates were denied a free run by the Liberals. As a result, they only won half a dozen seats, none of them in the large double-member towns and cities, and remained confined to a handful of strongholds. The major unions which had not yet thrown in their hand with the new party took note, and some even withdrew funding as a potential waste of money on an unproven venture. Others thought twice before affiliating. The LRC was looking like a stillbirth.

The Liberals, on the other hand, still won a landslide victory over the Unionists, scarcely affected by the opposition of the fifty LRC candidates. However, their awareness that the Labour Party, as it became later in 1906, was a potential threat led them to two new strategies. First, the social reforms brought in by Lloyd George and Churchill within Asquith's government after 1908 were even more radical and explicitly tailored to the demands of the working class and, in particular, the trade union movement. Plans for a national minimum wage were announced in the People's Budget of 1909, alarming the Unionists and more traditional Liberals, including the large employers still to be found within the party, but consolidating support among the large section of the labour movement which had not formally committed itself to the Labour Party. Second, a concerted effort was made by the Liberals to adopt more working men as candidates, realising that the electoral battle was to be drawn up increasingly along the lines of class.

Both 1910 elections were bitterly fought. The Unionists stridently proclaimed that the Liberals had introduced a new brand of sectional politics to Britain by dividing it into two nations. Labour could find the funds only for sixty-five candidates in January 1910, dropping to forty-five in December after their disappointment that they could once again win only a handful of seats. With the working-class vote in some marginal constituencies somewhat split by Liberal–Labour contests, the Unionists did manage to win around thirty more seats than the Liberals. The results of the two elections were almost identical: Unionist 295, Liberal 265 (including over twenty Lib-Labs), Labour 20, Irish Nationalist 80, others 10. However, after each election the Irish Nationalists offered their support to Asquith in return for the promise of the introduction of a bill to bring in Home Rule for Ireland, so the Liberals remained in government.

Following the taming of the Lords in the 1911 Parliament Act, the radicals in the government were emboldened; and with more than a corner of their eyes fixed on the potential challenge from Labour, the Asquith–Lloyd George government continued with an even more ambitious programme of social and tax reform in the years up to the outbreak of war in 1914 – including what might be called Lloyd George's 'People's Budget II', introduced in April 1914. This included the proposal that the right to a minimum wage, already granted to the miners in 1912 (thus precluding a potentially divisive and damaging strike threatened in that year[65]), should be extended to a range of other industries, including shipbuilding – regarded as vital as the clouds of war loomed – and some transport and engineering sectors. The 1913 Trade Union Act had also done much to reinforce the Liberals' links with the industrial wing of the Labour movement, not only nullifying the Osborne Judgment of 1909 (which had made it illegal for trade unions to raise a political levy) but facilitating its payment to any local or national party chosen by its officials; several unions, including the Nottinghamshire and Derbyshire areas of the Miners' Federation, opted to support local Liberal associations.

By 1914, thirteen million people were covered by the National Insurance Act, and Lloyd George promised that with finance from the Second People's Budget, benefit payments could be made more generous, extended to a period of twenty-six rather than fifteen weeks, applicable to workers outside those in domestic service and agriculture, who still gained relief under the old Poor Law.[66] It was also proposed that allowances would be made for spouses and children for the first time. Asquith backed these measures, leading to the defection of a 'cave' of right-wing traditional Liberals, such as the Liverpool magnate Richard Holt, but they were also supported by the bulk of moderate labour (although opposed by the syndicalists, who accused the Labour Party leaders of 'selling out' to the bourgeoisie).

When it became apparent that the Great War was not to be over by Christmas 1914, Asquith moved, in the following year, to invite the pro-war section of the Labour Party (including most of the unions, stirred by the same patriotism which had caused so many working-class men to volunteer) to become junior partners in a coalition government. They accepted Asquith's offer in order to acquire a share in office for the first time; Arthur Henderson joined the Cabinet. The anti-war Labour element, including Ramsay MacDonald, objected to the coalition strongly enough to split their party.

In 1916, the worst year of the war, Lloyd George ousted Asquith as Prime Minister, but the history and promises of the eloquent old radical persuaded the moderate Labour faction to remain in his grand coalition (which included Conservative leaders too). The decision of Henderson to take the 'coupon' offered by Lloyd George in the post-war 'khaki election' irrevocably split the Labour Party. The left-wingers formed the Socialist Party, with a new constitution firmly committed and dedicated to the public control of the means of production, distribution and exchange. The remainder, including most trade-union leaders, saw that their future lay with Lloyd George's radical Liberals in a new social democratic movement. In the 1918 election the Socialist Party and Asquith's independent Liberals were reduced to tiny rumps, while Lloyd George won by a landslide.

Four years later, in 1922, the coalition which had won the 1918 election split, as the Conservative Party reconstituted itself as an independent and confident force. Lloyd George and Henderson, realising that they must unite in order to avoid the fate of Asquith and the Socialists, declared a historic merger in the formal foundation of the Social Democratic Party (SDP). (A number of names had been considered, including Social and Liberal Democrats, and Liberal Democrats, but the union affiliates objected to the term Liberal being included, pointing to the names of many of the major left-of-centre parties on the continent of Europe, such as Germany. In any case, the rump of the old Liberal Party had threatened legal objections.) Although the Conservatives won the 1922 election, the SDP became the official opposition; the Socialists failed to make much headway, and the Asquithian Liberals rapidly disappeared from sight.

There followed decades of two-party politics, with government alternating between the Conservatives (in the 1930s, 1950s, and 1980s), and the Social Democrats, with their joint liberal and labour traditions, strongest in the 1940s – the decade of their greatest triumph, the welfare state thought up by the Social Democrat Beveridge and implemented by the government of the Social Democrat Attlee. The Socialists remained as a fringe party, confined largely to Scotland and Wales, and hampered by the operation of the first-past-the-post electoral system. After the alternations of the 1960s and 1970s, with the competent technocratic SDP governments of Wilson and Callaghan representing the intellectual and trade-union wings of the party, Conservative administrations governed throughout the 1980s and early 1990s, although with relatively slender majorities in the face of the moderate SDP and its allied modernising unions. In 1997 the SDP returned under their articulate new leader, an ambitious young barrister by the name of Tony Blair.

Blair won two terms easily enough, trumpeting his classical social democratic nostrums of a 'third way' between Conservatism and Socialism. However in 2005, the general election produced a hung parliament. In order to continue with what he promised would be his third, and final, term, Blair was forced into an uneasy accommodation with the Scottish leader of the small third party, the Socialists, a man representing one of the few areas which had stayed loyal to Socialism since the great Labour split of the First World war – the Fife coalfield. Blair had to offer the key role of Chancellor of the Exchequer to a man on whom he depended for office, but felt he could not fully trust, and whom he strongly suspected did not share his reformed social-democratic vision – Gordon Brown.

~

The author would like to acknowledge the kind comments and assistance of the members of the British Liberal and Political Studies Group, especially Russell Deacon, Richard Grayson, and Tony Little: a draft of this chapter was presented as a paper for discussion at the Group's conference at Gregynog Hall, University of Wales, in January 2006.

Notes

1   The reason for this location was that MacDonald had been admitted for a minor illness during a session of the TUC at Leicester.

2   *Daily News*, 6 July 1903, quoted in H. V. Emy, *Liberals, Radicals and Social Politics 1892–1914* (Cambridge, 1973), p. 91.

3   G. R. Searle, *The Liberal Party: Triumph and Disintegration 1885–1929* (Basingstoke and London, 1992), pp. 36–37.

4   G. L. Bernstein, *Liberalism and Liberal Politics in Edwardian England* (Boston, 1986), p. 64.

5   Ibid., p. 65.

6   Ibid., p. 67.

7   F. Bealey and H. Pelling, *Labour and Politics 1900–06* (London, 1958), p. 125.

8   *The Times*, 3 January 1903.

9   Bernstein, *Liberalism and Liberal Politics in Edwardian England*, p. 69.

10 Bealey and Pelling, *Labour and Politics*, pp. 152–53; P. Poirier, *The Advent of the Labour Party* (London 1958), pp. 199–203; Stephen Koss, *Nonconformity in Modern British Politics* (London, 1975), pp. 63–64.

11 *Leicester Daily Mercury*, 28 July 1903.

12 Searle, *The Liberal Party: Triumph and Disintegration 1885–1929*, p. 72.

13 Bernstein, *Liberalism and Liberal Politics in Edwardian England*, p. 76.

14 Ibid., p. 77.

15 Searle, *The Liberal Party: Triumph and Disintegration 1885–1929*, p. 73.

16 Derek Peaple and Tony Lancaster, *British Politics 1885–1910* (Ormskirk, 2000), p. 199.

17 Searle, *The Liberal Party: Triumph and Disintegration 1885–1929*, p. 174.

18 T. Wilson, *The Downfall of the Liberal Party 1914–35* (London, 1966) pp. 18–19.

19 See, for example, the persuasive analyses of K. D. Wald, *Crosses on the Ballot* (Princeton, 1983) and H. Pelling, *The Social Geography of British Elections 1885–1910* (London, 1967), pp. 431–33.

20 H. Pelling, *Popular Politics and Society in Late Victorian Britain* (London 1968), p. 120.

21 R. McKibbin, *The Evolution of the Labour Party* (Oxford, 1974), p. 39.

22 Ibid., pp. 70–77.

23 Quoted in Koss, *Nonconformity in Modern British Politics*, p. 76.

24 Ibid., pp. 228–30.

25 Bernstein, *Liberalism and Liberal Politics in Edwardian England*, p. 199.

26 G. Phillips, *Rise of the Labour Party* (London, 1992).

27 Roy Douglas, *The History of the Liberal Party 1875–1970* (London, 1971), p. 65.

28 Bernstein, *Liberalism and Liberal Politics in Edwardian England*, p. 200.

29 J. Ramsden, *The Age of Balfour and Baldwin 1902–1940* (London, 1978), pp. 98–99.

30 Emy, *Liberals, Radicals and Social Politics 1892–1914*, pp. 94–99.

31 G. R. Searle, 'The Edwardian Liberal Party and Business', *English Historical Review* 98, 1983, p. 34.

32 Emy, *Liberals, Radicals and Social Politics 1892–1914*, p. 99.

33 K. O. Morgan, 'The New Liberalism and the Challenge of Labour: the Welsh Experience 1885–1929', in K. D. Brown (ed.), *Essays in Anti-Labour History* (London, 1974), p. 164.

34 Ibid., p. 166.

35 Ibid., p. 167.

36 Ibid., p. 168.

37 Emy, *Liberals, Radicals and Social Politics 1892–1914*, Preface, p. ix.

38 Ibid., p. x.

39 Pelling, *Popular Politics and Society in Late Victorian Britain*, p. 2.

40 Ibid., p. 12.

41 Lloyd George, quoted in *The Daily Citizen*, 14 October 1912.

42 Searle, *The Liberal Party: Triumph and Disintegration 1885–1929*, p. 100.

43 Bernstein, *Liberalism and Liberal Politics in Edwardian England*, p. 201.

44 P. Thompson, *Socialists, Liberals and Labour: The Struggle for London 1885–1914* (London, 1967) p. 170.

45 P. F. Clarke, *Times Literary Supplement* 27 August 1976, p. 1044.

46 P. F. Clarke, *Lancashire and the New Liberalism* (2nd ed, Aldershot, 1993), p. 406.

47 Ibid., p. 407.

48 N. Blewett, *The Peers, The Parties and the People: The British General Elections of 1910* (London 1972), ch 12.

49 Martin Petter, 'The Progressive Alliance', *History* 58 (1973), p. 48.

50 Chris Cook, *A Short History of the Liberal Party 1900–2001* (London, sixth edition, 2002), p. 58, has a useful list of all by-elections 1911–14.

51 *The Nation*, 31 January 1914.

52 *Labour Leader*, 30 April 1914.

53 Poirier, *The Advent of the Labour Party*, p. 271.

54 S. H. Beer, *Modern British Politics* (London, 1965) p. 141.

55 Clarke, *Lancashire and the New Liberalism*, pp. 406–07.

56 Richard Grayson, 'Liberalism and Social Democracy: Ideological Sources of Liberal Democrat Policy,' paper presented to the conference of the British Liberal Political Studies Group (Gregynog, Montgomeryshire 2006), abstract.

57 Grayson, 'Liberalism and Social Democracy', p. 4, quoting C. A. R. Crosland, *The Future of Socialism* (London, 1956), pp. 116, 521–22, 524.

58 Liberal Democrats, *Our Different Vision* (values paper, 1989), pp. 9 and 14–15.

59 See, for example, Searle, *The Liberal Party: Triumph and Disintegration 1885–1929*, pp. 128–29; P. Lowe, 'The Rise to the Premiership' in A. J. P. Taylor (ed.), *Lloyd George: Twelve Essays* (London, 1971), pp. 95–133; J. M. McEwen, 'The Struggle for Mastery in Britain: Lloyd George versus Asquith, December 1916', *Journal of British Studies* 18 (1978), pp. 131–56.

60 M. Pearce and G. Stewart, *British Political History 1667–2001, Democracy and Decline* (3rd ed, London, 2002), pp. 217–18; Searle, *The Liberal Party: Triumph and Disintegration 1885–1929*, p. 129.

61 T. Wilson, 'The Coupon and the British General Election of 1918', *Journal of Modern History* 36 (1964), pp. 28–42; R. Douglas, 'The Background to the "Coupon" Election Agreements', *English Historical Review* 86 (1971), B. McGill, 'Lloyd George's Timing of the 1918 Election', *Journal of British Studies* 14 (1974), pp. 109–24.

62 Pearce and Stewart, *British Political History 1667–2001*, pp. 223–24; Searle, *The Liberal Party: Triumph and Disintegration 1885–1929*, p. 143.

63 Searle, *The Liberal Party: Triumph and Disintegration 1885–1929*, pp. 161–63.

64 Ibid., pp. 154–56; R. McKibbin, *The Ideologies of Class* (Oxford, 1990), p. 278; I. G. C. Hutchison, *A Political History of Scotland 1832–1924* (Edinburgh, 1986), p. 326.

65 D. Weigall and M. Murphy, *Modern History* (London, 1986), pp. 178–79.

66 These were the main features of the National Insurance Act actually passed in 1920.

Chapter 6

What if Franz Ferdinand's assassin had missed in 1914?

York Membery

It's the most famous bullet in history. The bullet that triggered not only the death of the Austrian Archduke, Franz Ferdinand, but also set in chain a series of events culminating in the Great War, the war supposedly to end all wars.

The fatal bullet was fired by Gavrilo Princip, a member of the Black Hand society, a secret nationalist movement favouring union between Bosnia-Herzegovina and Serbia. With his pathetic little moustache, shabby appearance and sad face, today he looks like a figure from a Chaplin film. But his mission was deadly serious: he was part of a team sent to assassinate Franz Ferdinand, heir to the Austrian throne, during his visit to Sarajevo on 28 June 1914.

Within minutes of the Archduke arriving in Sarajevo, two members of his cavalcade were injured in a grenade attack. When the Archduke decided to visit them at the local hospital, it was suggested that he should adopt an alternate itinerary. But unbelievably, his driver was not informed of the change of plan and so took the original route.

A fellow passenger, General Potiorek, remonstrated with the driver when he realised his mistake. The driver stopped and began to reverse back down Franz Josef Street. It was too late. Princip seized his chance, ran forward and fired at Ferdinand from a distance of just five feet. His bullets struck the Archduke in the neck and he died soon afterwards.

The world would never be the same again. Spurred on by a German 'blank cheque', Austria declared war on Serbia, which it blamed for the assassination. The Russians, determined not to let down Serbia, mobilised their army. The Germans ordered the Russians to cancel the order. When they refused, Germany declared war on Russia, and then on France, assuming that it would come to the aid of its ally, Russia. In order to land a knock-out blow and take France out of war quickly, German soldiers entered Belgium. Britain demanded their withdrawal. When Germany ignored the demand, Britain entered the war … and so it was that the lights went out all over Europe.

But what if Franz Ferdinand's assassin had missed on that fateful day? What if someone had possessed the foresight to notify his driver of the change of route? Would war still have broken out?

~

Some historians think war was inevitable, and believe that the Europe of 1914 was a powder keg waiting to explode. Some other event, if not Franz Ferdinand's assassination, would have triggered hostilities, they say, pointing out that by 1914 Europe was divided into two opposing camps: the Triple Alliance (Germany, Austria-Hungary and Italy) and the Triple Entente (Britain, France and Russia). They cite the string of incidents in the run-up to the First World War, such as the Moroccan Crisis (1905–06), the Bosnia Crisis (1908), the Agadir Crisis and the two Balkan Wars (1912 and 1913), any one of which could have sparked a European conflict. Another factor in the drift to war, they argue, was the Anglo-German naval race, the Kaiser's attempt to build up the German Navy, which posed a direct threat to Britannia's domination of the waves and soured relations between the two countries.

Others, such as the historian A. J. P. Taylor, have argued that Europe's continental nations were the victims of their own mobilisation timetables in August 1914, the heyday of the railway. Once they had started mobilising their mighty armies, to plans that depended on adhering strictly to railway timetables, the drift towards war acquired a fatal, irreversible momentum of its own.[1]

A third school subscribes to the German historian Fritz Fischer's argument that Germany's leaders were hell-bent on world domination and deliberately provoked war.[2]

Even if these historians are right (and it's a big if), had war broken out at a later date, it would have almost certainly been a very different war.

The first couple of decades of the twentieth century were a time of rapid technological progress. Great advances were being made in engineering and science, among other fields. One of the main reasons the First World War lasted as long as it did was the limited technology available at the time. The weapons available might have enabled the rival armies to bombard each other senseless and inflict untold slaughter; but they were insufficient to deliver a knockout blow to end the stalemate on the Western Front.

True, many of the military innovations of 1914–18 were made under pressure of war. But given some of the developments that had been made in the peacetime conditions of the previous years – the year 1901 alone saw the appearance of the first public telephones at railway stations, the first diesel motor, the mobile radio transmitter, and the launch of Britain's first submarine (*Holland I*) – technological progress would have continued even in the absence of war.

So if the conflict had broken out in, say, 1919 or later, advances in technology could well have resulted in the fighting of a different sort of war.

In fact, if war had not broken out until 1919 or later, the First World War might never have happened at all. For the influenza epidemic of 1918–19 would have broken out by then – an epidemic that would kill between twenty-five million and forty million people worldwide, more than died in the war. Some 200,000 died in Britain, 400,000 in France, 600,000 in the US – and fifteen million-plus in India. The pandemic was caused by an H1 virus (avian flu) making the leap from birds, possibly poultry, to humans.

It has been suggested that it made the jump at a military camp, possibly in the US or France, though no one knows for certain. However, while battle weariness, combined with the effects of gas warfare, may have weakened soldiers' immune systems and helped trigger the pandemic, it is probable that it would have broken out with or without war. In which case, is it really conceivable that Europe's great powers would have gone to war in the wake of the most devastating epidemic in history, one which killed more people than the Black Death?

Finally, the very fact that it was the assassination of Franz Ferdinand, and not some other incident, that triggered the war surely begs the question: was war really inevitable? For if Gavrilo Princip had missed, war would, quite simply, not have broken out in June 1914. And if it hadn't broken out then, it might not have broken out at all, even if the Austro-Hungarian Empire's days were clearly numbered.

Relations between Britain and Germany were actually better in 1914 than they had been for quite some time. Most historians accept that by 1912 Britain had won the naval race, and the vitriol of a few years earlier had gone out of the dispute. By 1914, as A. J. P. Taylor observed, 'The British had come to tolerate the German navy and were outstripping it without undue financial strain'.[3]

Furthermore, the argument that a 1914-era Europe divided into two opposing camps – the Triple Alliance and the Triple Entente – made war inevitable is also questionable. How else can one explain the fact that NATO and the Warsaw Pact did not go to war during the Cold War? Granted, the 1945–90 era witnessed a series of 'mini-wars' – in Korea, Vietnam, Africa and elsewhere – where America and its allies locked jaws with communist forces. But the existence of these two fearsome power blocs, each of which had the ability to destroy the world, in effect kept the peace for nearly fifty years.

The terrible truth is surely this: that the assassination of Franz Ferdinand could well have been the Edwardian era's 'Cuban missile crisis' moment – the Cuban missile crisis of 1962 of course being the moment when the world came closest to all-out hostilities during the Cold War; but Krushchev blinked, the moment of danger passed and the world heaved a sigh of relief.

~

If the First World War had not taken place, what would have been the effect on Britain, its Empire, Europe and the wider world?

Let's take Britain first. The Edwardian era is sometimes portrayed as a golden age when Britannia ruled the waves, the British Empire was at its zenith and the nation's upper and upper-middle classes enjoyed a blissful 'Upstairs, Downstairs' existence with an army of servants at their beck and call. However, while a sizeable minority had probably never had it so good, life was still hard for the vast majority of working people, poverty was widespread and Liberal reformers such as Lloyd George were just beginning to address the issues resulting from the shocking inequality in wealth. What's more, the ruling Liberal government faced a number of serious problems in the years leading up to 1914: a bitter battle with the House of Lords, industrial unrest, suffragette agitation, and the perennial problem of Ireland.

At first glance, things seemed to have reached boiling point. At least, so George Dangerfield argued in his 1935 book, *The Strange Death of Liberal England*, which painted an alarming portrait of 1914 Britain sliding into anarchy and revolution. In fact, for all Dangerfield's predictions, there are reasons for questioning his dramatic doomsday scenario.

Firstly, the constitutional battle sparked by the House of Lords' rejection of government legislation had, in effect, been won by the Liberals. Secondly, the pre-war industrial unrest, which had led to the use of troops in the 1911 railway strike, resulting in the deaths of two men, had largely subsided by 1914. And thirdly, by then the Liberal Prime Minister, Herbert Asquith, and his Cabinet, had largely accepted the principle of votes for women; though, perhaps mistakenly in hindsight, they did not want to be seen to surrender to suffragette militancy, hence their apparent hesitation.

The subject posing the greatest headache was Irish Home Rule, which the Liberal government was committed to introducing. Protestants in Ulster, led by Sir Edward Carson, a Unionist MP, were arming themselves along quasi-military lines and threatening to fight, under their infamous rallying cry 'Ulster will fight and Ulster will be right', to preserve their ties with mainland Britain. The Curragh Mutiny, in which sixty British army officers threatened to resign rather than force Ulster into accepting Home Rule, was another ominous development.

The Ulster Unionists' hardline stance was backed by the Conservative (Unionist) Party for largely political reasons – and to avenge its defeat over reform of the House of Lords which had resulted in the 1911 Parliament Act. In hindsight, its actions appear highly irresponsible. And while the Conservative leader, Arthur Bonar Law, may well have changed his tune if violence had erupted across the Irish Sea (as his defenders argue), by then it could well have been too late to keep a lid on things.

However, finding a solution to the Irish problem was surely not beyond the realms of possibility? Agreement had very nearly been reached at an all-party conference in July 1914. Indeed, John Redmond, the Irish Nationalist leader, seems to have been prepared to agree to the temporary exclusion of the four mainly Protestant counties in the north from Home Rule. But then the Unionists stepped up their demands and insisted that two more counties, with sizeable Catholic populations, also be excluded – something which Redmond could never have agreed to if he was to retain any credibility in his homeland.

Unfortunately, Asquith's 'wait and see' approach to the problem simply fanned the flames on both sides of the debate. If he had spent less time writing love letters to society beauty Venetia Stanley during Cabinet meetings and given the matter his full attention, perhaps it could have been solved without the spilling of blood.

And astonishing though it may seem today, the Liberal government was more worried by what was happening in Belfast than in Berlin in the summer of 1914. Still, it is debatable whether things could have any got worse than they did in reality – with the Easter Rising of 1916, the sending in of the 'Black and Tans', and the outbreak of a bloody civil war in Ireland following partition.

What is certain is that events in Ireland would have played an important part in the outcome of the general election due in 1915, had such an election taken place. How pivotal a part it is impossible to say.

The question of who would have been the likely winner of a hypothetical 1915 general election is an intriguing one: for the Liberals never again held outright power following the creation of the wartime coalition government, and their relegation to third-party status in the post-war era paved the way for the rise of Labour and changed the political landscape forever.

But was the Liberal Party hurtling towards some sort of predetermined oblivion, as Dangerfield argues?

It's debatable, to say the least. The Liberal government of 1906–14 boasted an impressive front-bench team, among them figures like David Lloyd George and Winston Churchill. It laid the foundations of the welfare state, and has gone down in history as one of Britain's great reforming governments. Intriguingly, analysis of local election and by-election results by the historian Peter Clarke[4] suggests that, if anything, Labour was losing ground to the Liberals after 1910.

The state of the Liberal Party in 1914 is hotly contested. But surely it is plausible to argue that it could have gone on to win a fourth successive election in 1915? For it was the Great War which fatally divided the party. As the historian Trevor Wilson has argued, the conflict acted as 'a rampant omnibus' which knocked down and then ran over the party.[5]

But for the war, British politics might well have continued in much the same Liberal versus Conservative vein as it had for the previous sixty-odd years – as it did, for example, in Canada, where the Liberal and Conservative parties remained the two main political parties of government for the duration of the twentieth century. Indeed, they remain the two main political parties to this day.

If the war had not broken out, Lloyd George – 'the most inspired and creative British statesman of the twentieth century', in A. J. P. Taylor's view[6] – would in due course have probably succeeded Asquith in less controversial circumstances. In reality, with the fall of his coalition government in 1922, the Liberal split, the collapse of his power base and the rise of Labour, Lloyd George spent the rest of his days on the sidelines of British politics.

On the other hand, had he been premier during the 1920s, and perhaps beyond, there may have been no General Strike; he had proved himself a good labour negotiator before the war. And his famous Liberal 'Yellow Book', *Britain's Industrial Future*, advocating a Keynesian approach to the economy, showed that he – and perhaps he alone among the era's leading politicians – possessed the imagination and boldness necessary to deal with the mass unemployment sparked by the Wall Street Crash.

The social and economic consequences of the war on Britain were profound. Some 750,000 British men – over 6 per cent of the male population aged 15–49 – were killed and a further 1.5 million wounded, many so badly that they never worked again. In all, the British Empire (taking into account those troops sent by the Dominions and India) suffered around a million dead. The war also cut a swathe through Britain's elite. Around one in four of those who went to Oxford or Cambridge in the years 1910–14 died too, depriving the nation of a future generation of leaders. Is it any surprise that people spoke of the 'lost generation'?

The economic repercussions of Franz Ferdinand's assassination, and the war it triggered, were just as momentous. Until 1914, the City of London was the world's undisputed financial powerhouse, bankrolling railways and mines, farms and factories around the world. Wherever the City could make money, it was willing to invest. But the war left Britain economically exhausted. By 1918 it had run up enormous debts, mainly to the US, which had to be repaid with interest. The loss of around 15 per cent of the country's assets reduced its invisible earnings and hit its balance of payments. To make matters worse, while Britain had thrown everything into the war, countries such as the US and Japan had taken the opportunity to seize long-time British markets in South America, China and the Far East. Last but not least, the war had turned America from a debtor into a creditor nation; from now on the global monetary system would be bipolar, centred on Wall Street as well as on the City of London.

But for the Great War, Britain would still have been the world's financial capital (although in time America's growing population advantage over Britain would surely have told); her economy would have been that much stronger and able to withstand the economic dislocations of the 1920s and '30s; the unemployment and consequent hardship resulting from economic dislocation that bit less severe. But for the Great War and its economic and social repurcussions, the 1926 General Strike, the biggest industrial action in British history, might never have even taken place.

The impact of the war on Europe, and further afield, was no less far-reaching. The main participants all suffered enormous loss of life – the total war dead (including those suffered by Britain and its empire) amounted to some ten million – and ran up huge debts. The political map of Europe was transformed by the post-war Treaty of Versailles. A new, shrunken Germany, saddled with huge reparations, emerged; while the Austro-Hungarian and Ottoman empires disappeared from the map altogether, to be replaced by a jumble of small, weak states.

But for the war, the Europe of the 1920s and 1930s would have almost certainly been a happier, more prosperous place. Its economy would have been in better shape and the post-war years would not have been so difficult. Crucially, Europe would have been more resistant to the malignant lure of fascism. Deprived of the bitterness that infected Germany after 1918, followed by the rampant inflation and mass unemployment of the 1920s and '30s, it is hard to envisage the Nazi Party gaining power in Germany, or Mussolini and his Blackshirts in Italy.

A key factor in the rise of fascism was the threat posed by communism following the October 1917 Revolution, which was in part triggered by Russia's inability to meet the demands of modern warfare. The Russian army suffered over five million casualties during the war and the population was soon running short of food. The war pushed Russia to breaking point. Cue the February Revolution, the abdication of the Tsar and the setting up of the Provisional Government. Later that year, Lenin, seeing his chance, ordered his Red Guards to storm the Winter Palace. The Bolsheviks triumphed, and Soviet-style communism was born.

But for the war triggered by the firing of that fatal bullet at Sarajevo, it is questionable whether the Tsar would have been forced to abdicate in 1917. A fast-industrialising Russia, ruled by an absolute monarch, could still, of course, have succumbed to some sort of revolution – but if it had, it could have just been the liberal Kerensky revolution of February 1917, not the blood-drenched Bolshevik coup that followed in October of that year.

The consequences of a world without Nazi Germany and the Soviet Union – a world without Hitler and Stalin, two of the twentieth century's greatest mass murderers – are far-reaching, to say the least.

But for Hitler, the Second World War would not have broken out. There would have been no Dunkirk, Stalingrad or D-Day. France would not have fallen. The cities of Britain and Germany would have been spared mass bombing. There would have been no Holocaust; the names of Auschwitz and Belsen would today carry no resonance. Twenty million Russians would not have perished. And the development of the atomic bomb would have happened later rather than sooner.

The rest of the world would also have looked very different but for Franz Ferdinand's murder. But for the pressures of war, it is hard to imagine Britain promising to create a Jewish national homeland in Palestine – as it did in the 1917 Balfour Declaration, a rash promise made largely in the hope that by doing so, Russian Jews would keep their country in the war despite the revolution.[7]

The collapse of the Ottoman Empire following the war created a power vacuum in the Middle East, sucking in Britain, among others. With the benefit of hindsight, the wisdom of Britain first promising to create a Jewish homeland, and then taking control of Palestine and Iraq, albeit under League of Nations mandates, appears debatable – although some historians would argue that the lure of oil in Iraq provided a compelling enough reason. Ever since, the contradictions inherent in the conflicting claims of Jew and Arab to the land once known as Palestine have contributed to today's complex, perhaps insoluble, impasse.

With or without the war, the Ottoman Empire's days were clearly numbered. However, if it had not been for the 1914–18 conflict, Britain may not have been sucked into the Middle East to the same extent. That being the case, it would also most likely have avoided being caught up in the terrorism that later (post-1945) erupted in the area, claiming many British lives. Perhaps the biggest irony of all is that but for the firing of that fatal bullet, and the war it triggered, a Jewish homeland might still just be a pipe dream.

And what of the British Empire? The post-1918 years saw the British Empire reach its territorial zenith following the acquisition of its Middle Eastern mandates and the occupation of German colonies like Tanganyika, the Cameroons and Namibia – despite their questionable value to the mother country. How would relations between Britain and its colonies have differed but for the war?

On the one hand, the First World War brought the Empire closer together. It saw the 'white dominions' of Canada, Australia and New Zealand, together with India, rally to the motherland in its hour of need, providing millions of troops (some 200,000 of whom would die in combat), and helping to ensure eventual Allied victory.

However, the First World War, and to an even greater extent, the Second World War (a by-product of the earlier conflict), increased demands among the Empire's subjects for a greater measure of self-government.

In effect, the Great War acted as a motor, speeding up the pace of change throughout the world, including the British Empire. The growth of nationalist sentiment in the dominions and elsewhere in the Empire would have almost certainly been slower but for the war – the one exception, perhaps, being India, with its 250 million people, where nationalist sentiment appeared to be on the rise, war or no war.

The 1914–18 conflict also affected the movement of people within the Empire. In the years immediately preceding the war, hundreds of thousands had left the United Kingdom to start a new life overseas, primarily in Canada, Australia and New Zealand. Over 400,000 emigrated in 1913 alone. The outbreak of hostilities brought such mass migration to a standstill and it never again achieved such levels. If it had, it would have perhaps created even stronger bonds of kinship between Britain and the white dominions – although whether a far-flung British Empire could ever have become the tightly knit federal structure envisaged by imperialists like Joseph Chamberlain is open to question.

The long-term effects of Franz Ferdinand's assassination would have been equally dramatic on East–West relations. But for the Bolshevik Revolution, and the establishment of the Soviet regime, relations between Russia and the West would have been very different.

The Bolshevik Revolution of 1917 sent shockwaves through the Western world. Britain refused to recognise the new Soviet government until 1924; the United States did not recognise it until 1933. The outbreak of the Cold War in 1945 was in some ways a consequence of the mutual suspicion that had long existed existed between Russia and West, exacerbated by actions like the imposition of the Berlin blockade.

In 1914, in contrast, Britain enjoyed better relations with Russia than she had for decades. The threat posed by the Russian bear to the Indian Raj had receded in British eyes following Russia's disastrous defeat in the 1904–05 Russo-Japanese War. Had it not been for the First World War and the Bolshevik Revolution, the freeze which characterised Anglo-Russian relations for much of the twentieth century might not have taken place. Having said that, given Russia's size and proximity to the Middle East, it was always likely to have been viewed with some ambivalence in London, whatever its type of government, capitalist or communist.

If it had not been for the rise of Hitler, and the unleashing of the German war machine on Europe in 1939, it is also less likely that Japan would have attacked Singapore and Pearl Harbor – although it still seems likely that Japan's aggressive military regime would have invaded China in the 1930s.

The close relationship – the much-vaunted 'special relationship' – that Britain and America have enjoyed over the last sixty-five years – a de facto military alliance cemented by the fight, first against fascism in Germany and Japan, then against the worldwide threat of communism, and more recently against terrorism – would have taken a very different turn but for the events at Sarajevo and the two world wars that followed.

The US might have begun life as a British colony but despite the two nations sharing a common language and certain core values, they were by no means friendly for much of the nineteenth and early twentieth centuries. True, they fought on the same side in the First World War but the US did not enter the conflict until 1917. And after the Treaty of Versailles there was a widespread feeling in America that the country had been sucked into a European war that was none of its business, and it withdrew into isolationism. As late as the 1920s, US admirals were playing war games in which Britain was cast as the enemy.

The Second World War changed everything. America and Britain needed each other, and so it was that Britain became America's best friend and foremost ally, a bond that endured through the long years of the Cold War, and still holds true today, bar the occasional hiccup. However, but for the military alliance the two nations forged when faced by the twins threats of fascism and communism, the relationship between Britain and the US would have surely been much cooler. Instead it may have continued in the pre-1939 vein, a relationship characterised by a surprising degree of rivalry and suspicion.

~

So what kind of a place would Britain be today if Gavrilo Princip had missed? It is of course an impossible question to answer with any degree of precision, but one can attempt to paint some broad brushstrokes.

Few commentators in 1914 doubted that Britain would still possess an empire a century later. But for Franz Ferdinand's death, perhaps parts of the map would still be painted pink, even if the dominions had become independent countries. Having said that, there were long-term social, political and economic forces at work that would surely have resulted in the Empire's eventual break-up.

As the historian David Reynolds observed: 'In retrospect the great British empire seems something of a con trick. How could so many be ruled for so long by so few?'[8]

One thing is certain: a Britain that had not fought two world wars, and 'lost an empire but not yet found a role', in Dean Acheson's much-quoted words, would be a profoundly different place.

Would such a Britain, for instance, even have considered joining an organisation such as the European Economic Community, let alone adopting a European currency?

British attitudes towards Germany would be very different. If the Battle of Britain, Dunkirk and Alamein – not to mention the Battle of the Somme – had never taken place, Germany would never have been seen as 'the old enemy'. If Winston Churchill had not become Prime Minister during Britain's darkest hour, would he have been voted the 'Greatest Briton' in a BBC television poll? Would he have even made the shortlist?

England's famous win over West Germany at the 1966 World Cup would carry none of the 'wartime' overtones it enjoys today. It would simply be seen for what it was: a great sporting triumph. What's more, but for the October Revolution, the rise of Hitler and the outbreak of World War II, the match would of course have taken place against Germany, not the Federal Republic of Germany (as West Germany was officially known until reunification).

The world of politics would most likely be dominated by a centre-left Liberal Party and a centre-right Conservative Party, although the Liberals might well govern with the support of a minority Labour Party. Perhaps Tony Blair and Sir Menzies Campbell would be sitting alongside each other on the Liberal front bench in the House of Commons, while a stony-faced John Prescott, the fiery trade-unionist-turned Labour leader, contemplated how different things might have been if his party had replaced those pesky Liberals.

But for the First World War, and the Second World War, would Britain have been humbled in a Suez-style crisis? And with a degree of rivalry and suspicion still characterising Anglo-American relations, would a British Prime Minister have been as ready as Tony Blair to join in a US-led military adventure in the Middle East? Would 'the special relationship', as we know it, even exist?

Of course, the more detailed a prediction one tries to make about how the world might look today, the more risky the prediction. Who knows whether an atomic weapon would have ever been used in anger? Whether South Africa would still be in the grip of apartheid, or China governed by a totalitarian communist regime? Who, if anyone, could predict how the Middle East might look today? Would Israel as we know it even exist – or Al-Qaeda pose the threat that it does?

It is impossible to say whether it would have been a better or a worse world. It would have been an altogether different world, although it is hard to imagine the twentieth century being any bloodier than it was in reality. Who could have guessed how much one bullet would change the world?

Notes

1 A. J. P. Taylor, *How Wars Begin* (Hamish Hamilton, 1979).
2 Fritz Fischer, *Germany's Aims in the First World War* (Chatto & Windus, 1977).
3 A. J. P. Taylor, *English History 1914–45* (Penguin, 1970).
4 Peter Clarke, *Lancashire and the New Liberalism* (Cambridge University Press, 1971).
5 Trevor Wilson, *The Downfall of the Liberal Party 1914–35* (Collins, 1966).
6 Taylor, *English History 1914–45.*
7 In a November 2002 interview with the *New Statesman*, Jack Straw, then Foreign Secretary, blamed Britain's imperial past for many of modern political problems, including the Arab–Israeli conflict. He said that the Balfour Declaration of 1917, in which Britain pledged support for a Jewish homeland in Palestine, and the contradictory assurances given to Palestinians, were not entirely honourable: 'The Balfour Declaration and the contradictory assurances which were being given to Palestinians in private at the same time as they were being given to the Israelis – again, an interesting history for us, but not an honourable one.' See http://news.bbc.co.uk/1/hi/world/europe/2481371.stm
8 David Reynolds, *Britannia Overruled: British Policy and World Power in the Twentieth Century* (Longman, 1991).

Chapter 7

What if Ramsay MacDonald had lost the 1922 Labour leadership election?

Jaime Reynolds

Ramsay, Ramsay, shout it;
Don't be shy about it;
Labour's day is sure to come –
We cannot do without it.

Labour song, general election of 1922

On 21 November 1922 James Ramsay MacDonald was elected chairman of the parliamentary party, a post that for the first time carried the title of Leader of the Labour Party. Was this the crucial event that decided the course of British politics in the 1920s and shaped the party system that has prevailed to the present day?

The contest was tight. MacDonald had been returned to Parliament only a few days before at the general election. He had lost his Commons seat in 1918 and had been humiliatingly defeated at a by-election in 1921. He was fortunate in his new constituency, Aberavon, to face the divided opposition of Tory and Liberal candidates,[1] unlike his rival, Arthur Henderson, who was temporarily out of the Commons having narrowly lost his seat in Lancashire to a Liberal-supported Conservative.

Henderson's defeat removed the favourite from the race and weakened the grip of the trade-union MPs who had dominated the parliamentary party since 1918. Their alternative candidate, the incumbent chairman, J. R. Clynes, was nonetheless confident of re-election. MacDonald was the outsider, in every sense of the word, and did not expect to win, but decided to stand in order to put down a marker for the future. He was greatly helped by the decision of the Independent Labour Party (ILP) MPs, who formed the non-union wing of the Labour parliamentary party, to support his candidature. Although some left-wingers were unhappy about this decision, no left-wing candidate came forward to split MacDonald's vote.

As the MPs gathered for the election of the chairman, Clynes blundered. He opened the meeting with a report on his negotiations with the Speaker, who had proposed that Labour and the Liberals should share the Opposition front bench, despite the fact that Labour had more MPs than the divided Liberals. Clynes's failure to assert the Labour claim drew a sharp protest from MacDonald. When the vote was taken MacDonald was just ahead by sixty-one to fifty-six, with many MPs – some twenty or thirty – absent or abstaining (according to one story, several of Clynes' supporters were in a taxi whose driver lost his way). As one authority has written 'this bare majority effectively structured the pattern of Labour politics for almost the next nine years'.[2]

MacDonald stood for an energetic and ambitious Labour strategy. Under Clynes and the other trades-union politicians Labour had followed a staid and timid course, using the Commons to push for piecemeal, incremental gains for their memberships rather than reaching for power. But MacDonald would play a different game. His goal was to transform the Labour Party from a parliamentary pressure group into a party of government, and within little more than a year he had succeeded.

Labour's forward march

The rise of Labour has customarily been seen as a natural process, a social movement that owed little to individuals, even to its own leader. As late as the 1970s, the 'forward march of Labour' was part of the mindset of many Labour activists and commentators. According to this powerful myth, the 1920s had seen Labour's inevitable breakthrough to power on the path that, despite setbacks and betrayals, led to the triumphant Attlee government of 1945. Much of this mythologising rubbed off on Labour's opponents. Many Liberals accepted that the decline of their party was predestined in the face of Labour's ascent and debated how and when – rather than why and whether – it had to happen. It is only in recent years that historians have begun to look more critically at the party politics of the 1920s and assess more objectively the obstacles and uncertainties that stood in Labour's way.

This reappraisal has been influenced by the contemporary politics of the last quarter-century. On the one hand we have seen the enormous inbuilt advantages that the political system, and especially the British electoral system, gives to the two leading parties. In spite of declining party allegiances, a return to the voting volatility of the 1920s, and the rise of powerful onslaughts on the two-party system, the grip of the Labour and Conservative parties on the House of Commons remains almost as tight as ever. We have also seen the astonishing resilience of the major parties, as despite severe ideological challenges, splits, and leadership crises, they have recovered and regrouped. Finally we have seen the enormous impact of charismatic leaders on the fortunes of their parties. First Margaret Thatcher transformed the Conservative Party and, many would say, the Labour Party also. And if Tony Blair had not been available as Labour leader in 1994, does anyone believe that his party could have achieved such a massive electoral recovery?

The biases of the system and the interplay of personalities were also present in the fluid politics of the 1920s. Could such factors have hindered or halted Labour's forward march and have provided a life-line for the beleaguered Liberal Party?

The political challenge which each of the parties faced in the early 1920s – and the task of its leader – was similar. Each had to overcome divisions in its own ranks, consolidate its core support and reach out to weakly aligned voting groups, including the new voters – mainly women – who had been enfranchised in 1918. The winners in this game would be the two parties that emerged in the lead and gained the benefit of the inbuilt advantages of the parliamentary and electoral system. The loser would be the party that fell behind and suffered the handicap of being a third runner in a two-horse race. That is why MacDonald was so incensed by Clynes's passivity over the question of the Opposition front bench in the Commons. As he wrote after his election as leader: 'the failure of the Party in the last Parliament was that it never was an Opposition and was never led as an Opposition. It never impressed itself as an alternative Government with an alternative national policy'.[3] For MacDonald it was imperative that Labour seize its chance to claim the role of official Opposition in order to push the Liberals into third place in the pecking order.

The conventional view is that the Liberals were already fatally crippled by 1922. They were split into two rival camps behind Lloyd George and Asquith, their organisation in the country had fallen into disrepair, and they were afflicted by an ideological malaise as a result of the collapse of traditional Liberal values in the face of the triumph of militarism and collectivism in 1914–18. But the Liberals also retained considerable assets. In Lloyd George they had the most formidable politician of the period, a man who contrived to keep himself at the centre of events, despite his dwindling political base, for almost ten years after he lost the premiership. When Lloyd George's drive and money engaged with the Liberal Party, as in 1923 and 1926–29, the impact was dramatic.

The Liberals also had a galaxy of star performers in comparison with the other two parties; some, like Asquith and Grey, past their prime, but others, such as Churchill and Simon, with their greatest successes still ahead of them. Even if the Liberals' organisation was weakened, their networks of support from business, local elites, the media and academia were still largely intact in the early 1920s. Their electoral strongholds had been seriously eroded, but with a fair wind they could build on their residual redoubts in some urban and rural areas, Nonconformist centres and the Celtic fringe. After all, there were no less than 250 constituencies that elected a Liberal at one time or another during the 1920s.

Moreover, the other two parties faced great difficulties of their own.

The Conservatives had been suffering from a long-term crisis since 1905, when they had split over tariff reform and lost power. They were caught in a strategic dilemma: the diehard Toryism of the pre-1914 period had little appeal to the modern and expanded post-war electorate. However, tariff reform, the Conservatives' alternative to New Liberal taxation and Labour's socialist rhetoric, was seen as a tax on food and was thus electorally unpopular.

They lacked charismatic leaders, so much so that after seven years of serving in Liberal-led coalitions they were forced to turn to the ailing Bonar Law, soon succeeded by the unknown Baldwin. This was accompanied by another split as a large faction of Tory MPs led by Austen Chamberlain opposed the Tory withdrawal from Lloyd George's coalition government and remained unreconciled to the Bonar Law–Baldwin leadership. In spite of the Tories' victory in the 1922 general election, when they won some 340 seats to 142 for Labour and 115 for the Liberals (split almost evenly between the Asquith and Lloyd George wings), their situation was much more fragile than it looked. They held the advantage of probably some 200 or so secure seats in normal times,[4] but they were not immune to the perils of the electoral system if they misplayed their hand.

We have touched on Labour's problems already. The lesion between the trade-union wing and the activists mostly grouped around the ILP remained raw into the 1930s. Neither faction on its own was attractive to the target voters that MacDonald sought. The trade unionist MPs, occupying a bloc of some eighty or so generally safe seats in mining and some other industrial areas, lacked political talent and many of them 'visibly hankered after their old client relationship with Lloyd George and saw themselves not as a potential governing party but as a glorified pressure group ...'[5] The ILP-ers were mostly fervent idealistic activists, driven by socialist commitment whether of the ethical or Marxist varieties. Some of them were pretty wild, prone to disrupting the Commons, singing 'The Red Flag' and spouting millenarian socialist slogans.

MacDonald's task was to bring these two arms of the party together, to inspire the trade unionists and to discipline the radicals. The target was primarily the 'Liberal' vote, the moderate and progressive-minded citizens who would enable Labour to break out of its unionised working-class strongholds and win seats in the non-unionised working-class, mixed and semi-urbanised constituencies that it needed to gain in order to displace the Liberals. This was the course MacDonald single-mindedly followed throughout the 1920s, for 'although he had no strategy for using power, he had an extremely clear strategy for gaining it ... In 1918 [Labour] had emerged as the strongest opposition party largely by default. Even in 1922, its position was weaker than it looked at first sight ... if the Liberal split were healed, the Liberals, with the dynamic figure of Lloyd George at their head, might yet regain their old position ...'.[6]

MacDonald knew that this task was urgent: the three-party balance of the early 1920s was unlikely to survive for long. But he could not have anticipated quite how narrow the window of opportunity was. Three general elections were held between November 1922 and October 1924. Processes of electoral change that might have been expected to extend over a decade were compressed into two years.

The indispensable man

A *Punch* cartoon from the late 1920s shows Ramsay MacDonald parachuting down from the sky over London, with Westminster laid out at his feet; it has the caption: 'the Indispensable Man'. He was, with Harold Wilson and Tony Blair, one of the very few Labour leaders to capture the public's imagination and to dominate his party for a decade.

MacDonald is principally remembered as the somewhat pathetic figure of the 1930s, nominal Prime Minister of the Tory-dominated National Government, having betrayed and destroyed his life's work, melancholy and increasingly mentally confused. His appeal as the charismatic leader of the Labour Party in the 1920s is easily forgotten. Yet his election to the leadership was greeted with joy by his followers: 'Mr MacDonald will infallibly become the symbol, and personification which we have hitherto lacked'.[7]

MacDonald was pivotal to Labour's success. This was partly because he was, within the Labour leadership group, uniquely able to bridge the factions and to impose authority. Of the other party grandees, Henderson was a stolid if reassuring 'Uncle Arthur' figure identified with the trade-union wing. Philip Snowden, MacDonald's long-standing ally and adversary in the ILP, was an acerbic ethical socialist whose mission was to keep the Labour Party on the straight and narrow path of fiscal orthodoxy. Both men shared much of their basic outlook with the Liberals: Snowden was a fanatical free trader and Henderson's outlook was similarly Cobdenite. Neither had MacDonald's magic. Clynes, the would-be leader, was a solid, worthy and experienced trade-union boss, a cut above his fellow bosses, and a competent parliamentarian, but lacking in any charisma.

MacDonald, by contrast, was handsome and distinguished, in his heyday an inspiring public speaker. He was highly image-conscious and looked and sounded like a potential Prime Minister. He had the political vision and ability to reach out to the target voters. He was inclusive in his approach, avoiding ideological clarity. His *Socialism: Critical and Constructive* (1921) emphasised the broad ethical appeal of socialism to overcome poverty and class conflict, played down the long-term role of state socialism and disowned the pursuit of narrow working-class interests.[8]

His range was wider than his Labour peers. He was fortunate, in 1923, that political attention was focused on foreign affairs issues where he could shine in debate and underline his credentials as a statesman in waiting. By the end of the year *The Times* could tell its readers that 'Mr Ramsay MacDonald has led his party with success and he has risen to the big occasions in a big way'.[9]

By the time of the 1923 general election MacDonald had stamped his personality on the Labour Party and the electorate and his tumultuous election tour attracted huge and enthusiastic crowds, while many moderate voters were reassured that the Labour Party was a safe alternative to the Conservatives.

The Liberals' Waterloo: the general election of 1923

It is election night in December 1923. In East Ham the Tory-turned-Socialist Susan Lawrence gains the northern division with a lead of just 416 votes over the Liberal candidate. A couple of miles away in Walthamstow the Tory MP holds off the Labour challenge by 244 votes, with the Liberal just a thousand votes behind.

These two results mark the distance by which the last great Liberal challenge of 1923 fell short of victory. A further swing of less than 1 per cent would have gained East Ham for the Liberals, along with twenty-five other seats that they lost by a similar margin. With these gains they would have nudged ahead of Labour in the Commons and formed the official Opposition. A further swing of just over 3 per cent and they would have won Walthamstow East and another thirty-three seats, making them the largest party in the House.[10]

1923 is often written of as an election that in some sense does not count. It is viewed as unnecessary, a miscalculation by Baldwin that went disastrously wrong – but then mysteriously worked out in his favour. Within less than a year the result was reversed and Baldwin was triumphantly returned to power, with British politics shifted in favour of the Conservatives for the next two decades.

Baldwin had called the election suddenly, in November 1923, to seek a mandate for tariff reform, which he had unexpectedly re-adopted as his party's policy a few weeks before. It was a bold move, designed to reunite the Tories and wrong-step Lloyd George who, it was suspected, might be about to declare for protection himself. Ostensibly it was a huge blunder: immediately, the warring Liberals buried their differences and rallied in defence of free trade, which proved to be far more popular with the electorate than Baldwin imagined. The nightmare of both Baldwin and MacDonald – a revived Liberal Party challenging for government – seemed a real prospect. The outcome was indeed very close, with the Liberals making remarkable gains in seats that they had not won even in their 1906 landslide victory. In the key 'battleground' region of Lancashire they won more seats than they had at any time in the period 1885–1900, and nationally their poll was a million and a half votes greater than in 1906. In total the Tories obtained 5.5 million votes, Labour 4.4 million and the Liberals 4.3 million. The seats were shared: Conservative 258, Labour 191, Liberal 158.

Although the 1923 election is frequently dismissed as an aberration or temporary blip in the pre-ordained decline of Liberalism, it was in many ways the most important and decisive election in twentieth-century British politics. It effectively established the Labour–Conservative duopoly and consigned the Liberals to third-party status and thus oblivion. But as the figures show, it was, like Waterloo, a very close-run thing. The gap in votes between Labour and the Liberals was insignificant, and a very small shift of support would have seen the Liberals emerge ahead of the Labour Party in terms of seats in the House of Commons.

By how far did the Liberals fall short of this outcome? There are various ways of calculating it. It is often said that many of the Liberals' wins in 1923 were very narrow, but in fact they also missed many seats by a whisker. A hundred or two hundred more votes in the right constituencies would have boosted the Liberal tally by a couple of dozen seats or more.

But for our purposes the most interesting way is to look at the Labour vote, and how it ate into the moderate and progressive 'Liberal' votes that MacDonald was targeting. If actual Labour votes had been just 4 per cent lower across the country, the Liberals would have exceeded the Labour seat total (Con 263, Lib 173, Lab 171). In other words, if, for every twenty-four votes that Labour attracted they had failed to secure the vote of one further Liberal supporter, the Liberals would have come out ahead.

If the ratio had been two votes lost to the Liberals for every twenty-three Labour votes secured, the Liberals would have opened up a decisive lead over Labour in the Commons of over thirty seats (Con 268, Lib 185, Lab 152). This would certainly have placed the political initiative in the hands of Asquith and Lloyd George. The Liberals could have claimed victory in view of the major Tory losses and the negligible Labour gains. The consequences would have been profound. With more seats than Labour, Asquith, not Ramsay MacDonald, would have been invited by the King to form a government on Baldwin's resignation as Prime Minister, either by choice or – as would have been inevitable before long – following the loss of a vote of confidence.

The Liberals would then have had three options. First, they could have done as MacDonald actually chose to do and formed a minority government, daring the other two parties to vote them down. In this way they would have retained the political initiative and could have used the power of dissolution (as MacDonald did) against their opponents.

Second, they could have sought a coalition or understanding with Labour. There would have been opposition to this from the Labour left, no doubt, but it is likely that many Labour moderates and trade unionists would have been attracted by such an opening. They would have argued that it represented a further advance in the forward march of Labour – another step towards establishing Labour's credibility and respectability, the goal so close to MacDonald's heart. But whether it would have been a move towards MacDonald's aim of replacing the Liberals seems more doubtful. Rather, it could have laid the foundation for a progressive alliance built around the Liberal Party, in many ways a revival and development of pre-1914 Lib-Lab Progressivism.

There can be little doubt that this would have been the strategy of Lloyd George in the likely event that he had succeeded Asquith as Prime Minister in 1925 or 1926.

The Liberals' third option would have been to seek a deal with the Tories, or at least those coalitionist Conservatives led by Austen Chamberlain who were open to this prospect. In the real world, the Chamberlainites delayed reunion with the anti-coalitionist Tories until the Liberals decided, on 18 December 1923, to vote Baldwin out of office and allow Labour to form a government. There is every reason, therefore, to believe that they would have been willing to contemplate a revived coalition with the Liberals in the scenario we are considering. This would have compounded Baldwin's difficulties: the Conservative split would have deepened and he would probably have carried out his initial decision to resign as leader.[11] The Tories would have been deprived of the man who was to be the architect of their hegemony in inter-war Britain. The rump of the party, tied to a tariff reform pledge that had been rejected decisively by the voters, would have faced a severe crisis.

Conclusions

The 1923 election challenges the orthodox interpretations of Liberal decline and the inevitability of Labour's forward march. A small movement of votes at the margins would have altered the outcome profoundly and unlocked wide opportunities for the Liberals.

Without MacDonald's achievement, in 1922–23, in establishing his credibility as a potential Prime Minister and Labour's credibility as a party of government, such a small shift of votes between Labour and the Liberals would have been entirely plausible.

If MacDonald had not been elected as party leader in November 1922, Clynes would have been the face of the Labour Party and, figurehead or not, this would have dampened any impact that MacDonald could have made from the sidelines. It might be argued that MacDonald would soon have outshone Clynes and become de facto leader anyway. This may well have been true in time, but time was in short supply. As it was, MacDonald had only twelve months to establish himself as leader in the public mind before the fateful election of December 1923.

A different result in 1923 would have altered the dynamic of British politics in the 1920s. It could have arrested the decline of the Liberals and slowed the growth of the Labour Party. It could have revived the alliance between them. Or it could have split the Tory party and reopened the possibility of a Liberal-Conservative centre party.

If just three Labour MPs had voted differently at that fateful meeting on 21 November 1922, Labour's forward march behind the indispensable Ramsay MacDonald could have been stopped in its tracks.

Notes

1 MacDonald polled 14,300 as against a total of 16,400 polled by his two opponents.
2 D. Howell, *MacDonald's Party* (Oxford, 2002), p. 28.
3 Ibid., pp. 286–87.
4 The Tories were reduced to 150 seats at the 1906 election and 200 in 1945; they held some 260 in their worst inter-war performances, in 1923 and 1929.
5 D. Marquand, *Ramsay MacDonald: A Biography* (London, 1997), p. 269.
6 Ibid., p. 289.
7 *New Leader*, quoted in ibid., p. 287.
8 Ibid., pp. 277–79.
9 Ibid., p. 295.
10 The Labour majority in East Ham North was 1.7 per cent. Liberals fell short of victory by 1.7 per cent or less in seventeen Conservative, eight Labour and one Independent seat. The Tory lead over the Liberal in Walthamstow East was 6.4 per cent: forty-one Conservative, eighteen Labour and one Independent victors led Liberals by this amount or less in 1923. The analysis of elections in the 1920s is difficult because of inconsistency in the number of candidates standing in constituencies and widespread shifting alliances between the parties at local level.
11 P. Williamson, *Stanley Baldwin: Conservative leadership and national values* (Cambridge, 1999), pp. 31–32.

Chapter 8

What if the Liberals had formed the government in 1924?

David Hughes

O n the evening of 22 January 22 1924, King George V wrote
in his diary:

> Today 23 years ago dear Grandmama died. I wonder what she would
> have thought of a Labour government?

His comment came nearly seven weeks after the results of one of the
most inconclusive elections in British history, an outcome which
had led to the canvassing of the merits of at least five alternative
administrations, and a potentially decisive role for the Crown.

The election itself had followed a period of multi-party turmoil
lasting since 1918, which the Lloyd George coalition's massive
majority had initially masked. The divisions in the Liberal camp
between the supporters of Asquith and Lloyd George were trans-
parent and well-known, but the other parties had also been subject
to intense factional manoeuvring while the party system was in
flux, a process which only really concluded with the Conservatives'
decisive victory in October 1924.

The Conservative Party contained three substantial factions.
The first were the former ministers who had served in coalition
under Lloyd George, who had contemplated fusion with the
Coalition Liberals in the early 1920s and who would have been
happy to continue the coalition into the future. They regarded
the rise of the Labour Party as a potential government with great
concern, and were worried that the trebling of the electorate since

1910 could sweep away the old order. Led by the deposed party leader Austen Chamberlain, and including prominent figures such as Balfour, Birkenhead and Horne, they also enjoyed the general support of key press barons such as Lords Beaverbrook and Rothermere; they had also been excluded from the Conservative government led by Bonar Law and then Baldwin, and they were far from happy about it.

The second group had come to regard both Lloyd George and the coalition as anathema and had formed the backbone of the majority at the Carlton Club meeting which ended the coalition in October 1922. They regarded squeezing out the Liberals as a priority, in order to create a new two-party system with Labour which the Conservatives would dominate, and had welcomed and encouraged Baldwin's sudden conversion to tariffs and his decision to call the 1923 election. They included Amery, Bridgeman, Hoare and Neville Chamberlain.

Finally, there was a smaller group of diehard Conservative members. Their careers predated the war and they were firmly hostile to both Liberals and Labour, believing that only the Conservatives unrestrained could guarantee the preservation of their society. Their concerns were Ireland, German reparations and Bolshevism, though they were also mostly supporters of free trade. They were dominated by Lord Salisbury and included Sir William Joynson-Hicks and Sir Edward Carson.

On the Labour side, the divisions were simpler, focusing on the issue of whether Labour should take office without a majority and, indeed, whether the party was yet fit to acquit itself creditably in office. Although the left tended to have doubts about taking office, it was their votes which had narrowly given Ramsay MacDonald the leadership in 1922, and it was MacDonald who most passionately believed that Labour needed to demonstrate that it could fulfil the responsibilities of government as soon as possible.

Baldwin's decision to call an election for 6 December 1923 caught all but his closest confidants by surprise. It was only a year since

Bonar Law had secured a Conservative majority of ninety, and it was only the rash confidence of Baldwin's entourage that the British people would embrace protectionism that blinded them to the dangers of going to the country again. The effect of calling an election on the free trade issue was to unify the two Liberal factions, who had spent most of the year wrangling about money, around one of their best-known historic causes, and it gave Labour, also a free-trade party, the opportunity to advance further.

The election result immediately highlighted what appeared to be a massive error on Baldwin's part. The Conservatives lost more than eighty-five seats, to be left as the largest party, though far short of a majority, with 258. Labour gained an additional fifty seats, taking them up to 191, whilst the reunited Liberals increased their numbers by more than forty-five to 159.

Even though twelve months later he was back in power, with the Liberals clearly condemned to third-party status, and any possibility of Chamberlain resurrecting a coalition out of the question, at the time only one thing was clear: Baldwin's brief administration was at an end. Yet rarely have so many alternative possibilities presented themselves. An alternative Conservative government, a Conservative-Liberal coalition and a non-party government were all canvassed by those determined to exclude Labour at all costs. But the two possibilities most frequently aired were a minority Liberal government and the actual eventual outcome, a minority Labour government. For much of December the outcome rested on a knife-edge.

A return to office by a reunited Liberal Party would have had enormous implications for the shape of British politics in the years ahead, and might have come about had the various meetings and discussions described below developed only a little differently.

The events and communications described below in italics did actually occur. Only the renewed (fictional) correspondence of Asquith and Lady Venetia Montagu[1] tells us what might have been!

8 December 1923: Diary of Lord Curzon, Conservative Foreign Secretary –

This is the price that we all have to pay for the utter incompetence of Baldwin and for the madness of his selection by the King … I hear he is minded to resign as both Prime Minister and party leader, and only his placemen are advising him otherwise.

9 December 1923: Papers of Vivian Phillipps MP, Chief Whip of the Asquithian Liberal MPs –

We held our first meeting since the election today – Asquith, Simon, Gilbert Murray and self. HHA strongly of the view that 'Labour not ready for office yet. MacDonald, Snowden, Thomas and Henderson alright … for the rest the less said about them the better.'

The conversation then turned to the possible make-up of a Liberal Cabinet. Would LG be Foreign Secretary? At the mention of becoming Chancellor of the Exchequer Simon began to purr like a contented cat!

9 December 1923: Diary of Herbert Lees-Smith, Labour MP –

Sydney Arnold and I have already advised MacDonald not to take office on the grounds that a Labour Government would be bound to fail and that the party would then be 'overwhelmed'.

10 December 1923: Papers of Lord Stamfordham, Private Secretary to King George V –

The King's first thought is of some form of Conservative–Liberal construct.

11 December 1923: Letter from H. H. Asquith to Lady Venetia Montagu –

I thought that the current excitement of political events would be an ideal, though long overdue, opportunity at which to resume the correspondence that was so precious to me during my years in office, particularly as events may rather surprisingly restore me to my former position.

It is clear that Baldwin's days in office are numbered, as many of his own party are furious with him for precipitating this extraordinary debacle. It is merely a question of whether it is we or Labour who are to come in. Of course, they have the greater numbers, but we can provide extensive ministerial experience at every level. Furthermore, it seems to me that there are in both the other parties quite a few members who might come our way if they see us once again as an instrument of government.

Of course, one immediate issue is the role of our Welsh friend in all this. As you know, there is still a great deal of hostility towards him in many quarters of the party, and we have spent a great deal of time this year negotiating over money and organisational issues, but equally our own personal relations have improved, and it might just be that we could come to terms.

11 December 1923: Diary of Sidney Webb, MP and leading Fabian, following dinner at his home in Grosvenor Road with MacDonald and senior Labour MPs –

What a joke, what a ludicrous adventure! None of them have held cabinet office before whilst only three of them have been in Government, not including JRM (MacDonald). Everyone has cold feet except Henderson who has just lost his seat!'

11 December 1923: Letter from Austen Chamberlain MP to his sister, Hilda[2] –

I will do nothing to help Baldwin after this fiasco. I have not forgiven him for my treatment last May when he invited me to Chequers and spent an hour and a half lacking the courage to tell me directly that he would offer me no place in his government. As I wrote to Neville at the time: 'The discourtesy shown to me down to the last detail ... was not expected and I profoundly resent it.'

12 December 1923: Meeting of Labour Party NEC; notes by Arthur Henderson, Party Secretary –

It is clear that many of our MPs are opposed, including Lansbury, Pethick-Lawrence and the Clydesiders, and this could further weaken our position in the House. Ramsay is also suggesting that I should not serve in any government but should look after the party in the country in expectation of another election, which my family are not happy about.

13 December 1923: Letter from Sir George Younger MP, Conservative Party Chairman, to Lord Stamfordham –

Following our defeat in the House, His Majesty could fairly ask Mac-Donald if he could guarantee to govern for a reasonable time, to which MacDonald would have to answer 'no'. He could then send for Asquith and ask him the same question, at which point the Conservatives could offer support.

16 December 1923: Article by Sir Robert Horne, Conservative MP and Chancellor of the Exchequer 1921–22 –

The Libs could pass legislation to create the alternative vote and then go to the country after a year of quietness. Such a development would start business again and cheer commerce.

17 December 1923: Article by Winston Churchill, former Coalition Liberal MP –

[A Labour Government would be] a national misfortune such as has usually befallen a great state only on the morrow of defeat in war.

17 December 1923: Letter from H. H. Asquith to Lady Venetia Montagu –

I thought I would let you know how events are moving apace.

As you know a major issue is the question of who shall lead if we are to form a government and whether the goat will accept second place. I felt that the issue could best be resolved if he and I could meet privately on a one-to-one basis – the situation always seems to deteriorate when our acolytes take the lead.

Consequently we agreed to meet well away from the House and settled on an obscure restaurant run by one of Margot's more bohemian friends in Islington. On arrival he took only water and then immediately announced he would defer to my leadership of a new government on two conditions. Firstly, that I would stand down in his favour half-way through the Parliament, and secondly, that in the meantime he would be Chancellor again but with an expanded role, responsible for all areas of domestic policy. Without over-committing myself, I confirmed that I was sure we could proceed on this basis. Slightly distastefully, he then suggested that we should publish a signed agreement to this effect, at which I demurred, citing the King's prerogative etc. He then said: 'Well as long as I have your word?' I ignored this impertinence (thank goodness Margot was not present!) and replied 'Solid as a rock.' 'Like Granite,' he said. 'Like Granite,' I confirmed.

He then rather excitedly expressed his confidence that we would succeed in attracting support from members of the other parties, thus creating what he called 'a big tent'.

I hope that this will not include too many of his shiftier coalition allies but I suppose we must accept support wherever we might find it.

The success of this meeting has quite strengthened my resolve prior to tomorrow's party meeting. I had intended merely confirming that we would vote down Baldwin and if that led to a Labour government, then so be it.

18 December 1923: Diary of C. P. Scott, Editor, Manchester Guardian –
It is quite clear. The Tories should be turned out, and then Labour rejected also.

20 December 1923: Diary of Beatrice Webb –
Henderson reports that there is likely to be considerable industrial action in the spring, involving the train drivers and dockers. Another argument against installing a weak Labour government.

23 December 1923: English Review *(Christmas edition) –*
Comment on possible arrival of Labour Government: 'The sun of England seems menaced by final eclipse'.

31 December 1923: Letter from H. H. Asquith to Lady Venetia Montagu –

It is now quite likely that we will form a government after Baldwin is defeated on the King's Speech. A considerable body of press and business opinion supports this outcome, and we may well get the tacit support on key votes of the Chamberlainite Tories. Austen has been reminding all and sundry that he was originally a Liberal Unionist, and with Ireland apparently resolved and tariffs dead, there is little that still divides us. LG thinks we should offer him and some of his colleagues office, but I have no real wish to reconstruct the entire coalition around me. Margot is already expressing her reluctance to living next door to the goat (and his secretary!) again.

Ramsay has taken himself off to Lossiemouth until the new year whilst the rest of his party draws back from taking the plunge.

22 January 1924: Letter from H. H. Asquith to Lady Venetia Montagu –

And so it is done. As expected Baldwin was overwhelmingly defeated on the vote on the Address, whereupon we moved on to a trickier resolution expressing Labour's unsuitability to govern, and the presence in the House of a clear majority opposed to Socialism. Baldwin had instructed his followers to abstain, which could have left us defeated by Labour by some thirty votes. However, some seventy Tories – mainly former supporters of LG – defied their whips and voted with us. The King then sent for me and I have undertaken to offer some places to a few of these Conservatives in order to create some stability, but this will lead to some awkward conversations on the morrow.

26 January 1924: Letter from H. H. Asquith to Lady Venetia Montagu –

Well, I have reverted to my former practice of easing the tedium of Cabinet by writing to you during this our first meeting, and my prediction of awkward conversations was something of an understatement.

I started forming the government from my room in the House – a great mistake, as will become apparent. First of all, I confirmed LG's appointment, who then offered to undertake the construction of the rest of the administration on my behalf as if he was relieving me of a minor household chore. Once I had disabused him of this idea, he produced with a flourish a list of his suggestions, which constituted a veritable rogue's gallery of contemporary England, at least two-thirds of whom had already received quite enough of the Welsh Wizard's patronage, as their ill-justified honours confirmed.

He seemed to accept my reluctance in good humour, before jauntily interjecting: 'But don't forget, we don't know how soon we might have to fund another election campaign!'

After this scene, it was quite easy to brace oneself to offer positions to Austen Chamberlain and a few of his associates, without letting them slip into any of the great offices. In fact, it was quite easy to restore some of my former leading colleagues to their former positions; as well as LG, Edward went back to the Foreign Office, Simon to the Home Office, Crewe to leading the Lords and Haldane to the Woolsack, even though I had heard some ludicrous rumour that he was preparing to fulfil the same function for Ramsay.

It was then time to be generous to the apostates. Buxton, Ponsonby, Trevelyan, Addison and Fisher all gratefully came in, not one of them alluding to their recent flirtations, to say the least, with Labour.

And then, of course, there was Winston. He bounded in, exclaiming: 'So good to see my true chief back where he belongs!' I stuttered out: 'Winston, I would like you to join us as Chancellor of the ...'

'The Treasury at last! How can I ever thank you! It is less than forty years since my own dear papa held this post. I still have his robes!' He straightened himself: 'I am delighted that you have chosen me to serve as the bulwark against profligacy and socialist excess at the crucial juncture in our nation's fortunes. You will, of course, have to find me a seat after my small misfortunes at the last two elections.'

At last there was a pause. 'Yes Winston we will find you a seat, but it is so you might serve as Chancellor of the Duchy of Lancaster.' At this, all hell broke loose. 'But I have already held that post. It is a low and meagre role. I have spent many years as a Secretary of State – and what about my father's robes?'

At this point he started to blub, so I pointed out a few home truths: he was so unpopular that he kept on losing seats; he was still blamed by many for the Dardanelles; and he had spent much of his recent period as Colonial Secretary running around the Middle East with that lunatic Laurence, abolishing the historic nation of Mesopotamia and creating something called Iraq with the divergent peoples who were left over, under a King who thought he had been promised Syria. I added that it was Edward Grey's opinion that this particular chicken would come home to roost with a vengeance at some point in the future.

What is more, I added, it was widely believed by many in the party that he was contemplating switching back to the Tories – in short that having 'ratted', he would shortly have 'reratted'. Although I did not personally believe this for one moment, I confirmed, he would nonetheless need to demonstrate his loyalty for a period before eyeing up any more lofty offices.

Winston was now uncharacteristically silent and looking at his shoes with a somewhat shamefaced expression as he accepted my paltry offering. No sooner had he departed, however, than my door was flung open by the most appalling mountebank, who had the effrontery to declare: 'Never fear, Prime Minister, your government will succeed for I am willing to serve.' I recognised this young man as the husband of Curzon's poor daughter, who is already being given such a runaround by him as would put even LG to shame. I also recalled that in his six years in the House, to which he was elected at the age of 22, he had already sat as a Conservative and an Independent, and was now thought to be about to join Labour.[3]

This he denied, stating that he had merely been waiting for a new disciplined force to emerge which would address the country's problems with a programme of dynamic action. He then asked if I had kept abreast of Signor Mussolini's latest policy initiatives for domestic reform in Italy.

Fortunately, at this very moment I recalled my agreement with LG that he would take charge of this area, and sent my unwelcome guest off to discuss these matters with him. I swear that as he left he clicked his heels together in the manner of some demented mid-European princeling.

But by yesterday the job was done. In fact, I only had one rejection. I had approached that delightful public-school major from the East End about a junior job. But he declined, quite curtly replying: 'Sorry. Can't do it. Really am a socialist, yer see.'[4] He then suggested I approach his friend, Herbert,[5] who was always banging on about how much he could improve our press relations if ever given the chance and that we should call ourselves New Liberals ... But I think I'll leave courting the press barons to LG.

~

And so it could have happened. Asquith had the people to form a government, and considerable potential tacit support from the Conservative Party, the press and much of the business community.

If there was one moment at which he let the opportunity pass it was the meeting of the parliamentary party on 18 December 1923, where he reaffirmed his commitment to Baldwin but added that he thought these were the safest conditions under which a Labour government could be tested. Lloyd George had reached a similar conclusion, but mainly because he did not wish to risk again being turfed out of office on the Tories' whim, and was wondering whether he could come to some working arrangement with Labour himself in the future.

But if Asquith's initial post-election inclinations had prevailed, how would this government have fared, and what would be the consequences for the future shape of the party system?

Perhaps an extract from King George's diary ten years later might have told us:

22 January 1934 –

Today 33 years ago dear Grandmama died. I am sure she would share my relief that our party system now seems again to be revolving around the Conservatives and Liberals, after the threat of a Socialist government ten years ago, though I don't think she would be very amused by the amount of time since her death that it has been the Liberals who have actually been in office.

Looking back, Asquith's last two years in office were quite a success, as he consolidated and broadened the appeal of his party. By 1926 he had drawn in both some of the most moderate Tories and some of the brightest young men who had looked as though they would settle on Labour as the party of the future. His calm lack of belligerence and appointment of the first women ministers also seemed to establish his party's standing with women voters, notwithstanding his earlier opposition to female suffrage (and notwithstanding LG's more disreputable antics).

His success in settling with the miners in 1926 was a great final achievement which did much to stabilise the economy and forestall class conflict. At the time I thought the government's promulgating a slogan 'Not an hour on the day, and a shilling on their pay' rather undignified, but it proved the perfect point at which to hand over to LG, and the consequent defection of 34 miners' MPs to the Liberals stabilised their position and finished off any possibility of Labour as a governing party.

I was also concerned when Winston's first act on taking over as Chancellor was to take us off the Gold Standard;[6] apparently he'd spent a lot of time with Keynes when he had nothing to do as Chancellor of the Duchy over the previous two years. But together with the proposals in Mosley's black and yellow book, *Dynamic Action Can Conquer Unemployment,* it seems to have minimised our economic problems – goodness knows how Labour would have coped. We'd have ended up with hunger marches!

As to the future, my only worry is that my idiot son, David, will plump for that adulterous charlatan Mosley as LG's successor, rather than that nice laird from Caithness,[7] when he comes to exert the Royal Prerogative. My father always said that you can trust a man with a lot of land not to upset the apple-cart – though how much land anyone will still have by the time LG has finished with his rolling programme of land taxes, I do not know. Winston would have been an older possibility for PM but he's much happier as Viceroy with an entire sub-continent to run.

It won't be long now before I slip the scene, but at least I'll leave behind a political system rather more like that of our Canadian cousins than the class-based conflict emerging all over the troubled continent. I still hate abroad!

Notes

1 Lady Venetia Stanley, though only in her twenties, had been the object of intense correspondence from Asquith when Prime Minister. He had broken off the correspondence when she announced her engagement to Edwin Montagu, one of his junior ministers who subsequently served Lloyd George throughout the coalition.

2 Austen Chamberlain and his half-brother, Neville, both bombarded their two spinster sisters, Hilda and Ida, with correspondence about their woes throughout their political lives.

3 During 1923 senior Liberals, including Sir John Simon, devoted much energy trying to persuade the 27-year-old Oswald Mosley to join the party. He contested the election as a free-trade-supporting independent, and only joined Labour a month after it had successfully formed a government, receiving a letter of regret from Margot Asquith expressing her belief that he could have been a future Liberal Party leader. In the late 1920s he advocated an essentially Keynesian programme of public works and, after resigning from the Labour government in 1930, co-ordinated his public statements with Lloyd George.

4 Clement Attlee surprised his contemporaries on arrival in the House of Commons as Labour MP for Mile End in 1922, as they remembered him as a committed Conservative at Haileybury and Oxford. He served as Under-Secretary of State for War in MacDonald's first government and then succeeded Mosley as Chancellor of the Duchy of Lancaster in 1930.

5 Herbert Morrison rose rapidly under MacDonald, entering the cabinet as Minister of Transport in 1929. His reputation for deviousness and duplicity prompted Ernest Bevin's famous reply to the statement 'Herbert's his own worst enemy', 'Not while I'm alive, he ain't!' He was Peter Mandelson's grandfather. The present author is unaware of any conclusive research demonstrating whether political behaviour has a genetic foundation.

6 Winston Churchill's decision to adhere to the Gold Standard as Baldwin's Chancellor in 1926 is widely considered to have been an important factor in the intensity of the economic depression in the UK in the 1930s.

7 Sir Archibald Sinclair did become leader of the Liberals in 1935, but in rather less propitious circumstances than those envisaged here. He led a party of only twenty-one members, but was given high office by his long-standing close friend Winston Churchill throughout the lifetime of the war coalition.

Chapter 9

What if Gustav Stresemann had lived beyond 1929?

Richard S. Grayson

In the subtitle of Jonathan Wright's brilliant biography, Gustav Stresemann is described as 'Weimar's Greatest Statesman'. There is certainly no other figure from Germany's Weimar Republic era for whom such a claim can be made. Although only briefly Chancellor, heading a grand coalition from August to November 1923, Stresemann was foreign secretary in several different coalitions until his untimely death, at the age of only fifty-one, in October 1929. Throughout his six years in office, while there was so much change around him, it seemed that Stresemann and the centre-right liberals of the Deutsche Volkspartei (DVP – German People's Party) were the glue which bound together the governments of the Weimar Republic.

It is no surprise then, that Stresemann's death in 1929 has been seen as one of the destabilising factors which contributed to the crises leading to the Nazi takeover in 1933. If nothing else, while Stresemann lived, Germany had the kind of 'strong' leader that it seemed to desire. The question that must therefore be asked is whether, if he had lived, Gustav Stresemann could have materially altered German politics? Ultimately, could Stresemann have stopped Hitler?

~

To answer the question, one first needs to establish Stresemann's credential for greatness. Born in 1878 to a middle-class Berlin family, Stresemann studied literature and philosophy, prior to taking a doctorate in economics, and then beginning a public career centred on trade associations. Politically, his first loyalty was to the Nationalliberale Partei (National Liberal Party). In the 1870s, the National Liberals had supported Bismarck, but they had broken with him when he opposed free trade. Eventually the party became closer to big business, which contributed to growing intra-party tensions over free trade versus protectionism. Stresemann was elected to the Reichstag in 1907, but lost the seat in 1912. For two years he worked in business, before returning to the Reichstag. Although generally seen, at this stage, as being on the left of his party, Stresemann became an enthusiastic supporter of German expansion after 1914, and was a leading supporter of unrestricted submarine warfare during the First World War. This put Stresemann out of favour with some left-wing liberals.

In the shake up of party politics which followed the end of the war, the Nationalliberale Partei was replaced by two liberal parties, the centre-left Deutsche Demokratische Partei (DDP – German Democratic Party) and the centre-right party which Stresemann founded and led, the Deutsche Volkspartei. Initially, the DVP was seen simply as an oppositionist party, but Stresemann began to work with other parties and in August 1923 gained broad enough support to form a coalition government, consisting of both left and right-wing Liberals, alongside members of the Catholic Zentrum (Centre) party and the Sozialdemokratische Partei Deutschlands (SPD – Social Democratic Party of Germany).

Stresemann's main challenge as Chancellor was to lead the country out of the Ruhr crisis after France occupied the Ruhr area because of Germany's defaulting on reparations payments. His response, avoiding a dramatic act of opposition to France, was a significant factor in persuading Britain and America that the French had gone too far. It was in this role as a negotiator and conciliator that Stresemann sought to advance German interests in foreign policy when his government collapsed and he remained as foreign secretary.

Stresemann held this post in seven coalition governments: four led by Wilhelm Marx (Zentrum), two by Hans Luther, a non-party financier who was nevertheless close to the DVP, and one by the SPD's Hermann Müller. Throughout this time, Stresemann had a difficult balancing act to perform in pleasing coalition partners on the highly emotive and controversial issues he faced in foreign policy. Zentrum was a constant presence in the seven coalitions, while the DDP joined six of them, along with the Bavarian equivalent of Zentrum, the Bayerische Vokspartei (BVP – Bavarian People's Party) in five. These three parties shared much common ground with the DVP on foreign affairs, but Stresemann also had to pacify the ultra-conservative and nationalist Deutschnationale Volkspartei (DNVP – German National People's Party) as a crucial coalition partner in 1925 and 1927–28, along with the SPD in 1928–29. The DNVP were a particular challenge given that they had aggressive intentions regarding revisions of Germany's eastern border with Poland; they eventually found common ground with Hitler in 1933 and joined his government.

The success of Stresemann's balancing act lay first in securing tangible peaceful gains for Germany in terms of treaty revision. Revising the terms of the Treaty of Versailles was the pressing need for any German foreign minister, as the terms of the 'Diktat' of 1919 were so despised. Stresemann's approach to this was to try to draw the British and the French into a new agreement covering Germany's western borders. In January 1925, therefore, the German government enquired as to whether Britain and France might be willing to make arbitration treaties relating to future disputes, along with guaranteeing the existing territorial status of the Rhineland as part of Germany. Although that proposal was rejected, both the British and the French were ripe for some kind of new agreement. Much political opinion in the UK agreed that the terms of the Treaty of Versailles were harsh, and many were alarmed by the French occupation of the Ruhr. There was a drive to reduce the numbers of British troops stationed in Germany for financial reasons.

Meanwhile, there was a need to develop an alternative to the Geneva Protocol, a policy which had emerged from the League of Nations to try to clarify the circumstances in which countries would assist other countries which were the victims of aggression. The Conservative government in Britain held that the Protocol was a dangerous enhancement of the League's power, but wanted to offer a constructive alternative. The line that therefore emerged from the British was that countries with specific security problems should make pacts to tackle those particular problems, rather than agree to wider ranging universalist schemes. This coincided with some French concerns. Ever since 1919, France had been trying to entangle Britain into a security pact which would ensure that if Germany again attacked France, Britain would come to France's assistance.

After much internal discussion in the UK, the British foreign secretary, Austen Chamberlain, was authorised to pursue a pact drawing in both France and Germany. The ensuing negotiations eventually led, in October 1925, to the Locarno Agreements. The main Locarno treaty saw France and Germany accept their shared border. Crucially, that pact was guaranteed by Britain and Italy, who agreed that if either Germany or France attacked the other, both countries would act against the aggressor. Given all that we now know about the following fifteen years, Locarno is seen to have been a failure. But we should not underestimate the enthusiasm with which it was greeted at the time; Stresemann, along with Austen Chamberlain and their French counterpart, Aristide Briand, received the Nobel Peace Prize for the work that led to Locarno.

The new era of détente which followed Locarno enabled Stresemann to put a number of issues on the table to further the cause of treaty revision. Over the next four years, he skilfully pressed the British and French governments to make concessions over the terms of Versailles, on matters such as reparations and the presence of British and French troops in Germany. The Cologne zone was evacuated soon after Locarno, and although neither the presence of troops in the Rhineland nor reparations were finally resolved until after Stresemann's death, there were steady reductions in the numbers of occupying troops. He also laid important foundations for progress after his death, both through Locarno and the diplomacy which followed. He also took Germany into the League of Nations (including gaining a seat on the crucial Council of the League), which gave it international respectability.

However, Stresemann's real diplomatic genius lay in his treatment of the eastern question – Germany's border with Poland. One of the Locarno agreements did concern German–Polish relations, but it was simply an arbitration agreement. By agreeing to it, Stresemann was able to present Germany as having come to terms with its western borders, so that it could then negotiate with Britain and France over issues such as reparations. Meanwhile, in the east, Germany could appear to have embarked on a path of peace, while at the same time keeping border revision on the agenda. Those Germans who regarded the Polish border as unacceptable – and there were many of them – could still see in Locarno the potential for gaining back land which was populated by German speakers and which they believed should be part of Germany.

In Stresemann's various efforts to sell Locarno to nationalists and those concerned about treaty revision, the language he used suggested that the possibility of revision of the eastern frontiers was one of the main benefits of the agreements. Talking to an association representing those Germans who had seen their lands divided or lost at Versailles, he argued that Germany's best chance of revision would arise from developing good relations with the western powers so that they would look favourably on German claims. That might especially be the case, Stresemann believed, in the event of an economic crisis. As he told his audience, he believed that:

> ... if the question arises as to whether the whole instability of Europe
> is not caused by the impossible way the frontiers are drawn in the east
> ... it may ... be possible for Germany to succeed with its demands, if it
> has previously established ties of political friendship and an economic
> community of interests with all the world powers who have to decide
> the issue.[1]

He made similar points in a meeting with his own party's national executive, showing that he was not simply tailoring his argument to his audience. The core of Stresemann's policy was that peace in the west could lead to treaty revision in the east.

This was not enough, however, to win the support of all the nationalists. The DNVP initially left the coalition over Locarno, believing that Stresemann had surrendered Germany's freedom of action. However, Stresemann's policy had two strengths regarding conciliation of nationalist opinion. First, it left him with room to manoeuvre regarding Poland. Whenever the issue of eastern frontiers came on to the agenda, he could say that he was actively taking steps to change those borders through a policy of good relations with western European countries. Second, the DNVP's initial hostility had faded by the start of 1927, when they returned to the coalition. A condition of their membership of the government was broad acceptance of Stresemann's foreign policy, and the DNVP even went as far as taking part in a German delegation to the League of Nations in 1927. Arguably Stresemann's strategy contributed to the DNVP's relatively poor showing in the 1929 Reichstag elections.

The reality of much of Stresemann's strategy towards Poland in 1926–28 is that he sought to keep difficult issues off the agenda. After a trade boycott failed to have any significant impact on the Polish economy, there was a general rapprochement with the Poles. Yet at key moments, he could use the Polish issue to shore up support at home. By the end of 1928, there was growing discontent within Germany over the status of 'minorities' – those Germans living in areas lost to other countries in the border revisions of 1919. Many felt that the minorities had been neglected by the German government, and such concerns were expressed not only by the right, but also by more moderate parties. At the League of Nations Council meeting in December 1928 Stresemann had a blazing public row with the Polish foreign minister, August Zaleski, over the schooling of children in Polish Upper Silesia. Although it is generally believed that the outburst made the resolution of the issue more difficult, it earned Stresemann plaudits at home, and was probably part of a plan to detach moderate nationalists from the DNVP, which had just elected the hardline Alfred Hugenberg as its leader.

An assessment of the policy actually pursued by Stresemann has to conclude that he secured tangible gains for Germany in the west through rapprochement with its Great War opponents. In Stresemann's time as foreign minister, there was a new mood – 'the Locarno spirit' – in diplomatic relations. This eventually manifested itself at the Hague Conference of August 1929, where Stresemann secured agreement for the withdrawal of all troops from the Rhineland by the end of June 1930, and there was also agreement on outstanding reparations issues. Not only did this policy provide tangible gains in the west, but Stresemann believed that such rapprochement was likely to put Germany in a position where it could secure its goals in the east by peaceful means, and there is evidence that this won him some friends at home. There was every prospect that this approach could have continued to deliver peaceful progress throughout the 1930s. Yet Stresemann was to have no part in it; in October 1929 he suffered two strokes, which proved to be fatal. His death was widely seen, even by opponents, as having removed from Weimar a central pillar of the Republic's stability.[2]

~

At this point, what we know Stresemann actually achieved has to be replaced by speculation, although his record is a good guide to his future policy. It is important to note that such speculation is not idle; there has been serious academic debate over what difference

Stresemann might have made had he lived. Much of this debate has revolved around the issue of whether there were continuities between Stresemann and Hitler which might have led Stresemann to behave in a similar way to Nazi policy in the 1930s.

There were, of course, obvious differences between Stresemann and Hitler on matters of style. Stresemann was no demagogue and, except initially, did not question the democratic basis of the Weimar Republic. Although he was crucial to the DVP's public appeal, there was also no sense in which he was ever presented as any kind of Führer figure. Yet there are issues which can lead to questions about Stresemann's outlook.

The first, surprisingly, is his attitude to Judaism. It is surprising that there should be any question over this because in his younger days, Stresemann had opposed refusing Jews membership of the student fraternity to which he belonged. Moreover, Stresemann's wife was the daughter of a man who had converted from Judaism to Christianity and was described as being of Jewish descent. Despite this, by 1919, Stresemann was expressing criticism of Jews as a group, though stopping short of advocating DVP participation in anti-Semitic campaigns. He was particularly opposed to Jewish immigration to Germany from the east, and was, on occasion, willing to pander to anti-Semitic sentiments when speaking to his audiences. For all this, it should be stressed that Stresemann never exploited anti-Semitic sentiments as part of a party platform, even at a time when the Nazis were already doing so. There is also no question of him ever advocating the Nazi policy towards the Jews. What does need to be noted though, is that Stresemann was capable of appealing to *some* of the same sentiments in German society that extremists also exploited.

It is in foreign policy that other writers have seen much greater similarities. In particular, Stresemann's aim of revising the Polish frontiers means that it is possible to draw a direct line between Stresemann and the Nazis on that core foreign policy issue. At this point it must be stressed that Stresemann did not support the concept of lebensraum (living space), in the pursuit of which the Nazis wanted to occupy parts of eastern Europe, in addition to those already with German populations, in order to build a new German empire on the east. Stresemann had no such colonial goals. However, his strong commitment to regaining former German territories in Poland means that he might have been able to detach some of the less militant opinion from the Nazis.

This means, as Jonathan Wright has pointed out,[3] that in assessing whether Stresemann could have made a success of politics in the early 1930s, and held back the Nazi flood, he would have had to have done two things. First, his overall strategy had to be to continue to make the centre ground of politics appealing enough so that extremists did not progress. Second, a crucial tactic in that approach had to be to make tangible gains for Germany, through foreign policy, to show that peaceful cooperation with the west was the best way forward.

Could it be done? To answer the question, we first need to understand what actually did happen, in order to identify the points at which Stresemann might have made a difference. The first crisis for the Weimar Republic following Stresemann's death was the collapse of Hermann Müller's Grand Coalition in March 1930. This had been in office for nearly two years, and fell apart due to a row over the funding of an unemployment scheme in the wake of the effects of the depression brought on by the Wall Street Crash. In very simple terms, the SPD (to which Müller belonged) wanted to fund the scheme by higher taxes, while the DVP and other coalition members wanted it to be financed more by contributions from those who might be affected by it. In the end the coalition foundered on a disagreement over 0.5 per cent in the unemployment insurance rate.

This led to Müller being replaced by Heinrich Brüning of Zentrum. When he failed to push measures including cuts in public expenditure (to help Germany meet its reparations payments) through the Reichstag, President von Hindenburg granted new elections. That led to gains for both the Kommunistische Partei Deutschlands (KPD – Community Party of Germany) and the Nazis, and the parliamentary arithmetic dictated against the formation of any viable centrist coalition. Hindenburg therefore decreed that Brüning should be allowed to rule without the Reichstag, according to Article 48 of the Weimar constitution.

Brüning implemented many unpopular austerity measures, but also had some foreign policy successes, presiding over the final withdrawal of British and French troops from the Rhineland and also the announcement by the American President Hoover of a moratorium on reparations payments, although the final agreement on reparations was not reached until after Brüning's fall. Despite these achievements, Hindenburg steadily came round to the view that a more right-wing government, including the Nazis, was necessary to save the Republic; when Brüning refused to head the new coalition, Hindenburg removed him from office, replacing him with his party colleague, Franz von Papen, in June 1932.

Papen held office for only five months, during which time two elections were held. In the first, in July, the Nazis became the largest Reichstag party with 230 seats, and although they fell back to 196 in the second set of elections in November, it had become clear that they would have to be part of any future government. Hindenburg, however, did not wish to appoint Hitler as Chancellor, and instead replaced Papen with Kurt von Schleicher, who tried to build a new coalition based on the support of social democratic trades unionists, and, if it is not stretching a point to use the label, the 'left' of the Nazi party linked to Gregor Strasser. But Papen was working behind the scenes to undermine Schleicher, and in January 1933 he persuaded Hindenburg to appoint Hitler as Chancellor. The rest is history.

From the events as they happened, there emerge two points at which Stresemann might have prevented the descent towards dictatorship. First, could he have prevented the collapse of Müller's coalition in March 1930? Second, could he have been a more effective foreign secretary than either Julius Curtius (1929–31) or Brüning (who combined the post with that of Chancellor in 1931–32)? There are then two further alternative realities which involve rather different events. One revolves around the possibility that Stresemann might have been an alternative Chancellor to Brüning. The other is the intriguing prospect that Stresemann might have become President, in place of Hindenburg, in 1932.

In terms of the immediate collapse of Müller's Grand Coalition, Stresemann might have been able to make a difference if he had been able to persuade the DVP that continuing the coalition was more important than the short-term issue at stake. Though as close to business as anyone in the DVP, it is possible that Stresemann might have decided that stability was more important than the 0.5 per cent difference in the unemployment insurance rate over which the government fell. It is at least plausible that Stresemann could have taken that view, given his long record in building coalitions and then working with the SPD.

What might have made more of a difference, however, both in March 1930 and in the longer term, was if Stresemann had been a more effective foreign secretary than Curtius or Brüning. How could he have done that?

In the first place, had Stresemann been foreign minister beyond October 1929, he would have been ideally placed to make the most of German gains on both reparations and the withdrawal of British and French troops from Germany. These both happened in any case: reparations, first through the Young Plan (actually while Stresemann was still alive) and then the Hoover Moratorium, and troop withdrawals as an end result of the process begun at Locarno. Had Stresemann still been foreign minister in 1930 he might have been able to present both (especially troop withdrawals) as the outcome of his policy. He could have celebrated them with a public fanfare, claiming them as evidence of the success of a policy of rapprochement with the west, arguing that further gains to Germany would come if it continued along the same path. At that point he might then have begun to open, by diplomatic means, the question of the Polish–German border, perhaps at first focusing (as he had previously done) on the rights of German-speaking minorities in Poland in order to destabilise the border.

At the same time, Stresemann could have responded positively to the idea, floated by Aristide Briand, of a form of European union based on political and economic cooperation within a League of Nations framework. This offered the potential for a federal Europe in which borders between nations would have become blurred. Given the potential for German economic dominance in eastern Europe, such a scheme offered some hope of Germany gaining influence over Polish affairs. That might have made border questions less important, or it might have made it easier for Stresemann to argue for relatively minor, but nevertheless significant, border revisions. In either case, the prospect of further closer cooperation with France and others might have given Stresemann enough to persuade many Germans that Germany was achieving the power and influence it desired through peaceful means.

Stresemann's narrative would thus have been to show that Locarno had led to the settlement of western European questions in Germany's favour, for example, through the withdrawal of allied troops from the Rhineland. Continuing, the narrative would have been able to argue that the new mood engendered by the Locarno policy had also led to the revision of reparations agreements, enabling the eventual moratorium in response to the economic crisis. From all of this, Germany had clearly won – so Stresemann could then have argued convincingly that he would be able to deliver the same in the east by being a responsible and conciliatory member of a new European union.

Clearly, that would not have persuaded all of those on the far right of German politics who believed that only the remilitarisation of Germany could lead to its increased influence. Those hardliners were unlikely to be persuaded by any case for moderation. But with steady tangible gains – presented as part of a coherent policy, in a way that both Curtius and Brüning failed to do – Stresemann might have been able to buy off at least the more moderate section of the DNVP. Crucially, he might have persuaded the German people that the Nazi approach would prove counterproductive, and that in turn might have prevented their leap from 2.6 per cent of the vote in May 1928 to 18.3 per cent in September 1930. Against a backdrop of German gains from Stresemann's policy, both in terms of reparations and withdrawals, one might have expected not to see such a growth in extremism. But with Stresemann dead, the lack of anyone to sell the policy to the public may well have been highly significant.

Aside from helping to maintain the governments that were actually in power, Stresemann might instead have led his own government. In seeking a guide as to how he might have fared as Chancellor, the brevity of his brief spell in that office from August to November 1923 means that that period is of little help. However, as Chancellor, it is reasonable to assume that he would have brought the same strengths to government as he did as foreign minister. It is quite possible, furthermore, that as Chancellor, Stresemann would have continued to exert significant influence over German foreign policy; after all, he had not only the experience but also the international reputation and the good relations with his counterparts abroad. Thus in considering whether Stresemann could have been a more successful Chancellor than Brüning, one can look towards what he might have done as foreign minister. In the same way as Stresemann the foreign minister could have benefited from progress over troop withdrawals and reparations, the same benefits could have accrued to Stresemann the Chancellor. Regardless of the office he held, these successes could have been presented as the successful outcome of his influence and his policy.

On the details of economic policy, it is more difficult to build a case for Stresemann being able to make such a difference. A significant part of the context of German politics after 1929 was the global economic depression which followed the Wall Street Crash. There was nothing that Stresemann could have done to prevent that; and nor is it likely that he would have advocated any policy different to that pursued by the Brüning coalition in which his DVP colleagues played a part. Stresemann was as economically orthodox as the rest of his party and it is unlikely that he would have come up with an alternative plan to cope with the economic problems faced by Germany. However, that does not mean that he would have been powerless to reduce their impact. Brüning was not the only German leader to have pursued a policy which has been labelled Primat der Außenpolitik, that is, one in which the needs of foreign policy are given primacy over those of Innenpolitik (domestic policy). In such a situation, a successful foreign policy can help to shore up governments faced with domestic problems, and Stresemann's foreign policy might have helped to overcome concerns about the economic position in Germany. He could have argued, for instance, that a successful foreign policy – especially a reparations agreement which had major economic repercussions – was a necessary precursor to any kind of economic recovery.

Not all of the ways in which Stresemann might have made a difference rested on the pursuit of a successful foreign policy. Jonathan Wright has identified the intriguing prospect of Stresemann becoming the German President in 1932.[4] Wright points to plans that Stresemann had made to take a break from politics after he had secured the evacuation of the Rhineland. The memoirs of Stresemann's son, Wolfgang, suggest that he had thought about returning to politics by running for the Presidency in April 1932, having restored his health, perhaps by spending time in Egypt. Buoyed up by a successful foreign policy, he would have been a powerful candidate for the Presidency. Had he been elected, he could have formed a powerful democratic bulwark against Hitler in 1933, securing the support of the democratic parties and acting as a more powerful symbol of the strength of German democracy than had President Hindenburg. In the post of President, Stresemann might never have appointed Hitler as Chancellor in 1933, and might have been able to form a new anti-Nazi government which could have led Germany peacefully through the 1930s and into a new era of European peace and security.

The prospects for Germany if Stresemann had lived might have been very different than the slow descent into the darkness of Nazism. Stresemann offered Germans the chance for peaceful revision of the Diktat of Versailles. In his own lifetime he had been able to deliver results. He had negotiated a new peace with the west, which, incredibly, brought Britain and Italy in as guarantors of *either* Germany *or* France should one attack the other. He had brought Germany into the League of Nations, with a seat at its Council as a fully fledged European great power willing to play a part in the work of peace-building in the late 1920s. He laid the foundations of the successes over reparations and troop withdrawals that came so soon after his death.

Clearly, there were powerful forces at work in the 1930s; the Nazis tapped into deep-rooted expansionist and anti-Semitic sentiments in German society and politics. It would be too much to expect just one man to have been able to prevent this single-handedly. But at least Stresemann offered a different, and plausible, path to that of Hitler. Like Hitler, he was able to tap in to the widespread grievances that Germans felt over the end of the Great War and the treaties which ensued, but he did it in such a way as to persuade them that it was best to travel on the path of peace. At the same time, he did just enough on eastern policy to reassure his people that there was a real prospect of regaining parts of Germany lost to Poland in 1919. While he lived and did all this, the Nazi party remained on the fringe.

Without Stresemann's policy on offer, the far right found it much easier to flourish. Had Stresemann lived, there is at least the chance that he could have continued to keep the Nazis at bay. If that had happened, Adolf Hitler would have been remembered as little more than an historical curio, consigned to the same pages of history as all those others on the radical right who tried and failed to make an impact on the course of German history. Gustav Stresemann would have been remembered not only as Weimar's greatest statesman, but as the father of democracy in Germany.

Notes

1   Quoted in Jonathan Wright, *Gustav Stresemann: Weimar's Greatest Statesman* (Oxford, 2002), p. 345.
2   Ibid., pp. 493–94.
3   Ibid., pp. 500–03.
4   Ibid., p. 521.

Chapter 10

What if Czechoslovakia had fought in 1938?

Helen Szamuely

The political structure of Central Europe that had been set up at Versailles in 1919, and by the subsequent treaties of St Germain and Trianon, was effectively destroyed in 1938, a year before the start of the Second World War.

The invasion of Austria in March, with the subsequent Anschluss, and the Munich Agreement of 29 September 1938, with the subsequent incorporation of the Sudetenland into the German Reich did more than just destroy the 'Versailles system'. (The destruction was completed, as the Soviet newspapers proclaimed gleefully in early October 1939, by the partition of Poland.) Not only did this sequence of events severely tilt the balance of power in Germany's favour – as Winston Churchill, Duff Cooper and Harold Nicolson, among others, recognised – but by opening up Eastern and South-Eastern Europe to further German expansion it made an eventual European war inevitable.

The counter-argument – voiced at the time and since – was that war had already become inevitable, possibly by the mid-1930s and certainly by the beginning of 1938; the Munich Agreement postponed that inevitability by a year – a year gained by Britain that was, at last, rearming. It could also be argued that it was worth making every possible effort to preserve peace, just in case it worked.

In other words, the Munich Agreement in itself did not make war inevitable, but Hitler's subsequent behaviour did. A contributing factor was the growing perception in Britain and, to a lesser degree, in France that Hitler had diddled and humilated Chamberlain and Daladier through the series of discussions and meetings that had culminated in the final one on 29 September – from which Chamberlain had returned with the infamous piece of paper bearing Hitler's signature, recognised by many by that time to have been worthless.

The Munich Agreement has acquired a political and emotional meaning that has no parallel in modern history. It has become a symbol of the West's humilation at Hitler's hands; of short-sighted British stupidity (despite the fact that rearmament was stepped up and a guarantee was given to Poland); and of the betrayal of Eastern Europe, particularly of Czechoslovakia, establishing that country's almost unique victim status. Curiously enough, the event that might be seen as a far greater betrayal of those countries, the Yalta Agreement, has not been regarded in the same light and its Western signatories (Churchill and Roosevelt) have been repeatedly exonerated by various historians and analysts.

In the Preface to his recent biography of Neville Chamberlain, Robert Self postulates that the shadow of Munich is one of the contributing factors behind the dearth of biographies of that politician (other factors, as he clearly explains, have to do with the complexity and secretiveness of Chamberlain's personality).[1] He also quotes from Patrick Gordon Walker's diary for 21 September 1938 (i.e. before the final agreement, at a time when hopes and fears were constantly see-sawing) a paragraph that sums up contemporary and subsequent attitudes:

> It is difficult to judge how the country will react to Chamberlain's sell out of Czechoslovakia. I think Blum [Léon Blum, the French socialist leader] has expressed the public feeling very well when he said his own feelings were a mixture of cowardly relief and shame. If this is so, it is to be expected that many people – to hide their cowardice from themselves – will vent their shame on Chamberlain ... People who would not want

a stand to be made, had it actually been made, may now damn Chamberlain for not making a stand.[2]

On the other hand, John Charmley points out in his biography of Duff Cooper, the fervent anti-appeaser and the only man to resign from the Cabinet on 3 October 1938, because of disgust with the agreement, that *his* name will always be asociated with Munich:

> When the name of that treaty and the word 'appeasement' were excoriated then Duff's reputation stood high; a reading of his obituary notices is enough to make that point. But as appeasement has come to enjoy a better press, then so too Duff's reputation declined.[3]

'Appeasement', as applied to the 1930s, has not enjoyed a particularly good press, despite various historians' efforts (including John Charmley's) to try to understand better what really happened in what W. H. Auden called 'that low dishonest decade'. The partial opening of the Soviet archives ought to contribute to this growing understanding.

It is, nevertheless, fair to say that 'Munich' and 'appeasement' tend to be castigated as symbols of betrayal and cowardice even by people who, in other cases, would proclaim that any surrender and humiliation is better than war. Writers and campaigners who detail the horrors of the First World War (an important consideration in 1938) and demand a posthumous and completely anachronistic pardon for deserters in that terrible conflict, refuse to acknowledge that those who had actually lived through it all might have been reluctant to unleash another war. Instead, they hiss, as at a stage villain, when Chamberlain's name or the Munich Agreement are mentioned.

After Munich and the occupation of the Sudetenland the descent into war became apparently unstoppable. The invasion of the rest of Czechoslovakia in March 1939, the invasion of Poland and the Nazi–Soviet Pact led to the European war, the horrors of the Eastern Front and the Holocaust. It is, therefore, reasonable to ask whether any of this could have been prevented; whether the process could have been stopped in the autumn of 1938.

~

Various 'what if' scenarios have been discussed, if somewhat half-heartedly, in the past. What if the French had been more forceful in supporting the Czechs, to whom they were bound by treaty? What if Chamberlain had put pressure on the French to stand by Czecho-slovakia, and had been consistently tougher with Hitler, instead of pushing the Czech government towards an acceptance of the deal? What if the Soviet Union had engaged more forcefully and had offered to fight on the Czech side, as Ambassador Ivan Maisky intimated in London and the Foreign Minister Maxim Litvinoff in Geneva (both sets of comments faithfully and uncritically reported by Harold Nicolson in his diaries)?[4]

These are all questionable suppositions even in the realm of counterfactual history. Edouard Daladier, the French Prime Minister at the time of Munich, knew that his country was neither militarily nor politically equipped to challenge Germany in 1938. (As things turned out, she was not to be so equipped a year later either.) In the spring of that year another political crisis had resulted in four months without a government. The support of the Com-munist Party for any government was always questionable and the fascist movement was considerably stronger in France than Mosley's rather ineffectual movement was in Britain.

Duff Cooper spent a considerable amount of time and energy in those September days trying to ensure that Chamberlain strength-ened the French resolve, but it was clear all along that both Daladier and Georges Bonnet, the Foreign Minister, saw their own position as hopeless and were looking to Britain to take on the role, firstly of the country which was to pressurise the Czechs into submission and secondly of the general scapegoat to be blamed for whatever might go wrong.[5]

The Soviet Union had its own problems. The Great Purge, seemingly unnoticed by politicians and political diarists in the West, had reached full pitch in 1938 with the trial of the 'right-wing bloc of Trotskyite deviationists', in other words Nikolai Bukharin, the former Prime Minister Rykov, the former head of the secret police Genrikh Yagoda, and various others. The mass arrests continued unabated. Stalin launched two devastating assaults on the armed forces, making them, in effect, unoperable.[6] Even if the Red Army did decide and was able to intervene it would have taken them six weeks, as estimated by the Czech general staff, to reach Moravia and Bohemia. In any case, at the end of September necessary transit across Poland and Romania had not been agreed.[7] (Again, if one looks at what happened in 1939 with Poland, one has to question whether Soviet assistance would have been quite what Czechoslovakia needed or wanted.)

Effectively it was left to Britain to play the role of the protector — if that could be done. Some discussions of Munich emphasise the inadequacy of the Chamberlain government and of the man himself. While the effect of personality must not be dismissed out of hand, the circumstances of the late summer and autumn were such that quite possibly nobody could have done better, not even Churchill. On 15 September 1938 Duff Cooper wrote in a letter:

There are now only three horses left in the race: 1. Peace with honour; 2. Peace with dishonour; 3. Bloody war. I don't think that no. 1 has an earthly. The other two are neck and neck.[8]

What popular opinion wanted was peace with as much honour as could be mustered. Failing that, peace would have to do for the time being. Descriptions of the anxiety with which people waited for each one of Chamberlain's three returns from Germany, and the hysterical relief that greeted the final one, confirm this. There was a widespread acceptance that eventually war would happen, but it was only human to hope for its avoidance.

The split was more marked in the political class (or, possibly, we just know more about it). The Conservative Party was divided, with the majority supporting Chamberlain and many, like 'Chips' Channon, overflowing with admiration for his ability to produce the rabbit of peace out of the mangy hat of his negotiations with Hitler.[9]

The left, both in the Labour Party and outside it, effectively put itself out of the debate by its continuous opposition to rearmament. Attacking Chamberlain's policy of 'appeasement' made little sense if the same people then attacked the policy of creating the possibility of standing up to the dictators. When, after the Anschluss, Chamberlain decided that there should be no repetition with Czechoslovakia and, possibly, other countries, he stepped up the rearmament programme. In order to do so, he had to negotiate with the TUC 'to appeal for their goodwill and the concessions necessary to accelerate the defence programme'.[10]

The Labour Party in Parliament could not make up its mind whether to join the rebels on the government benches, some of whom, like Harold Nicolson, were members of what they considered to be the treacherous National Labour group. The people A. J. P. Taylor describes as 'Dissenters' were in disarray:

> On paper the Dissenters were all for resistance. Labour and trade union delegations waited on the Prime Minister; firm speeches were made in parliament. Yet 'stand by the Czechs' had far less fervour in it than 'arms for Spain'. The Dissenters felt that supporting Czechoslovakia was realpolitik – inevitable no doubt in a wicked world, but far from the moral line that they were accustomed to. Every Dissenter felt a double twinge of shame when the New Statesman suggested that the German Bohemians should be let go to Germany – shame that the suggestion should be made, but shame also that these Germans were in Czechoslovakia at all. No doubt Czechoslovakia was the only democracy east of the Rhine; but this was a recent description – previously she had been 'the vassal state' of French Imperialism.[11]

There is no one quite like a left-wing historian to skewer the intellectual muddle and pretensions of the left. However, Taylor did not mention at this stage two other important aspects. 'Arms for Spain', like several other widely supported campaigns, had been manipulated and organised by the Comintern (the Communist International), which had no interest in Czechoslovakia and, therefore, did not bother to put up a show of a fight. Secondly, one of the left's persistent delusions, when it came to rearmament, was that it would be used against the Soviet Union, which, they firmly believed, was a force for peace. Neither of those beliefs was true.

For various reasons rearmament had been slow and Chamberlain was painfully aware of the fact that in September 1938 Britain was not ready to challenge Germany if it might lead to war. The contrary argument was that it is precisely by challenging Hitler and threatening him with war that conflict could be avoided. This would have been a high-risk strategy in the circumstances. Even after the collapse of all his hopes in 1939, and after his own forced resignation in 1940, but while he was still active in Churchill's government, Chamberlain considered that the time he had gained by his policy had been well used to make the British forces, and particularly the air force, more effective.[12]

The reasons for the strong reluctance to call Hitler's bluff were rooted in the First World War and the subsequent arrangements for peace. Obviously, the huge losses, and stories of the horrors, influenced people both in Britain and in France. The latter also suffered from a serious shortage of young men, the birthrate having fallen dramatically between the wars. The idea of going to war yet again to defend a country, which, as Chamberlain rightly noted in his 26 September broadcast, was far off and whose disputes were little understood, was unappealing.

It has been noted that the division between appeasers and anti-appeasers was not necessarily along the lines of who had and who had not fought in the First World War. Harold Macmillan, Duff Cooper and, to some extent, Churchill himself had fought.

Chamberlain and Baldwin had been too old. Then again, Harold Nicolson had spent the war in the Foreign Office. The anti-appeasers argued that this was not just a question of Czechoslovakia but of the general principles of freedom, not giving in to bullies and, more practically, preventing one country, in this case Germany, from acquiring complete power in Europe. It had always been a cardinal tenet of British foreign policy to maintain a balance between European powers.

The other problem was that there had always been wide-ranging doubts in Britain about the Versailles Treaty and subsequent agreements. While it was accepted that Germany must be punished and, on a more self-righteous level, the 'oppressive' multinational empires dismantled (one, Russia, had managed to fall apart by herself), many were uneasy with the sense of revenge that was written into the treaties. Nor was there much support for the French thirst for revenge and reparation, as shown by the occupation of the Ruhr and the occupiers' behaviour there. The latter probably contributed to the Germans' own desire for revenge.

Then there was Czechoslovakia itself. Few people knew anything about it in detail and it is odd how little the country itself seems to have been discussed in Britain in those August and September days. But those who did try to understand the problem found themselves presented with something of a conundrum. The treaties were supposed to have been based on the principle of national self-determination, a difficult principle to act on in Central Europe where dividing lines between national groups did not run straight. However, the structure that was finally put together had, at the heart of it, a multinational state, with little indication that all the participants were happy with the arrangement.

The problem was agonisingly voiced by Harold Nicolson, who was not only an anti-appeaser but also someone who felt an almost personal responsibility to the Czechs, as he had been on the Committee of the Paris Peace Conference which had prepared the clauses of the Treaty of St Germain, which had defined the frontiers of Czechoslovakia:

> How difficult it is to decide! Vita takes the line that the Sudeten Germans are justified in claiming self-determination and the Czechs would be happier without them in any case. But if we give way on this, then the Hungarians and Poles will also claim self-determination, and the result will be that Czechoslovakia will cease to exist as an independent State. Vita says that if it is as artificial as all that, then it should never have been created. That may be true, although God knows how we could have refused to recognise her existence in 1918. It all seemed such a reality in those days. Hitler has all the arguments on his side, but essentially they are false arguments. And we, who have right on our side, cannot say that our real right is to resist German hegemony. That is 'imperialist'. Never have conflicting theories become so charged with illusions.[13]

A difficult position to be in and a difficult case to argue. In fact, Chamberlain's final offer, when he flew to Munich on 29 September, was to have been that the fate of Sudetenland be decided under the auspices of an international commission. Even strong anti-appeasers like Duff Cooper agreed that this was a reasonable solution. In the event, Hitler did not accept it.

~

There is one counterfactual scenario that has rarely been discussed but is, nevertheless, a genuine alternative possibility, unlike the ones that have been raised over and over again. What if the Czechoslovak armed forces had resisted the German advance into Sudetenland? What if President Edvard Beneš had refused to sign the agreement that had been made in his absence and over his head and had ordered the forces that had been mobilised on 25 September to man the border fortifications and repel the invader? Was this a real possibility, and if so what would have been the outcome?

Part of the problem with historical discussions of the events is the separation out of themes. Thus, Munich and the events that led up to it are analysed largely as a problem for the Western powers, whose humiliation it encompassed. The opposite of that is the triumph of the German policy of ill-concealed bullying written about by historians of Germany and the war. But the parallel events in Central Europe and Czechoslovakia are rarely examined in the same framework.

It is not easy to find out exactly how prepared the Czechoslovak armed forces were in 1938. It is known, however, that Sudetenland was the heart of the country's industrial base, and included a large armaments industry of such high calibre that its products were used by the German army in 1939 against Poland and in 1941 against the USSR:

> Czechoslovakia was a major manufacturer of machine guns, tanks, and artillery, and had a highly modernised army. Many of these factories continued to produce Czech designs until factories were converted for German designs. Czechoslovakia also had other major manufacturing concerns. Entire steel and chemical factories were moved from Czechoslovakia and reassembled in Linz, Austria which, incidentally, remains a heavily industrialised sector of the country.[14]

Nor were the German demands particularly unexpected in the light of developments in Sudetenland, as we shall see, but also in the light of international affairs. In 1947 Beneš wrote that he had always understood that Hitler was working to a plan rather than taking advantage of events (the two are not, of course, mutually incompatible, but Beneš saw them as such). He also wrote that:

> As early as 1921 or 1922 one of the greatest struggles in the political history of Europe began. It concerned the revision of the peace treaties made after the end of the First World War, a process which Hitler sucessfully completed.[15]

Whether this represents 20/20 hindsight is not clear, but in any case this view contradicts to some extent the one about Hitler working to a plan. There is also the problem that other countries and politicians may not have viewed the revision of the peace treaties a year or two after they were all signed as 'one of the greatest struggles in the political history of Europe'. The creation of Czechoslovakia was clearly of overriding importance to Beneš and the Masaryks as well as to their colleagues and supporters. It was viewed variously as a necessary development, realpolitik, or even a not-very-happy compromise.

From the very beginning the problems of its multinational entity had become apparent, with the Czechs assuming not just a leading but a governing role. This was particularly galling to the Slovaks who were treated as a younger and less developed sibling in the family of Slav nations, and was also resented by the other minorities, Germans, Poles and Hungarians. T. G. Masaryk, himself a Moravian Slovak by birth, for instance, proclaimed that:

> Slovaks and Czechs formed a single nation separated only by differences in language, history and culture.[16]

It is reasonable to ask exactly what made them a single nation if they were separated in all its major attributes. Abby Innes who quotes this statement, provides a kind of an explanation for the assumption of a Czechoslovak nation, one that was to haunt the creators of Czechoslovakia in the late thirties:

> There were also international pressures for the creation of a unified Czechoslovak state, and, concomitantly, for a unified 'Czechoslovak people' to act as the bulwark against the strength of other minorities. Without the proclamation of a 'Czechoslovak people' Czechoslovakia would have been a state lacking an absolute national majority and the question might then reasonably have been asked why it should include 3 million Germans. Without the German territories, however, the Czechoslovak economy would have been considerably weakened. A strong Czechoslovakia constrained Germany, an obvious gain in the eyes of the Great War victors, and the ethnic German territories stood within the natural and historical border of the Czech lands, as was made all too clear in 1938.[17]

Though a glorious idealistic achievement to Masaryk and Beneš, as well as the negotiators of the time, like Harold Nicolson, Czechoslovakia to the rest of Europe was a political creation that had grown out of the problems created by the end of the war. The tensions within it were likely to cause other problems after a time. These were exacerbated by the fact that, although Czechoslovakia was probably the one complete democracy in Central Europe by the 1930s, the non-Czech population felt that it was largely excluded from the government of the country. The Slovaks, in particular, resented the fact that although, as they saw it, there had been agreements in Cleveland in 1915 and Pittsburgh in 1918 to create full autonomy for them within the country, this remained little more than a rather cynical exercise to garner support.

In reality the country's politics became more and more centralised, with little participation by Slovak politicians (and none at all by the minorities). There were few Slovak politicians anywhere near the top and these tended to be 'pro-Prague' rather than interested in the complaints voiced by their own countrymen. It was not until November 1935 that President Masaryk appointed the only Slovak Prime Minister in the history of the First Republic, Milan Hodža, in a response to the shock caused by the electoral success of the pro-Nazi Sudeten German Party and to the growth of strong demands for autonomy in Slovakia. This was probably too late, though a good deal might have been salvaged by more skilful politicians.

> [Hodža], however was in a clear bind; for Czechs his credibility partly depended upon his presumed powers in Slovakia, but if he accepted HSPP [Hlinka Slovak People's Party] demands for economic and administrative concessions and implementation of the Pittsburgh Agreement he would lose his place in Prague.[18]

The negotiations which began at the end of January 1936 failed conclusively in late March and, as Abby Innes says: 'Thereafter the

HSPP assumed its full potential as a major threat to the Czechoslovak state.'[19]

Meanwhile, the situation in the Sudetenland had become even more critical. The German national parties, which had started life as largely radical socialist parties linked to the trade unions, were understandably distrusted by the Czech authorities. That very fact, as well as the economic slump of the early 1930s, which, as ever, hit many of the national minorities disproportionately hard (or so they felt), increased their following.

> DNSAP [Deutsche Nationalsozialistische Arbeitpartei] leaders, in particular Rudolf Jung, who had written on the theory of national socialism long before Hitler, in the 1920s developed a programme of autonomy and self-administration for the Sudeten Germans within Czechoslovakia. The national socialist party benefited from the economic slump; DNSAP membership doubled, to some 60,000 members between 1930 and 1932. It began to achieve significant successes in municipal elections, its membership was becoming younger and ever more impressed by the Hitler movement.[20]

In 1933 many of the leaders of the existing parties disappeared to Germany, there to acquire positions in the Nazi hierarchy and to influence attitudes to the Sudeten question in particular and to Czechoslovakia in general. The parties were banned, but no attempt was made to channel Sudeten German politics into parties and organisations that might have been more acceptable and useful to Czechoslovakia. Although the Sudetendeutsch Heimafront, set up in October 1933 and led by Konrad Henlein, whose background was military rather than socialist, was clearly pro-Nazi and was covertly subsidised from Germany, there were still many Sudeten Germans who disliked its ideology and belonged to the older, more democratic socialist tradition. Even in 1935 the democratic German parties received about a third of the vote. (These people, too, would be at risk after the German occupation of autumn 1938.)

In the May 1935 elections, the transformed Sudetendeutsche Partei (SdP) polled 1,249,230 votes, more than the biggest Czechoslovak party, the Agrarian Party, which received 1,116,593 votes. This, as we have seen, sent a shock through the Czechoslovak political system but did not produce the necessary results. Hitler began to step up his campaign to 'help our German brothers' oppressed by the Czechs. Henlein himself was not a particularly able or charismatic figure but he was used astutely and ruthlessly by Hitler.

> The prospect of going to war with Germany came as no surprise to the Czechoslovak government of the 1930s. Prague had, in fact, been preparing for war seriously for years; by some estimates, over half of all government spending from 1936 to 1938 was for military purposes. Much of this went towards the construction of an elaborate system of bunkers and other defences in the Sudetenland, the border region shared with Germany.[21]

It has been estimated that there were 200 fortified artillery batteries and 7,000 bunkers along the border. The Czechoslovak army was the third largest in Europe and a few days before the Munich Agreement 1.5 million soldiers had been mobilised. The German mobilisation of August 1938 resulted in 2 million troops. In other words, this was not an ill-prepared little force facing up to the might of Germany (which was in any case overestimated by Britain and France at the time).

There is the question of how good those fortifications were. At the rather desperate meeting of the Cabinet and military chiefs on 30 September in Prague, the new Prime Minister and Minister of Defence, General Syrovy, maintained that many fortifications had not been completed, which meant that there was no chance of successfully defending the country until the Soviet forces could arrive – which in any case, as we have seen, was not really a very strong possibility. France, which had signed an agreement with Czechoslovakia, now accepted that Sudetenland must, in effect, be separated from the country and there would be no help coming from them should the Czechs decide to fight. The logistical problems would have been too difficult anyway. Britain and France could have opened up a western front, but they could not have come to the Czechs' assistance directly.

General Husárek told the meeting that the operational plan of the army was built on the assumption that a large part of the German forces would be tied down in France, and even perhaps by having to cover themselves against Poland. The plan also assumed that the Hungarian forces would be exposed to a concentrated offensive of the Little Entente.[22] In those circumstances it would have been reasonable to assume, Husárek said, that at least Moravia and certainly Slovakia could be defended against the initial superiority of Germany and to save a large part of the Czechoslovak forces until the arrival of the Red Army. Husárek also pointed out that its transit across Poland and Romania had not been agreed.[23]

At best this seems to have been a chancy and poorly thought-out plan, relying on uncertain factors with no attempt made to ascertain the reality of the situation. Poland had already responded to the Sudeten troubles by backing the Polish population of Czechoslovakia in its demands for autonomy. It was hardly likely to fight on the Czech side. The problems over the Red Army were colossal. And it is true that after the Anschluss the southern borders of Bohemia and Moravia had become more exposed, with the fortifications between the rivers Morava and Znojmo not ordered until the middle of April 1938.

Nevertheless, given the large defence spending in the previous years, the existence of a large, well-armed military force and of extensive border fortifications, as well as the presence of huge modern arms manufacturing industries, the defeatism of the generals – only one of whom, General Vojcechovski, maintained that the country should defend itself – seems remarkable. Their response to his solitary voice was that the army would, of course, acquit itself well but it was up to politicians to give the order.

It seems that the politicians and military (as well as the people outside the Castle, where the meeting was taking place) united in blaming Beneš for the situation, maintaining that he could have negotiated differently. It is also possible that they were blaming him for not ordering the armed forces to resist the German army. In the few days before his resignation, the President continued to insist that Czechoslovakia was being destroyed by its supposed allies rather than by the German aggressor. Kornil Krofta, the Foreign Minister, who on 30 September 1938 accepted the Munich Agreement, stated that it was made 'without us and against us', prophesying that the other countries had not actually saved themselves by their betrayal. Jan Masaryk (son of Thomas and later the famously defenestrated Prime Minister) was at this time the Ambassador to London. He described the negotiations in Munich as a 'unique bestiality in international relations'.[24] And so the myth was born, and the possibility of Czechoslovak resistance buried. The recently conscripted soldiers were sent home and German troops were allowed to occupy the fortifications and the whole of Sudetenland.

Part of the Munich Agreement was a guarantee by the signatories (Britain, France, Germany and Italy) of the borders of the Czechoslovak state minus Sudetenland. That guarantee was of little avail against further territorial demands by Poland and Hungary, and Slovak demands for autonomy, backed by Germany. In March 1939 the German army occupied the rest of the country. There were no defences left, as they had been handed over in October 1938.

Czechoslovakia was reunited in 1945. In 1947, under the Beneš decrees, the German and Hungarian populations were expelled regardless of whether they had welcomed the invaders or not and often under conditions of some brutality. The theory was that this would make the country more homogenous but, as Abby Innes points out, the expulsion of minorities in many ways destroyed the need for a Czechoslovak nation state. Three years after the Communist system fell the country ceased to exist.

What difference would resistance to the German invasion of the Sudetenland have made, bearing in mind the size of the armed forces, the high level of equipment and munitions industries and the existence of the fortifications (though, as we have seen, their efficacy seems to have been doubted at the time)?

It might be useful to look at what happened eleven months later, when Germany invaded Poland on 1 September 1939. The Polish army was not so well equipped and had a much smaller industrial base. It also suffered from the fact that the country was simultaneously invaded in the east by the Red Army. Even so, the campaign lasted over a month, ending on 6 October when Germany and the USSR occupied the whole of Poland. In that short period the Germans sustained high personnel losses – around 16,000 killed in action. Even more important was the loss of about 30 per cent of their armoured vehicles, as a result of which an immediate attack westward was discarded.[25]

It is not unreasonable to suppose that a larger, better armed and more modern Czechoslovak army, unencumbered by having to fight the Soviet invaders as well (though there is a good chance that the Polish and Hungarian armies might have attacked to claim territories that they considered to be theirs by right) would have inflicted greater losses, and may well have stopped the German army long enough for some new decisions to be taken.

Of course, there were the political problems. How reliable were the Sudeten Germans? What about the Slovaks, and the smaller Hungarian and Polish minorities? A war against an invader may well have pulled the Czechs and Slovaks, with few exceptions, together, restoring the idea of national unity, particularly if promises of genuine autonomy within one state had been kept. The reaction of the Sudeten population is more difficult to gauge. It was not entirely German, and the Czech and Jewish sections of it would obviously have supported the Czechoslovak army and state. Even among the Germans, not all were enamoured with the idea of a Nazi regime, though, once again, some promises would have had to have been made and to be seen to be kept. The psychological effect of the country actually fighting for its existence would have been enormous, especially as its population seems to have been prepared to do so.

Beneath the myth of the betrayal of Czechoslovakia runs a thinner and more elusive thread of dissatisfaction with the country's and the government's behaviour at this moment of supreme trial:

> The Munich crisis touched on the most sensitive spot of Czech national conscience. It was another disaster to be added to the many calamities of the past. It concerned the viability of the state as well as the reliability of its friends – its domestic and foreign policies. But most of all it concerned the capacity of the nation to defend the state. Beneš and his government decided to give in and by doing so, they confirmed the expectations of the enemies and the worst suspicions of their own people. In effect Beneš and his government said that the state would not be defended and that it was not worth defending. The troops which had been gathered together during the general mobilisation went home, the border fortresses fell into enemy hands. Some months later, in March 1939, Hitler's troops marched into Prague and the Czechoslovak state ceased to exist in any form whatever.[26]

Had Czechoslovakia defended itself, it is entirely possible that Britain and, especially, France, would have found it impossible to withstand popular pressure to go to its aid. This would have had to have consisted of a declaration of war and the effective opening of a western front. With his troops tied up in Czechoslovakia and his rear not protected by the Nazi–Soviet Pact, not to mention the lack of supplies from the USSR and of armaments produced in Czechoslovak factories, Hitler's position would have been very different from what it turned out to be in spring 1940. Chamberlain's fears that London would be in ruins within hours were probably misplaced, as the Luftwaffe could not send bombers effectively until it had seized bases in France and the Low Countries.

Even a threat to become involved on the Czech side as the fighting went on would have made a difference. One has to remember that Hitler's position was not as secure as he would have liked it, particularly with regards to foreign policy. As Ian Kershaw notes:

> The Sudeten crisis of summer 1938 again illustrates Hitler's direct influence on the course of events. Although traditional power politics and military-strategic considerations would have made the neutralisation of Czechoslovakia a high priority for any revisionist government of Germany, it was Hitler's personal determination that he would 'smash Czechoslovakia by military action' – thereby embarking on a high-risk policy in which everything indicates that he was not bluffing – that, because of the speed and danger rather than the intrinsic nature of the enterprise, seriously alienated sections of the regime's conservative support, not least in the army. Only the concessions made to Hitler at the Munich Conference deflected him from what can justifiably be regarded as *his* policy to wage war *then* against Czechoslovakia. As is well known, it was Hitler – learning the lesson of Munich – who rejected any alternative to war in 1939, whereas Göring, the second man in the Reich, attempted belatedly to defer any outbreak of hostilities.[27]

There is a strong possibility that a war against Czecholsovakia at that point might not have gone particularly well for Germany, and the doubts about Hitler's style and foreign policies would have been confirmed. It was the smoothness of the two operations in 1938, the occupation of Austria and the Sudetenland, that served to remove many of the doubts.

If the Czechoslovaks had fought, Göring would have been in a much better position to urge caution. He himself was:

> ... more concerned to establish Germany's economic dominance of central and south-eastern Europe as the base of continental political hegemony consolidated through alliance with Britain. Whereas Ribbentrop's anti-British stance pandered to Hitler's readiness to risk war with a Britain he regarded as fundamentally weakened, Göring, partly echoing fears expressed by his many contacts in business, military and

landholding circles, sought to work against the high-risk policy and especially to avoid the prospect of a war with Britain.[28]

Not only Göring but the many other doubters would have been strengthened. In particular the army might well have withdrawn its — always rather half-hearted — support for Hitler if it had found itself in a prolonged campaign in Czechoslovakia, with the prospect of a western front opening up behind it. Could the army have got rid of Hitler and replaced him with someone else, less certain of his aims, less adventurous, less charismatic, who would have pursued the reasonably popular domestic policies but been more careful of antagonising foreign powers? This possibility is not to be excluded, although it is unlikely that the rearming of Germany would have stopped. However, a prolonged or, at least reasonably prolonged campaign in the Sudetenland would have weakened Gemany's economic growth and this, too, would probably have put a stop to further military and foreign adventures for some time.

Eventually, there is no doubt, the question of Germany's economic hegemony in Central Europe would have had to have been faced up to as well as, possibly, her demands for the restoration of some of the colonies taken away in 1918. But that would have been very different from a Germany led by a triumphant Hitler who could show that his mixture of cunning and bullying worked; a Germany that added to its own munitions industry by taking over the Czechoslovak one; a Germany that had divided up much of Central and Eastern Europe with the Soviet Union, which also supplied it with essential raw materials and guaranteed its rear; in short, the Germany that Britain and France did have to face in 1939–40.

Notes

1   Robert Self, *Neville Chamberlain* (Ashgate, 2006), pp. vii–viii, 1–17.
2   Quoted in ibid., p. 327.
3   John Charmley, *Duff Cooper* (Macmillan Pbk, 1987), p. 113.
4   Harold Nicolson, *Diaries and Letters*, vol. 1 1930–39 (Collins Fontana, 1969), entries for 22 August and 26 August 1938, pp. 250–51; entry for 23 September 1938, p. 359.
5   Charmley, *Duff Cooper*, pp. 115, 118.

6   Robert Conquest, *The Great Terror: A Reassessment* (Hutchinson, 1990), pp. 182 –213.

7   Zbynek Zeman and Antonín Klimek, *The Life of Eduard Beneš 1884–1948* (Clarendon Press, 1997), pp. 135–36.

8   Quoted in Charmley, *Duff Cooper*, p. 117.

9   Robert Rhodes James (ed.), *Chips – The Diaries of Sir Henry Channon* (Penguin, 1970), pp. 203–16 passim.

10 Self, *Neville Chamberlain*, p. 294.

11 A. J. P. Taylor, *The Trouble Makers* (Hamish Hamilton, Panther, 1970), pp. 178–79.

12 Self, *Neville Chamberlain*, pp. 439–40.

13 Nicolson, *Diaries and Letters*, vol. 1 1930–39, entry for 15 September 1938, pp. 353–54.

14 http://en.wikipedia. Org/wiki/Occupation_of_Czechoslovakia.

15 Zeman and Klimek, *The Life of Eduard Beneš*, p. 119.

16 Abby Innes, *Czechoslovakia – The Short Goodbye* (Yale Univeristy Press, 2001), p. 4.

17 Ibid.

18 Ibid., p. 12.

19 Ibid.

20 Zeman and Klimek, *The Life of Eduard Beneš*, p. 118.

21 http://www.radio.cz/en/article/66381

22 An alliance formed by Czechoslovakia, Romania and Yugoslavia with France's support in 1920–21 to prevent Hungarian revanchism and the restoration of the Habsburgs; it was effectively finished by 1938.

23 Zeman and Klimek, *The Life of Eduard Beneš*, pp. 135–36.

24 Ibid., p. 117.

25 http://en.wikipedia.org/wiki/Polish_contribution_to_World _War_II.

26 Zbynek Zeman, *The Masaryks – The Making of Czechoslovakia* (I. B. Tauris, 1990), p. 164.

27 Ian Kershaw, *The Nazi Dictatorship* (Hodder Arnold, London, 4th edition, 2000) p. 148.

28 Ian Kershaw, *Hitler* (Longman, Harlow, 1991), p. 145.

Chapter 11

What if Mao had met Roosevelt?

John Gittings

In early 1945, as the war with Japan neared its end – and as efforts began to avoid a subsequent civil war within China – Mao Zedong asked to fly to Washington for secret talks with President Roosevelt, and spoke in glowing terms of future relations with the US.

This was a remarkable request, coming as it did from the leader of Asia's largest communist party, which owed allegiance, formally at any rate, to the Soviet Union; Stalin would surely have been furious if such a visit had occurred. In the event nothing came of the proposal and for a quarter of a century even the fact that it had been made was ignored. No one was interested in asking whether relations between a communist China and the US could have taken a better course than the mutual hostility of the 1950s and 1960s – until they did actually improve, in the 1970s.

More recently, a new academic consensus has concluded that these early overtures (and others made later by the Chinese communists) could never have changed the course of events. I believe this is too easy a conclusion and that the course of US–China relations might quite possibly have had less tragic consequences 'if Mao had met Roosevelt'. We can also draw an interesting – and perhaps disturbing – lesson from the shifts in scholarly opinion towards this affair.

~

Mao's proposal was transmitted from Yan'an (Yenan), the communist capital in north-west China, by the head of the US wartime mission stationed there (the so-called 'Dixie Mission') on 9 January 1945:

> [The] Yenan Government wants to dispatch to America an unofficial rpt unofficial group to interpret and explain to American civilians and officials interested the present situation and problems of China. Next is [a] strictly off the record suggestion by the same [government]. Mao [Zedong] and Chou [Zhou Enlai] will be immediately available either singly or together for [an] exploratory conference at Washington should President Roosevelt express [the] desire to receive them at [the] White House as leaders of a primary Chinese [political] party. They expressly desire that it be unknown rpt not known that they are willing to go to Washington in case Roosevelt['s] invitation [is] not now forthcoming. This [is] to protect their political [situation] vis-a-vis Chiang [Kai-shek].[1]

There were in fact two proposals being made from Yan'an. First, that an 'unofficial' group would be sent to the US to explain the position of the Chinese Communist Party; this would evidently have operated in public. Second, that Mao and Zhou would have travelled in person, and perhaps in secret. It would have been no ordinary journey (especially for Mao, who had at that stage had never travelled in a plane).They would have flown from Yan'an to Chongqing (Chungking), and then trans-shipped to one of the famous Pan-American China Clippers, embarking on the hazardous Cannonball Route, over the Hump of the Himalayas to India, probably on through Karachi, Abadan, Cairo, Tripoli and Casablanca, down on to Bathurst or Accra, across the Pacific to Brazil, up to Trinidad and on to Miami, before the last leg to Washington. It would have taken at least five or six days.

Once in the White House, what would Mao have wanted to discuss? He had already set out his agenda for a future relationship with the US in a number of interviews with members of the Dixie Mission, particularly though not exclusively with the Foreign Service officer John (or Jack) Service.

First, Mao wanted the US to treat the Communist Party (CCP) as an equal partner with Chiang Kai-shek's Kuomintang (KMT), including in the distribution of arms, and to put pressure on Chiang to cooperate with the CCP to avoid civil war. As he explained to Service:

> With Chiang you can be friendly on your own terms. He must give in to constant, strong and unified pressure ... There is no longer any need or any reason to cultivate, baby or placate Chiang. The US can tell Chiang what he should do – in the interest of the war.

Second, Mao would downplay his party's relationship with the Soviet Union:

> The Russians ... will have their hands full with their own job of rebuilding [after the war]. We do not expect Russian help ... Russia only wants a friendly and democratic China. Cooperation between America and the Chinese Communist Party will be beneficial and satisfactory to all concerned.

Third, Mao would hold out a tempting prospect of a future relationship which at last provided a real 'open door' (the unvarying goal of US policy in China) for the capital and goods of America.

> China must industrialise. This can be done – in China – only by free enterprise and with the aid of foreign capital. Chinese and American interests are correlated and similar. They fit together, economically and politically. We can and must work together.
>
> We will be interested in the most rapid possible development of the country on constructive and productive lines.

Finally, Mao would stress the need for dialogue and understanding:

> America does not need to fear that we will not be cooperative. We must cooperate and we must have American help. That is why it is so important to us Communists to know what you Americans are thinking

and planning. We cannot risk crossing you – cannot risk any conflict with you.[2]

Mao's proposal was held up in Chongqing by President Roosevelt's special ambassador, General Hurley, who saw it as an attempt by the Communists to bypass him (which it was) and as a plot against him by the foreign service officers in the Dixie Mission (which it was not). Eventually the request was forwarded to FDR by Hurley, but only on 'the fifth page of a six-page letter' in which he cited it as part of the alleged conspiracy.[3]

Hurley also regarded as part of this plot various proposals, made by officers under the US military commander in China, General Wedemeyer (with whom he had testy relations), for military cooperation on the ground with the Chinese communists. These included a plan, conveyed to Yan'an by an officer of the Office of Strategic Services, to place US Special Operations men with communist units behind Japanese lines for acts of sabotage. (The strategic context for this was the expectation that US ground forces would soon land on the Chinese mainland as a prelude to the invasion of Japan; in the end the war effort was focused instead on approaching Japan via the Philippines, and the Chinese theatre declined in importance.)

Did FDR have any knowledge of the offer from Mao and Zhou? Two months later, in March 1945, during a conversation with Edgar Snow (author of *Red Star Over China*) Roosevelt indicated that a US landing on the North China coast would take place and that he had no objection to cooperating with the communist guerrillas. 'I've been working with two governments there [in China]. I intend to go on doing so until we can get them together.' The President had just received a memorandum, drafted by most of the Foreign Service officers in Chongqing, arguing the need to supply the Communists on political as well as military grounds; otherwise, it said, the Communists might seek Soviet assistance and 'chaos in China will be inevitable'. Roosevelt's statement to Snow is suggestive – and Mao would have been delighted to hear that the US President had referred to his regime as a 'government' – but Roosevelt was almost certainly referring in much more general terms to his hopes of bringing the Communists and Nationalists together.[4]

American war priorities changed, however; Hurley ensured the downgrading of the Dixie Mission and President Roosevelt died. Brief and elusive as this episode was, we can hardly fail to be intrigued by it. Snow speculated that Roosevelt's death may have 'closed the chapter on our chance to find out how the Chinese communists would behave towards us – and towards Russia – if treated as our ally in the common war against Japan'. And Carolle Carter, author of a recent study on the Dixie Mission, suggests that 'The journey by Mao and Chou to Washington would probably have placed additional distance between Yenan and Moscow while making the Communists appear less like an insurgent group than like an equal player in the joint war effort'.[5]

If this episode is taken seriously, it raises similar questions about subsequent moments in the US–China relationship which might have had different and more hopeful outcomes. These would include the mediation mission by US General George Marshall to China in 1946–48, a brief diplomatic overture from the new Communist government to US Ambassador Leighton Stuart in 1949 and, most significantly of all in my opinion, renewed efforts made by Beijing to entice Washington into a dialogue from 1955 to at least 1957, through the ambassadorial talks between the two countries in Warsaw.

What might have happened?

So what might have happened if Mao had met Roosevelt, or – in a more realistic scenario – Zhou Enlai had met him or, more modestly still, if it was Zhou, or even a less high-ranking delegation, who had made the long journey to Washington but had only met the Secretary of State?

Whatever the level of the visitors, the mere fact of such contacts taking place in the US capital – rather than in the remote loess highlands of Yan'an – could have improved significantly the chance of further and more fruitful dialogue between the CCP and the US, and would have put Chiang Kai-shek on notice that he could no longer take Washington's support for granted. This would then have created a different atmosphere for the efforts made by General Marshall to bring the two Chinese sides together and avert a civil war. Contrary to the arguments of many scholars today, such a conflict was not inevitable as far as the Communists were concerned. They had been at war, either with the Nationalists or the Japanese, and at times with both, for nearly twenty years. Mao himself believed that if civil war were to break out it would take 'ten to fifteen years' for his forces to prevail. Even in June 1946, by which time Marshall's mediation had almost certainly failed (although it dragged on into the following year) the Central Committee still concluded that 'without jeopardising any of our basic interests, [we should] pursue peace; a long period of war is not in our interest'. As the Chinese historian Zhang Baifa has commented, 'From our present perspective, it is quite hard to believe how optimistic the mood [for peace] of the Chinese Communists was at the time'.[6]

Mao clearly wished to create a good impression on Marshall, telling him that 'Chinese democracy must follow the American path, because the conditions for bringing about socialism in China are presently lacking'[7] – a statement of the obvious in the immediate post-war period. The CCP's preference for peace and desire for outside mediation was well attested in internal documents even as its prospects diminished and failure became more likely, as was recognised by Mao by mid-1946. As their hopes faded, Mao and Zhou even considered 'whether to raise the issue of the Chinese civil war at the UN to induce international intervention'.[8]

It is true that the Chinese communist forces were helped by the Soviet Red Army's occupation of north-eastern China, and that the Yan'an leadership kept in close touch with Moscow. But the history of relations with Moscow had not been smooth, and Stalin's commitment to the Chinese communist revolution was ambiguous – as it would continue to be until Mao had actually won. A diplomatic tilt towards the US would in this context have had a definite tactical value. As Zhou Enlai observed at the time:

> The key is that China must not subordinate itself to another country's influence or become another country's instrument. China's role should be to bring together its allies, and at the very least serve as a bridge promoting cooperation between the US and the Soviet Union.[9]

If 'Mao had met Roosevelt', this might have led to one of two outcomes. First, US mediation could have forced Chiang Kai-shek to accept a coalition government. This development could paradoxically have (a) delayed the CCP victory in 1949; and (b) resulted in an effective division of China into spheres of influence between the US and the Soviet Union. However, such a result – which was Stalin's goal – might then have exacerbated CCP–Soviet tensions, resulting in a weaker and more fraught relationship than actually emerged in the Sino–Soviet Alliance signed by Mao in Moscow in February 1950.

Second, and alternatively, on the assumption that civil war still broke out, the more favourable climate already created in US–Communist relations could have influenced Washington to take a more neutral line:

(a) The US might have been more reluctant to airlift Chiang's forces to Manchuria to accept the Japanese surrender, or to use US Marines to occupy key installations such as railways and coal mines until the Nationalist troops arrived in sufficient strength, or to maintain its naval base at Tsingtao until the end of the civil war.

(b) The US might have been less willing to provide surplus equipment and military aid to the Nationalists, which reached over $2 billion in the post-war period.

(c) If the US had maintained a position of at least half-way neutrality, then the offer of diplomatic negotiations made in 1949 by the incoming communist government might have been less equivocal, and the US response less negative.

(d) And if the Nationalists had received less US support, then Chiang Kai-shek might have failed to escape to Taiwan – and the biggest issue to bedevil US–China relations for the next sixty years would have been removed!

(e) Mao might also have been more reluctant to back the North Korean invasion of the South in 1950. We know that the argument in Beijing over whether or not to intervene was finely balanced. A continued US–Communist Chinese dialogue (even if only through back channels) could have reduced the danger of miscalculation on both sides. Thus the US under such circumstances might have refrained from crossing the 38th Parallel, or at least from penetrating deep into North Korea. The Chinese advance, if it had taken place, might in turn have been more measured, halting at the same parallel.

Shifts in Western scholarship

Historical judgement is never value-free nor divorced from the political culture of the time. The episode described above, and the questions it raises about alternative outcomes in what became a crucial theatre of the Cold (and sometimes hot) War, were ignored for two decades. It was then rediscovered by Western scholars who concurred in their judgement that this was indeed a missed opportunity. More recently a new body of scholarship has reached exactly the opposite verdict, concluding, in effect, that it would have made no difference at all if Mao had met Roosevelt.

These three phases coincide, and not by accident, with very substantial shifts in the intellectual climate within which Western scholarship towards China has operated. The first period, when the historical evidence was ignored, was that of the 1950s and 1960s, when US–China policy was a political minefield dominated by the McCarthyite question of who had 'lost China'. The second period was that of the 1970s and 1980s, when Communist China was rediscovered, and to some extent rehabilitated, by the US political establishment, with much agonising over the mistakes of the past which had caused such a long rupture. The more negative conclusions in recent scholarship (i.e. that there was no opportunity to be missed) are based partly on the analysis of new diplomatic documents, particularly from the Soviet archives. These have been taken to show that Mao was determined to 'lean to the (Soviet) side' and to humble the imperialists who had humiliated China in the past, thus precluding any possibility of meaningful relations with Washington. However this judgement also reflects a post-Cold-War consensus which is generally less willing to attribute responsibility, not to say blame, to the West for the Cold War confrontations of the past.

(1) **1950s and 1960s.** Mao's request to visit Washington, although kept secret at the time that it was made in 1945, was on record by the early 1950s in several accessible sources. The episode was referred to in the memoirs of Admiral Leahy, Roosevelt's Chief of Staff, published in 1950; General Wedemeyer, Leahy reported accurately, had been 'asked to secure passage to Washington for Mao Tse-tung and Chou En-lai, the top Chinese Communists, for conferences with the President'.[10] The actual dispatch from Hurley to Roosevelt, reporting the proposal from Yan'an, was then reproduced in the official Department of State volume known as the *Yalta Papers*, published in 1955.[11] This collection of documents received huge publicity and was extensively used by both sides in the recriminations over who had allegedly 'lost China' – yet this particular nugget of information was apparently ignored. Both Admiral Leahy's memoirs and the *Yalta Papers* were used as sources for the monumental volume *America's Failure in China, 1941–50*, by Tsou Tang, published in 1963 and for many years the standard work on this subject. Yet though Professor Tsou actually quoted from Hurley's dispatch, he failed to mention the proposal which it contained for Mao to visit Washington.[12]

A later study of US–Chinese relations by Michael Schaller notes that 'the Communist effort to reach the President directly appeared in certain published material as early as the 1950s. However, they were completely overlooked by historians'. We can share Professor Schaller's puzzlement, and wonder whether 'overlooked' is too weak a description.[13]

(2) **1970s and 1980s.** Extensive reports from the Dixie Mission in Yan'an describing the communist movement, often in favourable terms, relaying interviews with Mao and other leaders, and recommending a more positive approach towards them, eventually appeared in the Department of State's archive series *Foreign Relations of the US*, in the China volumes for the years 1944 and 1945. But publication of these was delayed in order to avoid giving offence to the Kuomintang government on Taiwan; the 1944 volume was finally published in 1967, the 1945 volume in 1969.[14] By this time, with the Vietnam War and the Cultural Revolution both in full spate, their contents attracted little attention; yet within a couple of years, when US–China relations had taken a dramatic new turn, what happened or failed to happen in 1945 suddenly seemed very relevant indeed. An article by Barbara Tuchman, with the compelling title 'If Mao had come to Washington', was published in the flagship *Foreign Affairs* journal (October 1972). The eminent American historian concluded that:

> If, in the absence of ill-feeling, we had established relations on some level with the People's Republic, permitting communications in a crisis, and if the Chinese had not been moved by hate and suspicion of us to make common cause with the Soviet Union, it is conceivable that there might have been no Korean War with all its evil consequences.

Professor Tuchman made her own visit to China and was much impressed by what she saw. Her *Foreign Affairs* article was reprinted two years later in a small volume of *Notes from China* in which she concluded that the elimination of poverty and corruption under the Communists was 'so striking that negative aspects of the new rule fade in relative importance'.[15]

Also in 1974, the wartime dispatches of John Service, the Dixie Mission officer who had developed the closest relationship with Mao, were published under the title *Lost Chance in China*. Its editor, Joseph Esherick, concluded that 'the United States lost its chance to forge a policy of friendship and cooperation with the Chinese Communists', and argued that 'if we had tolerated the Chinese Communists' rise to power, there would have been little need to so threaten China as to draw her into the Korean conflict, or to prop up military dictators in South Vietnam in order to "contain" China'.[16]

(3) **1990s to today.** The revival of the 'lost chance' debate from the beginning of the 1990s onwards has, as indicated above, taken advantage of new materials which had not previously been available. These include the memoirs of Chinese generals, more complete editions of Mao, and volumes of diplomatic documents – such as those of Zhou Enlai's negotiations with Marshall – and Soviet archives, particularly those concerning Mao's Moscow negotiations with Stalin and the Korean War.

However, this new scholarship also reflects a new mood of revisionism following the end of the Cold War. With the collapse of the Soviet Union and China's so-called 're-entry' into the world (and particularly the world economy), questions of Western responsibility, or shared responsibility, for the Cold War and for China's isolation seem less relevant and even naive. The enthusiasm for a more positive interpretation shown by Tuchman (and by others, including John King Fairbank, the father of modern US–China scholarship) looks embarrassing and even partial. Thus John Garver, a strong critic of the Lost China hypothesis, argues that Fairbank was 'writing for his time' and sought 'to challenge the then-dominant "China threat" thesis in order to open the door to better US–PRC relations'. Garver claims, to the contrary, that the new China did pose a real threat to US security in 1949, that any tensions between Mao and Stalin were subsidiary, and that there was never any alternative to the rupture between the Communists and Washington.[17]

Myth or possibility?

So was the 'lost chance' of the 1940s – ignored for two decades and then perceived in the 1970s by Barbara Tuchman and others, including myself, to have been a real possibility – really a complete myth? Were we all 'writing for our times'? While accepting that we were influenced by the contemporary intellectual climate (just as our critics are today), I would still argue that the episode and the questions raised by it cannot be so easily dismissed.

First, we should recognise an element of *post hoc propter hoc* in the view that better US–China relations at that time were never on the cards. The diplomatic record certainly shows that by 1949 Mao was extremely wary of the US and committed, in spite of long-held reservations about Stalin's autocratic style, to seeking alliance with the Soviet Union. This by itself tells us nothing about what might have been achieved if 'Mao had met Roosevelt', or if there had been some other comparable breakthrough at an earlier date. Indeed, most of the arguments raised against the 'lost chance' hypothesis focus entirely on the events of 1949–50, while ignoring altogether the questions raised by the Dixie Mission. These arguments can only be sustained if one believes that Mao was driven by anti-imperialism and the pursuit of Soviet-led socialism to an extent that would have ruled out any possible accommodation with the US in 1949 *whatever might have happened in the preceding years*. Thus Chen Jian, the foremost scholar of the 1949–50 period, argues that the CCP's adoption of an anti-US policy then had 'deep roots in China's history' and that 'from a Chinese perspective, the most profound cause ... lay in its connection to Mao's grand plans of transforming China's state, society, and international outlook'.[18]

Yet it can be argued instead – and more plausibly, in view of Mao's behaviour both earlier and later in his political career – that he was driven at least as much by circumstance as by dogma, and that he was never averse to 'seizing the moment' and changing course if the opportunity arose. In this view, 'circumstances rather than ideas have been the principal force shaping Chinese communist behaviour in international affairs'.[19] Ideology was a factor, sometimes paramount, sometimes subordinate and often confused. Yet for Western governments (and many academic specialists) faced with the 'new China', ideology was too easily seen as the 'magic weapon' which Mao in his more dogmatic last years claimed it to be. As the thoughtful Michael Hunt has observed, there was a tendency during the Cold War 'to denigrate ideology as a peculiar deformation of the socialist bloc, a tendency that carried over into the China field ... In [the accounts of Western international relations specialists] a persuasive, powerful Marxist-Leninist ideology came to offer an important key to understanding Chinese policy'. Hunt suggests correctly that we need a 'more subtle and expansive notion of ideology', as 'a complex, unstable amalgam drawn from a wide variety of sources and varying significantly from individual to individual'.[20]

There is no reason to regard Mao's professions of loyalty to the Soviet Union in 1949–50 as more or less sincere than his tempting offers of cooperation to the US five years earlier. Certainly he announced that China must 'lean to one side', argued strongly within his Politburo for alignment with the Soviet Union, and praised Stalin as a 'great leader'. But in retrospect Mao took a more cynical view of his own warm words: 'When I was in Moscow [in December 1949] to celebrate his birthday, what else could I have done if I had chosen not to congratulate him? Could I have cursed him instead?' Underlining the point, he claimed that two other famous articles he wrote about Stalin – one in 1939 and the other on Stalin's death – 'had come out of [political] need, not my heart, nor at my will'.[21]

Patriotism, nationalism and national interest could be factors as potent as Marxism or Leninism or internationalism and could lead to different conclusions at different times. This had been true of

Mao's attitude towards the outside world and its effect on China from the 1920s onwards, and would continue to be so – with one significant exception – until the end of his life. The exception was the extremist 'closed-door' policy of the early Cultural Revolution, when Mao allowed China to be virtually isolated from the world. Even so, we now know that as early as 1969, three years after the Cultural Revolution began, Mao was encouraging the 'Four Marshals', led by foreign minister Chen Yi, to ask serious questions about China's isolation and to recommend an opening to the West. That opening came very soon – in tandem with the more flexible approach of the Nixon administration – and was displayed to an amazed world with the Kissinger–Nixon visits to China within a couple of years.

Footnote: the mid-1950s ambassadorial talks

We could have been amazed nearly two decades earlier if another neglected episode in US–China relations had borne fruit. This was the ambassadorial dialogue of the mid-1950s, when Mao and his fellow leaders once more sought to test the possibilities of negotiation with Washington. As in the mid-1940s, we can see in retrospect a brief window of opportunity in which a Chinese initiative was neglected or repulsed by the US, causing Beijing to reassess its relatively more conciliatory attitude and adopt a harder line.

The time again seemed propitious for some improvement in US–China relations, following the death of Stalin, the end of the Korean and Vietnam wars, and Beijing's adoption of the 'three principles of peaceful co-existence'. Taiwan was the obvious stumbling block: in 1954 Eisenhower announced his intention of signing a mutual defence treaty with the Nationalist regime on the island and Beijing responded by shelling the Nationalist-controlled Offshore Islands. Yet it was this crisis that paved the way for the talks between the US and Chinese ambassadors which began in Geneva in August 1955. It was significant too that the initiative came from Beijing, which preferred a bilateral dialogue with Washington to a Soviet proposal for an international conference on Taiwan. This was one of several signs at the time of China's desire to emerge from under the shadow of Soviet diplomacy.

The talks were initially promising and resulted in agreement on the first item on the agenda – the mutual exchange of civilians detained on both sides. Negotiations then moved on to the second item, defined as the consideration of 'other practical matters at issue between the two parties'. Here the US simply stonewalled while China made a number of positive proposals, including one for a meeting of foreign ministers at which, Beijing suggested, 'practical and feasible means' could be found to defuse the Taiwan situation. As Kenneth Young, a former State Department official familiar with the negotiations, later concluded, a hopeful opportunity was missed. If Washington had broken the deadlock by conceding a foreign ministers' conference, this might have led to a high-level negotiation in which China continued to talk about 'easing tensions' in the Taiwan area rather than demand immediate US withdrawal of support for Chiang Kai-shek. Instead the US 'did not want diplomatic relations or continuing negotiations with Peking. Washington wanted to isolate, not enhance, Peking'.[22] Young's conclusion is supported in a more recent study of the talks; the aim of Secretary of State Dulles was simply to keep the Chinese talking, to 'beat [China] at its own game by out-sitting and out-talking them'.[23]

In essence, the US was prepared to explore the opportunities for detente with the Soviet Union but not with China: this became an important factor in the emerging Sino-Soviet dispute and in Mao's defiant resolve to 'go it alone' – with disastrous consequences for China. Ironically, when Washington finally began to make its own tentative overtures in the early 1960s, it was Beijing which responded at first with an 'all-or-nothing' rejection. Only after the chaos of the Cultural Revolution and the threat of Soviet military action would Mao finally 'seize the chance'. Chinese historians now acknowledge that this was a tragic mistake – but it had been preceded by equally tragic lost chances on the US side.[24]

One more footnote from history: in October 1971, when Henry Kissinger was paving the way in Beijing for the Nixon visit, he had to find a form of wording to describe the unity of China which would be acceptable to Beijing but would not support either the mainland's or Taipei's claim to be the sole Chinese government. Eventually, as he relates in his memoirs, Kissinger put forward an 'ambiguous formula' which both Beijing and Washington were able to live with. He did not invent this formula himself. It was 'adapted from a State Department planning document for negotiations, which aborted in the Fifties'.[25] We can only speculate how different the course of history might have been if those negotiations had not been 'aborted' by John Foster Dulles.

Notes

1 Text in Carolle Carter, *Mission to Yenan: American Liaison with the Chinese Communists, 1944–1947* (University Press of Kentucky, Lexington, 1997), p. 147.

2 All quotes from Service's 23 August 1944 interview with Mao, in Joseph W. Esherick (ed.), *Lost Chance in China: The World War II Dispatches of John S. Service* (Random House, New York, 1974), pp. 295–307.

3 Carter, *Mission to Yenan*, p. 148.

4 Edgar Snow, *Random Notes from Red China, 1936–1945* (Harvard University Press, 1957), pp. 125–30.

5 Carter, *Mission to Yenan*, p. 149.

6 Zhang Baijia, 'Zhou Enlai and the Marshall Mission', in Larry Bland (ed.), *George C. Marshall's Mediation Mission in China* (George C. Marshall Foundation, Lexington, 1998), pp. 11, 18, 24.

7 Ibid., p. 12.

8 Ibid.

9 Ibid., p. 24.

10 William D. Leahy, *I Was There* (Victor Gollancz, London, 1950), p. 340.

11 Historical Division of the Department of State, *The Conference at Malta and Yalta, 1945* (State Department, 1955), pp. 346–51.

12 Tsou Tang, *America's Failure in China, 1941–50* (University of Chicago Press, 1963), p. 178.

13 Michael Schaller, *The US Crusade in China 1938–45* (Columbia University Press, 1979), p. 332, n.12. Schaller lists p. 1903 of the *State Department Loyalty Investigation* (State Department, 1950) as another early source.

14 James Thomson, 'On the Making of US China Policy, 1961–1969', *China Quarterly*, no. 50, April–June 1972, pp. 224–25.

15 Barbara Tuchman, *Notes from China* (MacMillan, London, 1972), p. 2.

16 Esherick, *Lost Chance in China*, pp. 391–92. I dealt with this issue in my own early study of Chinese foreign policy, *The World and China, 1922–1972* (Eyre Methuen, London, 1974).

17 John W. Garver, 'Polemics, Paradigms, Responsibility and the Origins of the US–PRC Confrontation in the 1950s', in *The Journal of American–East Asian Relations*, spring 1994, p. 6.

18 Chen Jian, 'The Myth of America's 'Lost Chance' in China', *Diplomatic History*, winter 1997, p. 86.

19 James Reardon-Anderson, *Yenan and the Great Powers: The Origins of Chinese Communist Foreign Policy, 1944–1946* (Columbia University Press, 1974), pp. 109–27.

20 Michael H. Hunt, *The Genesis of Chinese Communist Foreign Policy* (Columbia University Press, 1996), pp. 247–49.

21 Minutes of Mao's conversation with a Yugoslavian delegation, Beijing, September 1956, transcribed in *Cold War International History Project Bulletin: 6–7*, p. 151.

22 Kenneth Young, *Negotiating with the Chinese Communists* (Council on Foreign Relations, New York, 1968), pp. 112–13.

23 Steven Goldstein, in Robert Ross & Jiang Changbin (eds.), *Re-examining the Cold War: US–China Diplomacy, 1954–1973* (Harvard University Press, 2002), pp. 213, 217.

24 In 1962 senior diplomat Wang Jiaxiang was castigated by Mao for arguing that Chinese foreign policy was in error. Looking back, Ambassador Wang Guoquan concluded that 'we lost a favourable opportunity', Ross & Jiang, *Re-examining the Cold War*, pp. 61–62, 193.

25 Henry Kissinger, *The White House Years* (Weidenfeld & Nicolson, London, 1979), p. 783.

Chapter 12

What if Britain had entered the Common Market in 1957?

Peter Riddell

Harold Macmillan was always ready to change his mind when faced with new circumstances: 'events, dear boy, events', as he said in what became his posthumous catchphrase. After all, he had reversed himself over Suez, first in and first out, in being the earliest and strongest advocate of military action, and then the first to demand that the operation be halted. But, now, as Prime Minister, Macmillan realised that he would have to initiate a far more fundamental change of policy to give himself, his party and his country a new direction after the Suez debacle of 1956. What he did not, could not, know then was that his decision would not only reshape British politics but that – after many squalls and difficult adjustments – it would also inaugurate a period of sustained economic growth. So Macmillan would be remembered, like Peel over a century earlier, as a great radical Tory Prime Minister, one of the few who had changed the direction of their nation.

Within days of becoming Prime Minister in January 1957, Macmillan had decided that Britain could not remain outside the emerging European Economic Community. As always with Macmillan, at first his true intentions were carefully concealed. He had to manoeuvre round the opponents in his own Cabinet, and placate the powerful agricultural and Commonwealth lobbies.

Admittedly, before then, Macmillan had agreed with the rest of the Eden Cabinet in rejecting the proposals for a Common Market

Treaty being developed by the six members of the European Coal and Steel Community – France, West Germany, Italy, the Netherlands, Belgium and Luxembourg. As Foreign Secretary, he had stood aside when the Six met at Messina in June 1955, despite their urgent requests for Britain to join from the start. Like Eden, Macmillan still saw Britain in wartime terms as one of the global great powers, and he did not want a six-power Europe with a customs union. The prevailing view in London, not least in the Foreign Office, was that that the Six would not succeed in agreeing the proposals for a customs union. And, even if a treaty was signed, it would not be ratified – particularly by France, whose National Assembly had rejected the European Defence Community with a rearmed Germany only two years before.

However, as the Six pressed ahead, from the initial talks at Messina to a detailed plan for a Common Market in March 1956, British doubts about its practicability were offset by worries; as an official committee in early 1956 put it, 'should the Messina powers achieve economic integration without the United Kingdom, this would mean German hegemony in Europe'. Nonetheless, further overtures from the Six were rejected by the Eden government, including Macmillan, by now Chancellor of the Exchequer. Realising the potential vulnerability of the British economy to the proposed Common Market's tariffs, however, he pushed for an alternative plan. Produced in late July 1956, the day that the Suez crisis began, Plan G, as it was known, represented a major change in British trade policy. It proposed a move to a free trade area and away from the protection of industry through the high tariffs which had existed since the 1932 Import Duties Act, and even earlier. But Plan G also proposed continuing with duty-free food imports from the Commonwealth into Britain, as well as low tariffs on Commonwealth industrial goods.

The retention of these Commonwealth preferences was not acceptable to the Six, though Macmillan had hopes of reaching a compromise. In early October 1956, he wrote to Paul-Henri Spaak, the Belgian Foreign Minister and architect of the Common Market, urging him 'to keep things as fluid as possible at the meeting of the Foreign Ministers of the Six on 20 October so as to permit us and other countries to associate with the Customs Union in a wider Free Trade Area if you can do so'.

The problem was agriculture. The British were at this stage determined to exclude farm products from any European Customs Union, in order to look after Commonwealth interests. But the Six had decided to include agriculture. Faced with this response, the British Cabinet decided, that November, to negotiate with the Six for a free trade area. However, despite Labour Party support for Plan G, there were warnings from strong pro-Europeans, like the rising Labour backbencher Roy Jenkins, that the Six would not 'swallow' this.

So it looked as if Macmillan's hopes would be dashed and the Six would go it alone without Britain. But, as we now know, a major change occurred in January 1957, just after Macmillan became Prime Minister. He had always been a committed European, one of the generation of British politicians who had travelled regularly to Strasbourg in the late 1940s to discuss how to achieve a more united Europe. He was not like those faint-hearts and anti-Europeans, Anthony Eden and R. A. Butler. But what really changed Macmillan's mind was the combination of the Suez crisis of autumn 1956 and the pleas of leading European figures such as the strongly Anglophile Paul-Henri Spaak and the pro-free-trade Ludwig Erhard, the West German finance minister.

The first lesson that Macmillan drew from Suez was the urgent priority of rebuilding relations with Washington and with his old colleague from the Mediterranean in the Second World War, now the President of the United States, Dwight D. Eisenhower. Britain would, in future, never act in a way which conflicted with Washington on a major global issue. But, at the same time, Macmillan recognised, reluctantly, that Suez had exposed the dangers of being too dependent on the US. The crisis had also exposed the vulnerabilities of sterling and the sterling area to pressures on international currency markets. This shift in thinking was reflected in a discussion by Cabinet ministers in January 1957. They concluded, according to the minutes, that:

> There must be a sea change in the basis of Anglo-American relations. It was doubtful whether the US would now be willing to accord to us alone the special position which we had held as their principal ally during the war. We might therefore be better able to influence them if we were part of an association of powers which had greater political, economic and military strength than we alone could command.

After all, the US, and particularly the State Department, always claimed that they wanted a more united Europe, including Britain. Hence, in the view of Macmillan, and an increasing number of influential official advisers, Britain's future lay in Europe, but a Europe closely allied with the United States, not least to counter the threat of the Soviet Union which had again been underlined by the Soviet destruction of Hungarian independence in autumn 1956.

How were these objectives to be reconciled? How could Macmillan look after Commonwealth agricultural interests, or, at least, appear to do so, while at the same time securing Britain's place in the new Europe? The answer came from within the Six. Most of the countries wanted Britain in, not least because of their own perceived sense of economic weakness, understandable given the experience of West Germany, France and Italy over the previous half-century. The key meeting occurred only two days after Macmillan became Prime Minister in January 1957, when he met Spaak. The differences over agriculture were all too apparent. However, the two saw a possible way forward by linking the proposed European Free Trade Area and the Six.

Ludwig Erhard in Bonn was also keen, since he had always been suspicious of an inward-looking European Community without Britain, which risked being pushed in a protectionist direction by France. Meanwhile, the ever-ingenious Guido Carli in Italy had a plan for reconciling variable external tariffs with free circulation of goods within the area. Macmillan, for his part, recognised that, after earlier British misgivings, the Six were determined to press ahead and he would have to be conciliatory. The draft treaty prepared by Spaak and his colleagues left a good deal open about how the proposed Community would develop in practice; it contained outlines and objectives, but few concrete details. So Macmillan concluded that if his commitment to join was accepted as sincere, the Six could be flexible over the detailed arrangements.

Macmillan also recognised a unique political opportunity which might not last for long. While he could not hope for much from that old rogue Konrad Adenauer, the West German Chancellor, whom he disliked, Erhard would back a fresh British initiative, as would most of the Benelux governments, under Spaak's lead. Italy also was sympathetic. Meanwhile, the French were divided and absorbed by the agonies of their war in Algeria, and unable on their own to oppose the rest of the Six. Thank heavens, thought Macmillan, that Charles de Gaulle was safely out of the way, out of power, as he had been for over a decade. He would have been a real thorn in the side of any last-minute deal.

The negotiations were difficult and delicate. Macmillan stated that the intention was to prevent a division of Europe and to create a broader free trade area, including the Six. Following their talks in January 1957, Spaak, however, understood that Macmillan really intended to join the proposed Common Market. Accordingly, he persuaded his colleagues, including even a reluctant France, to go along with British wishes and to give Macmillan time.

Macmillan needed time, both to win over British public opinion and to placate the Commonwealth. So his was a bold strategy cloaked in cautious tactics. The outcome was a complicated deal which provided transitional arrangements for Commonwealth food imports and for changes in the system of British farm support. New Zealand proved stubborn over its farm products, and eventually won special terms, but most of the other Commonwealth countries had already concluded that the days of special preferences from Britain were anyway going to end before long, and were adjusting their trading patterns accordingly. These arrangements were balanced by strict limits on Community-wide subsidies to agriculture. Macmillan proved to be a master of reassurance, convincing British farmers and Commonwealth countries that he had safeguarded their interests and the rest of Europe that he was a true European.

In political terms, the whole exercise was a tour de force. There was a major row within the Conservative Party. Butler threatened to resign, but, as always, he backed down at the last minute; Macmillan always knew how to get the better of his old rival, and called his bluff. Salisbury, Macmillan's old friend from Eton and the Guards, made one of his regular threats to resign, and then did so, prompting another of the Prime Minister's bon mots about the Cecils always resigning. Salisbury had the support of some of the more nationalist and pro-Empire Tory MPs, who went so far as to resign the whip. An effigy of Macmillan was burnt on a bonfire in Bournemouth and eggs were thrown at him at a fete in his constituency in Bromley. His remark that 'they would never have done this in Stockton' went down rather badly with his local Conservative activists in south London. Hugh Gaitskell, Labour's still relatively new leader, pledged to defend the Commonwealth, while the trade unions protested about threats to British jobs. A group of pro-European Labour MPs voted with the Conservatives and Liberals in favour of entry into the Common Market.

Macmillan's deft and successful shift in British foreign policy in 1957 not only took his opponents by surprise, but gave him the opportunity to win a substantial majority in the 1958 general election, which he called eighteen months early so as to give his government and Britain a fresh start. The small band of pro-Empire Tories who had resigned the whip was annihilated. Labour was defeated for a third time, having a fought a 'we'll pull out, defend the links with the Commonwealth' campaign. In fact Labour was deeply divided, not just between the Gaitskellite right and the unilateralist left, but along pro- and anti-Europe lines. Many of Gaitskell's natural allies were bitterly disappointed in him, and were even more disillusioned when he resigned and was succeeded by Harold Wilson. The strongly pro-European Liberals under Jo Grimond gained a couple of dozen seats and, after the general election, the Liberals' numbers were boosted by a dozen defectors from the Labour Party, who had voted against their party whip in the historic Commons division. So began the era of multi-party politics, which led, after Macmillan's retirement in 1965, to the long premiership of Edward Heath and his Con–Lib coalition.

Looking back from the perspective of nearly half a century, Britain's entry into the European Economic Community at its start had three main consequences: for the development of the EEC itself; for the performance of the British economy; and for the shape of British politics. The three were interconnected. Britain's participation as virtually a founding father – the patronising standoffishness at the Messina conference in 1955 was soon forgotten – ensured that the EEC, later the European Union, developed in a way much more in line with long-term British interests and instincts. When British ministers claimed that Europe was going in 'our direction', it was self-evidently true. That, in turn, gave fresh opportunities to British companies over the long term. And after considerable upheavals in the late 1950s and early 1960s, membership came to be accepted by all the main parties. Europe ceased to be a divisive issue in British politics for all but a few on the fringes.

While the Macmillan government only leapt aboard the European ship just as it was starting to set sail, Britain had a major and lasting impact on the shape and development of the new EEC. As noted above, the welcome by most countries to Macmillan's last-minute change of heart gave Britain an advantage in the negotiations over the shape of the Community. Britain was able to build alliances with several other countries, notably Germany and the Benelux states. That was hard for France, especially as the dying Fourth Republic was preoccupied by Algeria. Charles de Gaulle returned to power in 1958, a year too late to prevent the arrival of the English Trojan Horse, as he repeatedly claimed in speeches and interviews lamenting the lack of French influence in Brussels. By the time the Fifth Republic was established and de Gaulle had become President, the key decisions over the shape of the future Community had already been taken.

The Macmillan–Erhard view on the primacy of a free trade area in the new Europe was predominant. A Common Agricultural Policy was established, but it was very limited. The costs of agricultural support never exceeded a quarter of the Community's overall budget, and national governments had to bear most of the costs of reducing the size of their farming sectors and protecting the rural way of life. There was a lot of moaning from France and Italy, but their protests did not count for much against the weight of the north-west European axis, including six of the eight founding countries (Denmark entered along with Britain).

It was not long before France was being described as the awkward partner in Europe, for ever agonising about whether signing the Treaty of Rome had been correct or not. French diplomats often talked about trying to create a troika at the top of Europe. Although Macmillan, and later Heath, was always careful to consult de Gaulle and his successors, no one doubted that the British–German relationship was at the heart of Europe – its motor, in the favourite phrase of the time. This in turn had two main results: a strongly free-trade and free-market economic approach, both in external relations and internally; and an effective European voice in discussions with the United States.

Moreover, British and German leadership ensured that the EEC developed primarily as a group of nation states – with increasingly common policies on the economy and trade, but relying on co-operation in many other matters. This reduced tension over the necessary pooling of sovereignty without creating anxieties about creating supranational structures. In turn, the British were more relaxed when the post of foreign affairs spokesman – not high representative or any such grandiose title – was created to speak on behalf of all the foreign ministers. A directly elected European Parliament was established in the 1970s, but it had a limited remit and was required to work with national parliaments in approving new regulations and directives. So there was never any danger of the Parliament losing touch with voters in the member states. When a group of anti-EU politicians – led by Norman Tebbit, under the banner of 'Chingford not Charlemagne' – campaigned against a European superstate, few listened to their bizarre complaints. The reduced French influence meant there was little high-flown integrationist rhetoric or objectives and, instead, a more pragmatic approach.

The absence of significant Community-wide agricultural sub-sidies made it much easier for Europe to place itself at the forefront of initiatives to reduce international trade barriers. These free-trade drives helped offset the impact of the two oil price shocks in the mid and late 1970s. The London–Bonn partnership was also behind the launch of the internal market, intended to reduce internal barriers to competition. Heath's decision to appoint Margaret Thatcher as one of Britain's Commissioners, with the brief of push-ing through the measures associated with the Single European Act, was later regarded as particularly inspired. Her legendary success in late-night meetings in Brussels in implementing the single market programme not only won her the Charlemagne Prize but also led to the renaming of a square near the Commission building as the Place Thatcher. Her relations with Commission President Roy Jenkins were, however, less harmonious, as she revealed in her later account, *A Housewife in Brussels*.

The lasting result of this emphasis on free trade and internal competition was a faster rate of economic growth and a lasting reduction in unemployment. That made it easier for governments to limit the entitlements, and hence the costs, of some of the gener-ous pension and other welfare provisions introduced in the imme-diate post-war era. Labour regulations were also cut back to make it easier both to hire and to fire. The opposition of trade unions in most countries, apart from France, was reduced by the general prosperity at the time. Observers talked of a European social market model, with the market being as important as the social aspect. Differences still existed between the US and European approaches, but Europe was able both to afford a modernised welfare state and to be competitive.

The success of the internal market led inexorably by the 1990s to the creation and acceptance of a single European currency. Following the strong period of growth in the 1970s and 1980s, Britain, along with Germany (united as one country after the fall of the Berlin Wall), led the call for a single currency – called the ducat, with a nice historical touch, looking back to an earlier period of close cross-European co-operation and prosperity. The Bank of England led the campaign for its introduction, and, appropriately, the new central bank for Europe was based in London. There was a short-lived problem when France stayed out for the first three years following a referendum campaign led by the anti-ducat leader of the Gaullists, Jacques Chirac. But faced with the prosperity of the ducat area, the new left-of-centre French government, headed by President Jacques Delors, bowed to the inevitable and joined.

Another lasting consequence of British participation from the start was the fostering of a close and collaborative relationship with the US. The Eisenhower administration had strongly supported Macmillan's decision to join the Common Market, not least because foreign policy-makers in Washington had believed, rightly, that a strong British voice in the emerging European Community would be sympathetic, and helpful, to US interests. This was important during the Cold War and its messy aftermath. Britain also successfully pressed for increased co-operation between the European Union, as it had then become, and NATO. The distinction between the two became gradually irrelevant after the expansion of the EU following the end of the Cold War.

But there was also a subtle, and initially under-appreciated, shift in the British government's approach. Talk of a 'special relationship' between London and Washington, common during the immediate post-war decade, disappeared. Instead, British Prime Ministers sought to work through Europe in their dealings with the US. Heath was the first to suggest close collaboration between the leaders of the main European countries to consort their views and positions before these were presented to Washington. At first, the State Department was disconcerted by not having an exclusive channel to the Foreign Office and 10 Downing Street. But, in time, American policymakers accepted that their interests were better served by negotiating with European leaders as a whole. This did not mean that the British were hostile to Washington or anti-American − far from it. Rather, the new British 'euro-realism', as it was called, was intended to recognise that the UK's place was now primarily in Europe, while in no way repudiating the close transatlantic links between Europe and the US. The British influence, presented in a European context, managed to stifle not only suggestions of London being Washington's 'poodle', but also incipient anti-US feelings among European nationalists and advocates of an accommodation with Moscow.

This transatlantic harmony reduced tensions over the deployment of nuclear missiles in Europe in the 1980s and, later, over the rise of Islamic fundamentalism and associated terrorism from the late 1990s onwards. After the 9/11 attacks on New York and Washington, President John McCain warmly welcomed the joint offer of European help in combating terrorism − 'a long-term intelligence and police operation, rather than a short-term war', as he and European President Chris Patten put it in a joint statement. This spirit of co-operation was underlined by the later successful joint operation to isolate and intensify sanctions against Saddam Hussein's Iraq. This led to his removal by a palace coup at the start of what became known as the Purple Revolution in Baghdad, as a people oppressed for over thirty years took control of their country. But the Middle East miracle is another story ...

Joining the Common Market from the start also had a positive impact on the British economy, as a result of a sharp reduction in tariffs and other barriers to internal trade. At first, there were awkward adjustments, particularly for companies which had enjoyed privileged, and protected, relationships with the old British colonies and with Commonwealth countries. But the lengthy transitional period negotiated by Macmillan with his European partners limited the damage. At the same time, British manufacturing industry faced increased competition from across the Channel from European companies now fully into their stride after the decade of post-war recovery. There was a lot of talk of 'cold baths' and 'shock' treatment. Some companies went under. Other companies were taken over and reorganised during the wave of takeovers which fuelled the stock-market boom of the late 1950s and early 1960s. One of the great success stories was the motor industry, which, shaken out of its post-war complacency, established itself as a leader in quality, in time setting up collaborative ventures with Japanese and American groups. 'Made in Longbridge' became a prestige selling point in the German and Italian markets.

Writing at the end of the century, in a speculative work wondering what would have happened if Britain had stayed out of the EEC until the early 1970s – *From Empire to Europe: The Decline and Revival of British Industry since the Second World War* – Geoffrey Owen concluded that: 'The decision to opt out of European integration was the biggest missed opportunity of the 1945–60 period, more important than any mistakes in macro-economic policy'. Owen, a former editor of the *Financial Times*, or *European Times* as it became in the 1980s, gave the example of the paper industry, where West Germany benefited hugely from the reductions in tariffs and increased competition. In order to survive, the German paper industry had had to invest heavily in modernisation, as well as in the reorganisation of its operations. But if Britain had initially stayed out of the

EEC, its industry would have been placed under no such pressures: 'At a time when the British paper industry was stagnating, German mills were investing in modern machines to serve an expanding European market. If Britain had joined the Common Market at the start, the paper industry would have avoided the sudden lurch from protection to free trade brought about by EFTA. It would also have been exposed at an earlier state to competition in a large and dynamic market.'

This boost to productivity and performance lasted for over two decades. But more than a hint of complacency crept in during the 1980s over what was glibly described as the Anglo-German economic miracle. The revival of the American economy in the 1980s and 1990s, especially as the internet and information-technology revolution spread towards the end of the century, proved a profound shock. However, the flexibility of the main north-west European economies – including those in Scandanavia and the new entrants to the EU from the former communist countries – proved equal to the challenge. The slowdown in growth was short-lived, though factory closures and redundancies did encourage the growth of some fringe extremist parties.

These competitive pressures also affected Britain's industrial relations. Governments in the 1960s recognised that Britain could not hope to compete if unions were able to disrupt production by calling wildcat unofficial strikes. So the Con–Lib coalition of the late 1960s pushed through a series of sweeping changes to the laws affecting trade unions, banning the closed shop and secondary or sympathy strikes, and requiring ballots before any strikes or disruptive actions. This law was strongly opposed by the trade unions and by Labour. However, the credibility of Labour as the main opposition party had been severely weakened by the breakaway of the pro-Europeans in the late 1950s and early 1960s. So the government prevailed and defeated a number of threatening strikes, notably in the newspaper industry. Heath was helped by the support of *The*

Sun, the strongly anti-union but pro-European tabloid; 'Our Future lies across the Channel', as it proclaimed above its editorials.

Amongst the most striking consequences of British entry into the Common Market from the start has been the changes in British domestic politics. Macmillan not only seized the initiative for a revived progressive Conservative Party during the late 1950s and early 1960s, but he also paved the way – after his departure in 1965 – for the dominance over a decade of an alliance between his party and the Liberals. The latter were renamed Liberal Democrats after the defection from Labour in the late 1950s and early 1960s of a group of pro-European social democrats headed by Roy Jenkins, as well as talented younger politicians like Shirley Williams and Bill Rodgers. These upheavals in the party structure, with the Liberal Democrats as a pivotal third force and coalition partner for much of the time, led to far-reaching changes in the electoral system, towards a continental form of proportional representation. So coalitions, and co-operation, became the norm. This in turn led to wide-ranging constitutional reform in the 1970s and 1980s, with a reformed House of Lords, or House of the Nations as it was called after the introduction of widespread devolution within the United Kingdom. These arrangements were all linked together within the framework of a written constitution.

After a series of electoral defeats, Labour was also forced to reform itself, abandoning the remaining vestiges of its 1918 programme and the old Clause Four commitment to public ownership. Labour's model was the Bad Godesberg programme which the West German Social Democrats adopted in 1959. The traditional link with the trade unions was also broken. This led to the creation of a broadly social democratic party, able to form coalitions with the Liberal Democrats from the 1980s onwards.

The Tories lost power, not over Europe but because of economic problems. This inaugurated the rumbustious era of the Denis Healey premiership, to be followed, after a Conservative interlude under Michael Heseltine, by the Tony Blair–Paddy Ashdown coalition. Eventually, the changes in the electoral system led to a splintering of the party structure, with the rise of both far right and far left parties, confusingly called the English Nationalists and English Internationalists respectively. These parties achieved some minor successes during the economic downturn of the early 1990s.

Apart from these fringe groups, however, there has been no real dissent over British membership of the Europe Union as such. Membership has been accepted as part of the normal political landscape for decades. The European argument – and the debate about Britain's role in the world after the end of the Empire – had been settled by Macmillan in 1957.

~

As in all works of counterfactual speculation, this chapter mixes fact and fantasy. Everything up to January 1957 did happen as recorded, and Harold Macmillan did meet Paul-Henri Spaak just after becoming Prime Minister. But the outcome of their meeting was different from what I suggest above, as, of course, were all subsequent events. However, the views of political leaders like Spaak and Ludwig Erhard were as I record, and there was a Carli plan which might have resolved European differences on agriculture. Moreover, Sir Geoffrey Owen, my former editor at the *Financial Times*, did write a book of the title and theme I report, though he, of course, was discussing the adverse consequences of the failure to join the Common Market, rather than speculating on the reverse.

This chapter is dedicated to the memory of Sir Roy Denman, a lifelong pro-European as well as a distinguished public servant in London and Brussels, who died while this chapter was being written. He believed that Britain missed a crucial opportunity by staying out of the Common Market at its start in the 1950s. I hope that he would have enjoyed my musings, and jokes, and I am sure he would have suggested several of his own.

Chapter 13

What if the Scots had voted for devolution in 1979?

Rab Houston

On the morning of 1 July 1999 the members of the Scottish Parliament convened in the Parliament House, off Edinburgh's High Street, to begin what the late Donald Dewar called 'a journey without an end'. The journey continues.

It could have started earlier – on 2 March 1979 – and with worse outcomes. An earlier beginning does not necessarily mean a better end.

On 1 March 1979, 51.6 per cent of voters in the referendum supported a Scottish Assembly. However, London Labour MP George Cunningham had proposed that 40 per cent of the electorate must vote 'yes', thus effectively counting abstainers as 'no' voters. By this narrowed criterion just 32.9 per cent of the electorate were in favour, 30.8 per cent opposed and 36.3 per cent did not vote. Devolution was dead.

But suppose James Callaghan's Labour government had delivered on devolution instead of stacking the deck against it? The 1980s is viewed as the Thatcher era, and most Scots blame her for the country's past (and many present) ills. Devolution in 1979 would have proved that this was only partly true.

~

As Callaghan had warned his squabbling followers in the run-up to the general election of 3 May 1979, oil would keep whoever won it in power for a generation. It did. That much we know. But devolved government for Scotland in 1979 meant its fortunes were in many ways worse, for Toryism in England was matched by a different, though equally sterile, Labour government in Scotland. What is more, a change in representation at the Westminster Parliament, which followed directly from devolution, meant that British politics moved strongly to the right for twenty years. It took Labour more than a decade after Thatcher's fall in 1990 to reinvent itself as a party of government in England. When it finally emerged, 'New Labour' came out of a very different context of British politics.

How would this counterfactual scenario have played? The fundamental difference lay in a combination of three factors: how politicians worked out the implications of devolution; how international economic forces affected Britain; and how Scotland's particular social problems and cultural ethos mediated politics and economics.

In his 1977 book *Devolution: The end of Britain*, Tam Dalyell, MP for the Scottish constituency of West Lothian, near Edinburgh, claimed the following:

> If the United Kingdom is to remain in being, then there can be no question but that the Scottish constituencies must continue to be represented at Westminster ... Yet once the Assembly had come into being, and was legislating for those areas that had not been reserved to the United Kingdom Government, the position of the seventy-one Scottish Westminster MPs would become awkward and invidious. Their credibility – like those of their counterparts in the Assembly – would be deeply suspect, simply because there would be so many areas of concern to their electors on which they could not pronounce.

Dalyell wrote to stop the break-up of Britain. His words were construed rather differently by Enoch Powell, who suggested mischievously, but with his characteristic piercing intelligence, that Scotland could not be represented twice. This was the clincher for Thatcher when she swept to power. No lover of devolution, she nevertheless recognised that most English people, who viewed Scots with a curious mixture of incomprehension, condescension and envy, would find it inequitable to have MPs representing Scotland at Edinburgh *and* at Westminster. Thus she turned the 'West Lothian question' on its head by denying Scottish MPs a say on 'English' matters (very broadly construed) in the Westminster Parliament. Scots therefore ended up with even less say over their own affairs than they had before devolution. In one deft political move, Thatcher cemented the ascendancy of the Conservative Party in England and then used North Sea oil revenues to fund a benign personal taxation regime that assured its continued hegemony for another two decades.

In some respects Scotland came off lightly. Thatcher sometimes appeased, but had no need to discipline, Scottish voters and the poll tax experiment was conducted not in Scotland, but in some uppity inner-city English constituencies that had the nerve to resist gerrymandering. Most noteworthy were some in north and east London with persistently high levels of rates and irritatingly populist local officials. The poll tax failed, but Thatcher's attempts fostered deep dislike and led directly to the creation of the office of Mayor of London in 2000.

North of the Border, support for the Tories held up among the British-thinking middle-class 'haves', but they were not numerous enough in Scotland to give Conservatism any significant political presence after 1979. The Tory vote slumped sickeningly, from 30 per cent in 1979 to 24 per cent in 1987 and just 15 per cent in 2000, by which time they had no Scottish seats at Westminster. Support for Labour held up well, and at first that for the SNP waned, as Labour had hoped. Behind the nods towards democracy and regional self-government was Labour's profound lack of enthusiasm for devolution in 1979. Its one redeeming feature, that it would 'kill the SNP stone dead', proved in the long term to be a profound misjudgement. The SNP took 18 per cent of the vote in 1979, but this fell to 11 per cent in 1983. However, it had risen to 14 per cent in 1987 and continued to improve under the shrewd leadership of Alex Salmond. The removal of their Scottish MPs also had a serious impact on the Liberals south of the border and this really did kill the Liberal Democrats stone dead. Roy Jenkins won the Hillhead by-election in 1982 – for Labour.

In time Salmond positioned himself to the left of Labour and built on its many weaknesses: sleaze in Labour's one-party states in west central Scotland, the limited powers of the Edinburgh parliament, tension over the level of its block grant (eyed enviously by the English regions), and the incompatibility between Labour's easy lip-service to regional power and the harder realities of dependence. Given cerebral support by bright young Labour men like Robin Cook, Salmond spoke out convincingly against intervention in Yugoslavia (soon to become 'the former Yugoslavia'). At first his views were not popular, but he had the luxury of standing little chance of becoming Scotland's First Minister. His stance established the intellectual agenda for a Labour attack on the disastrous Iraq war of 2003–04. From the mid-1990s the wider effect of Salmond's measured, consistent approach was to drive the Labour-dominated Scottish Assembly selectively towards more radical, almost Bennite, social policies which had, nevertheless, a much wider political appeal than the barrel-thumping socialism of the 1970s. 'New Labour' came to govern Britain in the early years of the twenty-first century, but it first emerged out of productive relations with Nationalist politicians in Scotland in the 1990s.

The Labour Party in England was emasculated by being deprived of its huge Scottish cohort. Without a chance of government it floundered, steadily losing seats and going through a succession of lacklustre leaders, of whom Michael Foot was only the most incredible. It adapted, but in Scotland first of all rather than in England, where Neil Kinnock's purge of the hard left did little to stem its ebbing support. In Scotland Labour and Nationalists found more in common than they had imagined in the tense days of early 1979. It was around social policy that the parties united, though strains remained as Nationalists aspired to full independence, while Labour continued to adhere to notions of 'Britain'. Gradually, however, the Nationalists surrendered their stated wish for full independence – or, as they preferred to put it, placed it 'beyond use' – secure in the knowledge that across Europe the winds of political decentralisation were blowing their way. New Labour emerged as a left-of-centre party dedicated to a social democracy that borrowed the best from its Scottish roots. It was moral, committed to educational opportunity for all (including no student tuition fees), socially inclusive, and accommodating of international capitalism while protective of its victims.

There were plenty of those. Jim Callaghan had been right about oil, but the impact of the price of crude, and many other aspects of international capitalism, gave Scotland (and Britain) a rocky ride. Sterling's sharp rise in the early 1980s was partly because it was a petro-currency, and partly because of the crippling interest rate and VAT rises introduced by Geoffrey Howe. Its strength wiped out much of Scottish (and British) heavy industry: the mines, the steelworks, shipbuilding and more. Of eighteen deep coal mines in 1979, only one survived the vicious 'efficiency drive' instituted by the Scots-American Iain MacGregor, whom Thatcher appointed to the Coal Board. The tonnage of coal extracted declined by half between 1979 and 1997. Car-making, the ultimate virility symbol of any successful regional economy, started and finished abruptly at Linwood (Chrysler-Peugeot) and Bathgate (British Leyland). The Ravenscraig steel works were razed to the ground in July 1996.

At the first of its two peaks, in 1986, oil production made up 5 per cent of British GNP, and at its second, in 1995, a massive net £27 billion was paid in Petroleum Revenue Tax to Whitehall. Where the Norwegian state slowly exploited its oil reserves and built an infrastructure that would last for generations, the British surrendered too much control to the multinational corporations, and the Tories squandered what bounty there was on toadying to the Americans in foreign policy and on short-term party interests.

By the mid-1980s the amount of capital controlled by Scottish commercial and industrial firms had halved. Foreign ownership made closing manufacturing plants easier and this, coupled with dependence on oil and defence contracts, ruined Clyde ship-building. Exports were choked off and a fifth of manufacturing employment evaporated. Massive unemployment followed, with Scotland, under a Labour government, helpless to do anything about it. Scotland (and Britain) continued to ride the rollercoaster of international capitalism without any safety harness, just as it had in the 1970s.

Scottish politicians could toady with the best of them and they bowed low before the Americans, who seemed to be the only ones who could create employment, in oil and computers. Grants to potential employers were handed out ad lib; John De Lorean was feted as a potential saviour of Scottish car manufacturing. Employers wanted docile workers, and union membership was eroded by American hard-cop-soft-cop management techniques. Scotland's future was shaped by economic forces that governments hardly understood and barely influenced.

Yet the one thing Scottish politicians had that the English seemed to lack was moral principle. In 1982 Gordon Brown and Robin Cook set out a socialist message in *Scotland – the Real Divide: Poverty and Deprivation in Scotland*. Steps were taken to bridge the 'great divide'. An example was the sale of council houses. Just as George Younger had suggested selling council houses in England, to build new political allegiances amongst the new house-owners, the Scottish Assembly reached the opposite conclusion in Scotland, and agreed to maintain a substantial public rented sector. For the 'have nots', housing, at least, really was affordable. Other examples of signally constructive social policies were in healthcare and in care of the elderly.

The productive relationship between the parties in Scotland also bore fruit over political participation. The steady decline in membership of parties and in numbers voting at elections that began in the late 1970s was stemmed, as people saw that politicians could, after all, work towards a common goal. Scots had always *believed* that they had a sense of community and, paradoxically, the excesses of free-market capitalism helped them to realise a vision of social corporatism that changed the face of British politics. Derided in the English media for their slipper-wearing and nose-picking, Assembly members all knew and generally liked each other; they drank in the same Edinburgh wine bars and pubs; some shared, albeit unknowingly, the same lovers. The world of the Scottish Assembly was a long way from the bear pit of the House of Commons.

Westminster retained Britain's oil. However, to stem the continuing tide in favour of the SNP, Thatcher brought in various measures to devolve further the administrative government of Scotland and allow special treatment of Scottish business in Parliament itself. One of these prevented Westminster exploiting other resources. It allowed the Assembly to legislate on issues affecting 'the culture and environment of Scotland'. Faced with dwindling oil and gas stocks and spiralling world prices for fossil fuels, the Westminster government decided to build a number of new nuclear power plants. But it had to do it in the north of England. Disused mines in the north-west were filled with spent atomic fuel. The dockyards of Tyneside decommissioned tired, but still all too potent, nuclear submarines. The effect was further to encourage the break-up of Britain by making it clear to northerners what they had long suspected: that they were second-class citizens.

Decentralisation enhanced insularity. Without the goal of devolution to crave and without the bogey of Thatcher to unite against, Scots turned in on themselves and outwardly against those towards whom they had traditionally felt antipathy. Culturally the consequences were dire. The anti-European sentiment of the 1970s, only partly dulled by the 1975 Common Market referendum, revived with a vengeance as jobs disappeared. The number of Scots pupils studying European languages fell by two-thirds between 1980 and 1995. The Scots became bad Europeans, too busy strutting or cringing to make the best of what the EEC/EU had to offer – while the Irish cleaned up.

The Edinburgh Festival folded in the mid-1980s. It had never really been accepted by the citizens, for whom the Fringe in particular represented an often noisy, scarcely comprehensible and sometimes scandalous intrusion into their measured, polite and predictable world. Anyway, decent folk could hardly get on the buses for puzzled foreigners, clutching £20 notes, too stupid to read 'exact fare please'. Edinburgh's bourgeoisie preferred the ordered pageantry of the Military Tattoo on the Castle Esplanade. If they wanted to see naked women on stage the 'haves' could go to Amsterdam, paying full whack for scheduled fares to travel (via London) from the two viable airports at Edinburgh or Glasgow Prestwick; only oilmen used Aberdeen, while Inverness airport (along with the Fort William rail line) closed when the English had their second homes taken away from them. Flights to North America were business-class only and cost the equivalent of three months of the average Scottish wage. Most Scots stayed at home, too poor to participate in the mass tourism boom sweeping Europe. They rationalised this behaviour, in the words of the Tourist Board that presented 'Scotland the brand' to the world as a formula of heritage, landscape and something called culture: 'Why go anywhere else?' But Glasgow never did realise Sir William Burrell's project for a great arts museum and the proposal for a National Museum of Scotland in Edinburgh never got off the ground.

For many the future seemed increasingly bleak. One in ten families had lived on below half the average UK income in 1979, but the figure had risen to three in ten by 2006. A third of Scotland's children grew up in poverty at the start of the new millennium, compared with less than one in ten in Germany. Among the large numbers of 'excluded' Scots, who made up the soaring unemployment and crime statistics, there was a sullen hatred that spilled over into sectarianism, reminiscent of the 1930s, and racism. Many Scots lacked a voice and when they broke their silence it was with a knife or a gun. Reported crimes nearly doubled, to 600,000, between 1977 and 1992 and doubled again in the following decade. Multiculturalism became a dirty word. Scots hardly accepted the presence of ethnic minorities and remained comfortable with terms like 'Chinky' in Chinese restaurants or 'Paki' at the local newsagent. Most foreigners were instantly written off as a worthless 'asylum-seekers'.

The main beneficiaries were those who worked for the multinationals or who made money by moving money – the financial services industry. From their offices in and around Charlotte Square the besuited professionals discreetly obliged their international clients. Scottish financial management was viewed as boring, but proper: a safe pair of hands in a world where most had sticky fingers. Edinburgh became the Zürich of the Atlantic archipelago – a bit less discreet than the gnomes, but a long way removed from the Tory-worshiping wide-boys who wheeled and dealed and bent and pocketed in the City of London. By 2006, 20 per cent of Scotland's labour force worked in financial services.

One upshot was the announcement in 1999 of a massive joint business venture between the Bank of Scotland and the US right-wing fundamentalist Pat Robertson. Under the deal, a new direct banking subsidiary was set up in the United States, majority owned by the Bank of Scotland and most of the rest by Robertson. Gospel preacher and founder of the Christian Coalition, Robertson was described by civil rights campaigners as 'the most dangerous man in America'. Anti-Muslim, anti-Hindu, anti-women and anti-gay, he liked the board of the Bank of Scotland and they liked him. The joint venture was a roaring success and consolidated the international standing of Scotland's financial services industry.

Of the bleeding stump of manufacturing little remained. Electronics was the leading sector, though again almost all owned by Americans (like Honeywell) or Koreans and other once dimly understood 'third-world' countries turned capitalist beacons. However, Scotland struggled to get past the stage of 'screwdriver' operations, assembling the hardware, and largely failed to develop the more lucrative software and research sides of the industry that had powered the Irish economy through the 1990s and into the next millennium. The Scottish plants remained vulnerable to sharp fluctuations in demand for microchips and the products they powered, and to price competition from the emerging low-wage, high-skill economies in India and south-east Asia.

The new technology Scots built helped, among other things, to shift service employment from the office to the home. Banks were turned into pubs and restaurants. After all, cheap shoes could be imported from China, but it was hard to outsource an order of steak and chips to Vietnam. Underemployed female home workers eagerly staffed the international call centres of US companies, whose North American customers loved the Scottish accent, even if they could not always understand it.

Divided by a common language, the Scots nevertheless tolerated their Anglo-Saxon brothers on the other side of the Atlantic. They were less accommodating about the frailties of the English. Tensions had existed between Scotland and England since the days of Edward I and William Wallace. Seven centuries of relations between the countries had left a legacy of distrust, double-dealing, broken promises and betrayal. But the Scots did not need long memories to dislike the English. Thatcher's successor, Alan Clark, was also heir to her ignorance of and insensitivity towards what made the Scots tick. With The Lady out of the way, he appointed to the DTI in 1992 former Guinness chairman Ernest Saunders, who made a miraculous recovery from Alzheimer's Disease not long after his early release from jail for his part in the scandalous take-over of Distillers in 1986. Prime Minister Clark later went on record as saying that Scotland was only good as a place to have a second home, dismissing its 'whinging' about the economic malaise of the 1990s as 'worse than the Irish'.

Scots had nothing if not a sense of their history, and what was dubbed 'the land question' had been an undertow of politics since the Clearances and Crofters' Wars of the nineteenth century. It was emotive because, whatever the historic realities of social and economic inequality, Scots thought that they had once had rights to land that had been taken away. Ownership was undoubtedly highly polarised. A 1975 survey found that 1,400 families owned 60 per cent of Scotland. In the 1980s and early 1990s a number of high-profile cases of foreign buying of islands and estates caused a public outcry.

Thus the Scottish Assembly used its powers over culture and environment to repay Clark and his kind in spades. Following a model well established in Norway, Switzerland and the Netherlands, the Scottish government put a stop to any non-Scot buying domestic property there – unless, of course, employed by a foreign multinational that created employment. It became almost impossible to buy a house in rural Scotland unless one had been born in the area. Sales too were closely monitored. Clark's family estate at Eriboll in the Scottish Highlands was compulsorily purchased before his death in 1999. Like other former second homes, it was made available to local people or to other Scots who chose to settle in rural areas – at a price set not by the market but by Assembly-appointed valuers. The policy was called: 'Scotland first'.

At the time of writing, Eriboll is owned by a 'new-age' co-operative that rents out holiday cottages, produces organic honey and makes candles and soap. Cynics say that the choice had been motivated by a desire to spite Clark. But with crippling levels of rural unemployment, politicians really did see a future in the atavistic mix of farming, tourism and artisan production that such latter-day crofting seemed to offer. The truth was that people did not want to work on the land any more than they wanted to speak Gaelic, other than as an antiquarian hobby or a 'Braveheart' statement.

Large-scale farming offered no refuge, for changes had finally been made to the EU's Common Agricultural Policy and, with the high pound, the only enterprises that could survive were highly mechanised factory-farms, mostly run on ruthless business lines by off-shoots of foreign multinationals. In 1800, 80 per cent of Scotland's people had worked on the land. By 2006 the figure was down to 8 per cent. Despite attempts at social engineering, memories of the land were all that most Scots had left.

Clark's cavalier likening of the Scots to the Irish touched a nerve. For all that Scots prized the ethos of egalitarianism, there had always been an edge of intolerance towards those who did not fit in. That included gays, as Robertson showed, but also Irish Catholics. In a throwaway remark at the Tory party conference in 1997, Clark advocated a 'night of the long knives' to rid Britain of the threat of the IRA. Many Scots (and not a few English) approved of that idea, not least the ones that participated in Orange marches in Scotland and Northern Ireland. Clark's success had been attributable in part at least to a continuing move to the right in European politics. In Germany neo-Nazis successfully challenged the law forbidding denial of the Holocaust. Where in the 1980s Clark had been an 'old Tory' of the right, his views on many topics became much more centrist in the 1990s, incorporating, among other new political forces, an organised and effective, though strictly orderly, animal rights movement, of which he was the champion. The equivalent in Scotland was a renewed anti-Catholicism that had festered within Scottish society since the Reformation half a millennium earlier.

Membership of trade unions withered — down from a half to a third of the workforce between 1979 and 1997 — as it did across Britain, but in Scotland it became normal for (white Protestant) men to join Masonic lodges in pursuit of employment, just as they had done in the 1930s. The model for the Protestant establishment was Sutherland, where 90 per cent of adult males belonged to lodges in 1979; the goal was never achieved nationwide, but by the close of 2006 it was 50 per cent.

No lodge would take women. In any case, they had other roles to fulfil. By the year 2006, Scotland's Labour government, alarmed by persistent unemployment and by the fact that the population, 5.2 million in 1981, had dipped below 4.5 million, suggested radical steps to encourage women to stay at home and have more children. There was something to be said for Catholics after all; just look at Ireland, where birth rates continued to be high. There were other causes for envy. Irish economic performance had been astutely advanced by full membership of the European Union, billions of ECUs in subsidies and the attraction, through tax incentives, of software, pharmaceuticals and 'artists' (if you could use that epithet of rock bands).

More self-congratulatory proponents of the pro-natalist project argued that it could be funded by the (purely hypothetical) half a billion pounds the country had saved since 1979 by siting the Assembly in that fine symbol of nationalism, the Royal High School on Edinburgh's Calton Hill, rather than in what some had proposed – a flash new building, like a peasant hovel on steroids, designed by some foreigner.

Scots continued to influence Westminster politics and to provide its most original minds. Tony Blair at the Foreign Office, and Gordon Brown as Home Secretary, still had a part to play in shaping England's destiny, but they remained firmly under the thumb of the new Prime Minister, Ken Livingstone. Building on populist moves, like a separate time zone for London and the Home Counties, this one-time socialist (dubbed 'Red Ken') had become an astute middle-of-the-road politician who quickly used his London mayoral power base to become leader of the Labour Party. Resisting, on the one hand, the prejudice against Scots in positions of power, he was able to use the talents of those who had opposed him in the leadership contest. But on the other hand he was able to prevent further leadership challenges by playing to mass dislike of 'Jimmys on the make': not hard, considering centuries of English antipathies to Scots in the south, topped up by judicious reminders that the lineage of the poll tax included the Adam Smith Institute and George Younger. Livingstone conveniently forgot that he was of Scots descent himself.

In the free-market Thatcher era, Adam Smith had featured highly among newspaper surveys of the most important Britons in history, even if most English had never heard of Kirkcaldy. Vaguely aware of being its victims, Scots were nevertheless deeply proud of their history – not that many of them actually knew much about their nation's past. History in the schools collapsed as pupils flocked to 'vocational' courses in competition for what few jobs there were. In the 1980s the writer Sydney Wood found that out of a sample of sixteen-year-olds, 50 per cent had heard of William Wallace and Robert the Bruce, but just 3 per cent recognised the name of Ramsay MacDonald (a Scot and the first Labour Prime Minister, in 1924). Hollywood filled the gap. In 1995 Scots found solace for their difficult relations with England in 'Braveheart'. Maybe King Edward I had tried to shaft their country, but William Wallace had paid him back by screwing his queen. The theme of submission pervaded Scottish culture. In his novel *Poor Things*, Alasdair Gray made the heroine an amoral but likeable nymphomaniac who became a symbol of Scotland. His book was required reading for all final-year school pupils and a touchstone for after-dinner jokes at American-style management courses.

Against a background of rampant technological and other consumerism among the 'haves', deprivation and debt afflicted much of the population. Housing policy might have stopped the English having second homes, but it also meant that the Scots who inhabited their own homes often had no jobs. The British Social Attitudes survey found that more Scots (three-quarters) than anywhere else in Europe put job security as their highest priority, with job satisfaction a long way behind. After a quarter of a century of the 'freedom' they had craved (so they thought) since William Wallace, there came a dawning awareness that very little could be changed by talking in Edinburgh rather than in London. Many Scots had become like native Americans on a reserve: they were certainly different, but no one wanted to share their unfortunate combination of poverty, immobility, short life and poor health. By 2006 the best known Scottish food was not haggis, but the deep-fried Mars bar; the national drink was not the multi-billion pound export, whisky, which many Scots could not afford, but EU wine-lake plonk that even the Swedes refused to make into ethanol for their buses.

Rates of obesity, alcohol abuse and heart disease were the highest in Europe. In Germany people were encouraged to eat nine items of fruit and vegetables a day, in England medical authorities suggested a more realistic five, and in Scotland Professor Philip James of Aberdeen University thought three was too optimistic. Scotland became the only 'developed' country where tobacco smoking continued to increase in the 1990s. The romantic mists of Scotland were made of exhaled smoke. Visitors still came to Scotland, but they were steered around the 'multiply-deprived' urban ghettos, like visitors to Johannesburg, and viewed from a distance the handful of rough, dreadlocked people among the machines in a raw rural landscape.

Tourism was helped by a political prioritisation that made Scotland into arguably the world's largest theme park. In 2003 the Assembly toyed with the idea of appointing a figurehead to replace the increasingly unpopular House of Windsor, headed by a cold, distant monarch who seemed to expect rather than earn loyalty, and her son, on whom the kilt looked not so much like fancy dress as just plain silly. The Scottish Assembly decided to appoint the actor Sean Connery as life president of Scotland. The marketing people had told the Assembly that no one was better suited to further 'Scotland the brand' and to fill the 'ceremony gap' lacking in the package. His 'traditional' attitudes to women also counted in his favour with the male-dominated Assembly.

Yet important changes were occurring from the late 1990s. Never a people who liked to be given anything, the Scots strengthened their sense of community and identity by using a deal, finally brokered by UNESCO in 1996, to give the Elgin Marbles to Greece, to seize back the Stone of Destiny, removed from Scone Palace in Perthshire to London by Edward I in 1296. 'Haves' and 'have nots' were also united by a shared experience of the chill economic wind of the late 1990s. The economic depression of 1998 saw tumbling oil prices and contracting demand for whisky and computer hardware; the financial services industry caught a cold when world stock markets fell. In England, as in Scotland, the 'haves' had less.

When the Labour Party eventually morphed into 'New Labour' the beast was very different. Labour eventually came to power in England in the early years of the twenty-first century. Support for the Tories in England had been on the wane in Clark's latter years. His old-Tory paternalism was seen as no longer enough to protect the people of England against the vagaries of capitalism. There were personal issues too. Clark had been a philanderer, but at least he was a heterosexual, and the Tories' fortunes were not helped by the election of Michael Portillo as party leader in 1999. But it was revulsion at an illegal, prolonged and unpleasant war in Iraq, during which many came to see Britain's relationship with America as 'special' only in the sense of being particularly taken for granted, that finally brought 'New Labour' to power in 2004.

Political pundits recognised the contribution that Scotland had made to the rise of New Labour. After a rocky start its Assembly had shown the way for British politics in a world dominated by North America and by global capitalism: constructive political dialogue built around an ethos of social corporatism. Scottish devolution in 1979 changed the future of Scotland, but England too could not escape its implications. As had been happening for centuries, the fortunes of one part of the British Isles had influenced those of the others. And, as Tam Dalyell realised, it also affected the idea of Britain. After five hundred years of building themselves up, nation states everywhere were crumbling back into their component parts. Like Humpty Dumpty, putting Britain back together again was more than even New Labour could manage.

Chapter 14

What if President Mitterrand had imposed first-past-the-post instead of proportional representation in 1986?

Byron Criddle

Francois Mitterrand was elected as the first Socialist President of the French Fifth Republic in May 1981. Promptly using his presidential power to dissolve the National Assembly, he called new parliamentary elections, in which his Socialist Party secured a substantial majority of seats – only the second time since the Republic was created in 1958 that a single party had so controlled the Assembly.

With this control in place he was able to appoint a Prime Minister and government in his own image, with the government comprising all elements of the left, including the Communist Party, even though the votes of Communist deputies were not needed to sustain the government in the Assembly. Thus was formed what was effectively the first government of the left in France. (The much-vaunted Popular Front government of 1936–38 had been a Socialist and Radical government without Communist participation, and the post-war three-party coalition, whilst including Socialists and Communists, had also seen the participation of Christian Democrats and was led initially by General Charles de Gaulle. Not until 1981 did the left comprehensively acquire executive power.)

The origins of this 1981 victory lay in the failings of the right. Centre-right parties – the Gaullists and non-Gaullist conservatives – had run France for much of the previous thirty-four years, and without interruption since Charles de Gaulle's regime was set up in 1958. For twenty-three years the same faces had governed, under the presidencies of de Gaulle (1959–69), Georges Pompidou (1969–74) and Valéry Giscard d'Estaing (1974–81). By 1981 this centre-right coalition was suffering from wear and tear, with stalled economic growth, rising unemployment, high inflation, and serious personal rivalries between the non-Gaullist President Giscard d'Estaing and the Gaullist leader Jacques Chirac. On the death of President Pompidou in 1974 Chirac had split the coalition in Giscard's favour; in 1981 he split it again, but this time in order to end Giscard's presidency. By running against Giscard in the 1981 presidential election and polling 18 per cent to Giscard's meagre 28 per cent, and then refusing properly to endorse Giscard in the decisive second ballot, he helped open the door for Mitterrand's victory.

Mitterrand, meanwhile, had built his long-run quest for the presidency, starting in 1965 with a strategy of left union, involving an electoral and programmatic alliance of the Socialist and Communist Parties. To some observers, notably on the right, this implied a Socialist move to the left, putting the party in hock to Marxist-Leninists. It was the right's habitual tactic to perpetuate its monopoly on power by waving the Communist scarecrow. In reality, Mitterrand – a man of notoriously opaque ideological commitments – created this alliance in acknowledgement of the Communist Party's sheer electoral bulk. For thirty years after the war the Communists had commanded an electorate of five million – between a quarter and a fifth of the votes at every general election – and controlled the biggest trade union federation. It was the presence of this dominant Communist phenomenon that barred the creation of any left government. In the traditional rhetoric of the right, if the left governed it would be Communist-dominated, there would be no foreign policy, a new economic order would be installed, and the government would never retreat from power.

Mitterrand recognised, however, that in the directly elected presidency of the Fifth Republic lay the makings of Communist decline. Under the presidential electoral system of two ballots, with only the top two candidates at the first ballot going through to the second, there was the opportunity for the Socialists to marginalise the Communists, since a Communist President of France was perceived as entirely unrealistic, even by Communist voters. Indeed, the Communist Party connived at such a perception by not running candidates in two of the earliest presidential elections, in 1965 and 1974.

But Socialist access to the second ballot required the poaching of Communist votes at the first ballot, as well as the mobilisation of the remaining Communist electorate at the second. Mitterrand's left union strategy had therefore been designed to position the Socialists close to the Communists with a left-sounding Common Programme designed to convince Communist voters that a Socialist President could be trusted to govern from – as well as to be elected on – the left. It was a purely tactical manoeuvre to neutralise the Communist Party's power to use its veto; the aim was, as Mitterrand stated, to show that of five million Communist voters, three million could be made to vote Socialist.

Naturally enough, the Communist leadership was not unaware of the trap, and caused the alliance to founder in the late 1970s as election results and polls increasingly revealed Socialist growth at Communist expense. In 1981 the Communist leader Georges Marchais ran against Mitterrand in the presidential election. But his candidacy also helped Mitterrand, as the gap between the Socialist and Communist candidates' first ballot vote share – 26 per cent Mitterrand, 16 per cent Marchais – served to confirm the rebalancing of electoral strength on the left in the Socialists' favour. This in turn de-radicalised the image of the left, shot the right's Communist fox, and helped Mitterrand to his historic victory.

So in 1981 the right lost and the left, because moderately led, won. Here at last was the historic swing of the pendulum, or as the French prefer, 'alternance' (alternation) after twenty-three years of right government. But for how long?

The new government moved quickly to apply a programme of public sector enlargement, decentralisation to the regions, higher social spending and abolition of the death penalty. But a Keynesian policy of inflating demand whilst France's trading partners were deflating caused a run on the currency and three devaluations in as many years. By 1984 high unemployment and the withdrawal by Mitterrand of a totemic policy to incorporate the private Catholic schools into the secular state system, brought a change of Prime Minister, the exit of the Communist ministers, and an economic U-turn involving a switch to economic orthodoxy — austerity, privatisation, and job shake-out. All of this was reflected in bad poll ratings, but even as early as 1982 it was clear that the electoral honeymoon of 1981 was over, and that the Socialists would lose their parliamentary majority at the next Assembly elections due in 1986, leaving Mitterrand without the means to govern.

Under the parliamentary electoral system of two ballots in single-member constituencies, it was predicted that the Socialists would be reduced to a rump of fifty or sixty seats in the 577-seat Assembly. At that time, given the assumption of presidential dominance of government that had become the hallmark of the Fifth Republic, such an outcome would be seen as such a humiliation for the President that he would — in a phrase dating from a constitutional crisis of the 1870s — be expected to 'submit or resign'. With two years of his seven-year presidential mandate remaining after the election, however, it was clear that Mitterrand would have no intention of resigning. Equally, however, the French had, at that point, no experience of the cohabitation of a President of one party and an Assembly, and thus government, of another — experience which they were in due course to acquire in 1986–88, 1993–95, and 1997–2002. Consequently the looming Socialist parliamentary meltdown looked like precipitating a major crisis of the regime.

Mitterrand thus reached for electoral system manipulation in order to alleviate his difficulty, and selected a proportional system expected to minimise Socialist seat losses and split the right. The system involved competition between party lists in multi-member constituencies based on the French départements (counties) with voting in a single ballot.[1] Whilst the workings of the system discriminated somewhat against smaller parties, it was sufficiently proportional to allow larger parties to discard tactical alliances with other parties, as under the discarded two-ballot single-member constituency system, so permitting the Communists to survive independently of the Socialists and to allow the National Front (FN) to occupy seats that would otherwise have gone to the orthodox centre-right.

The system did deliver some of Mitterrand's objectives: it greatly reduced the scale of expected Socialist seat losses and held Chirac's centre-right alliance to an overall Assembly majority of two seats. The Socialist vote, at 32 per cent, satisfactorily contrasted with the Communists' 10 per cent, but the proportionality of the system delivered thirty-five seats to the Communists instead of the virtual extinction they might have faced under the old system. As important for the future of bipolarised electoral choice – encouraged at the second ballot of presidential (and hitherto of parliamentary) elections – was the awarding of thirty-five seats to the National Front. This exemplified Mitterrand's 'divide and rule' tactic, of releasing the extreme right genie in order to split the right.

The use of proportional representation certainly minimised the inconvenience facing Mitterrand in 1986, but at the cost of giving oxygen to the extreme parties of left and right – notably legitimising the National Front. In this sense it damaged the long-term prospects of Mitterrand's Socialist Party, and of the centre-right alliance of Chirac, becoming – as presidential election second ballots encouraged – the basis of a solidly bipolarised two-party system.

~

Ignoring the admittedly serious immediate-term damage Mitterrand would have done to his political career by sticking to an electoral system promising him a parliamentary rout in 1986, the hypothesis advanced here is that had he looked beyond short-term political survival in 1986 and introduced the British electoral system of single-member constituencies elected by first-past-the-post in a single ballot, he would have set French politics on course for the eventual atrophying of the extremes, to the benefit of the big governing parties. He would have set in train the erosion of a political culture rooted in a tradition of constitutional instability.

It has been suggested that 'a nation's party system is determined far more by its political institutions and traditions and by the social cleavages that underpin its politics than by the electoral system', and that 'due to the traditions of political conflict in France the introduction of the Anglo-American plurality system in the Third and Fourth Republics would probably have had hardly any effect on the party system and its consequences'.[2] By inference, however, the authors of these statements seem not to rule out the application of the British system in the Fifth Republic; but in any event, since the system was not applied to France at any time, the comments on its inapplicability are mere conjecture.

In Britain the tendency has been – as, indeed, approvingly noted by the French political scientist Maurice Duverger – the reinforcement of a two-party duopoly over time, even after the appearance of third parties, such as the Irish nationalists in the nineteenth century and the Labour Party in the twentieth.[3] In due course, as a consequence of the complex impact of these two incursions into the Liberal–Conservative duopoly, a new duopoly was formed based on the Conservative and Labour Parties. Nor was it impossible to imagine at the turn of the twenty-first century that the Liberal revival in the final decades of the twentieth century presaged a realignment of the party system around a different duopoly.

France has, even without the single-ballot British system, seen a bipolarisation of the party system under the Fifth Republic. Since the 1960s two large parties have come to dominate both centre-right (the Gaullists) and centre-left (the Socialists). A multi-party system covering a wide ideological spectrum has been shoehorned into a bipolarised choice at second ballots, the electoral mechanism in presidential elections precluding anything other than a straight fight of, normally, right and left. This process was admittedly prompted by a cultural factor as well; de Gaulle's charisma was an agent in the federating of the right, which in due course stimulated an imitative operation by Mitterrand on the left. By such means was the traditional fragmentation of electoral choice mitigated in France.

There remains, however, the damaging impact of the disaggregating effect of first-ballot competition between a full range of parties. In parliamentary elections, first-ballot candidates failing to clear a 12.5 per cent (of the registered electorate) hurdle are excluded from the second ballot; at the second ballot, whether by electoral strength or though the withdrawal of allied parties, a straight fight usually ensues. In presidential elections, as already stated, a straight fight is mandatory. The difficulty lies in assembling bipolarised blocs out of the fragmentation of the first ballot. For example, there is the problem on the right of getting National Front voters back into line, with evidence from past presidential contests of half of all FN voters, when denied a second-ballot candidate, dispersing either into abstention or to voting for the left. Mitterrand had fully realised the wrecking propensity of the FN on the right, and indeed was helped by it in his re-election to the presidency in 1988.

To the disaggregating impact of first ballots has to be added the damaging effect of proportional representation, which was introduced at various lower-tier elections under both the Giscard and Mitterrand presidencies. Thus Giscard introduced PR for the 1979 European Parliamentary election, and in subsequent elections for that parliament, in 1999 and 2004, no fewer than eight parties secured seats. In 1983 and 1986 Mitterrand introduced PR for municipal and regional elections. All these electoral sites, as mid-term contests which do not have any bearing on national government, are purpose-built for protest voting, and it is precisely at such lower-tier elections that the rise in support for fringe parties has registered most since the 1980s.

Additionally, all the major parties (Socialist, Gaullist, the Giscardian UDF) and even the FN, have suffered splits under the encouragement offered by PR. Bolstered by PR at peripheral elections, the size of the National Front's vote in the important general election of 1997 would, had that election been held under PR, have yielded eighty-six seats. As it was, it obtained only one seat, but by gaining access to many second-ballot contests it split the right and handed the election to the left. The disaggregating impact of proportional representation has been termed by the political scientist Jean-Luc Parodi, the 'accordion effect' – the pulling out of the party spectrum to its fullest extent, whether by PR or at first ballots, thereby making difficult the squeezing back (of the accordion) to the middle.[4] This problem would be obviated by single ballots under first past the post, and no use of proportional representation.

The deficiency in French politics before the 1980s was the absence of alternation, with the right permanently in power. But since 1981, alternation has not been a problem; it has occurred at every conceivable electoral opportunity, offering governments no more than a short-term incumbency. Thus in 1986 the governing Socialist President Mitterrand had to cede power (if not office) to a governing Gaullist Prime Minister, Chirac. In 1988 that governing Gaullist Prime Minister lost a presidential election to Mitterrand, who removed Chirac's parliamentary majority by dissolving the Assembly and restoring (almost) a Socialist majority with which he could again govern. In 1993 the governing President Mitterrand suffered a parliamentary rout of the sort he avoided only by PR in 1986 and ceded power to a right Prime Minister, Balladur. In 1995 that right Prime Minister lost the presidential election to Chirac, and in 1997, the governing President Chirac in turn lost a general election to the Socialist Lionel Jospin's 'plural left' alliance, which governed for the next five years. But in 2002 the governing Prime Minister Jospin was eliminated at the first round of the presidential election, and a governing right President Chirac was restored. This was a pattern of government change at every election; from a stuck pendulum, France had moved to a frenetic metronome.

One cause of the serial eviction of governments from office is the curious French arrangement of an executive split between President and Prime Minister, with the latter emanating from an Assembly majority usually elected at some point during a presidential septennate. That particular Gallic eccentricity is beyond the scope of this essay.

Another cause is the fragmented party system. On the left, the Socialists, with under 30 per cent of the vote and consequent dependence on a variety of Marxists and environmentalists, either to augment their total of parliamentary seats or to secure second-ballot presidential victories, have had to rely on the divisions of the right, primarily delivered, as in 1988 and 1997, by the National Front. The decline of the Communist Party has not resolved the traditional weakness of the Socialist Party, because the anti-capitalist tradition has merely found expression elsewhere, in a range of gauchiste, mainly Trotskyist, alternatives. Herein lies the centre-left's most intractable problem: the need to treat with a revolutionary tradition that refuses to 'manage capitalism', which required the Socialist Party to approach power in 1981 with the formal pledge of a 'rupture' with capitalism, and that saw the Socialist Prime Minister Jospin (1997–2002) invoke 'a market economy, but not a market society'.[5]

No better illustration of the problem was there than Jospin's elimination in the presidential election in 2002,[6] when the two-ballot mechanism provided the opportunity to indulge a range of exotic leftist predilections at the first ballot, followed by the hand-wringing consequence of an absent Socialist candidate at the second. Sixteen candidates – a record in the history of the regime – contested the first ballot, eight of them on the left. In aggregate, 10 per cent voted for three Trotskyist candidates, 5 per cent for a dissident left-wing Socialist, 5 per cent for a Green, 3 per cent for a Communist, and 2 per cent for a left Radical. This dispersal of the left vote over wholly unelectable candidates ensured the exclusion of the outgoing Prime Minister Jospin – reduced to a meagre 16 per cent share of the vote, behind the National Front leader Jean-Marie Le Pen – from the second ballot run-off with President Chirac. There followed Chirac's victory with 82 per cent of the vote, much of it contributed by first-ballot leftists who hurriedly found themselves having to vote for the 'crook' in order to stop the 'fascist', whereas had Jospin confronted Chirac in the run-off, he might well have won. As it was, the accordion had been extended further than at any previous presidential election, and then jammed in the vicinity of its rightward end. Here was an electoral system delivering a wholly specious victory to the Fifth Republic's most insubstantial leader.

It does not take an Anglo-Saxon pragmatist to perceive the self-indulgent folly of the double-ballot system, made worse by use of proportional representation in lower-tier elections. Maurice Duverger's admiration for the British model has already been noted. The French system is one which enables the voters to indulge, in President Giscard d'Estaing's words, their 'Latin passion for extremes',[7] and in the spring of 2006, when persistent street 'manifestations' destroyed the right government's attempt to impose the most modest labour market reforms, a Sorbonne professor, Jacques Marseille, noted the French 'anti-reformist' culture, and an inability to proceed other than by 'rupture'.[8]

One way of modulating such cultural deficiencies over time would be an electoral system that denies oxygen to non-governing protest parties and encourages the aggregation of interests within large parties of centre-right and centre-left. For those inclined to argue that multiple parties in France reflect multiple issues, and even a congenital resistance to consensus, it may be asserted that there are electoral systems permissive of such fissiparousness, and those which are not. The presidential electoral mechanisms of the Fifth Republic have shown how a countercheck to fragmentation is possible (at the second ballot), with the creation of what has been termed 'bipolar multipartism', but over the past thirty years presidential first ballots have registered a decline in the major (centre-right and centre-left) party candidates' vote share. Thus, where Giscard and Mitterrand aggregated 76 per cent in the first ballot in 1974, the same two candidates together polled only 54 per cent in 1981; in 1988 Mitterrand and Chirac aggregated only 54 per cent, and in 1995 Chirac and Jospin polled only 44 per cent. In 2002 Chirac and Jospin, the leaders of the two alternative governing coalitions, together polled a mere 36 per cent of the vote.

This pattern of declining support for governing parties is not, admittedly, a specifically French phenomenon; the two-party duopoly has also been in decline in Britain over the same period. But French electoral mechanisms have exacerbated the inability of the major parties to retain electoral approval over time and facilitated regular government evictions. To sustain the legitimacy of parties in office, electoral mechanisms are needed that constrain rather than indulge those aspects of French political culture finding expression in support for parties, whether of left or right, whose policies are either resistant to reform or simply inapplicable. A single-ballot non-proportional system would eventually entrench on the centre-left a party released from Marxist pretensions and able to reduce the state, and a party on the centre-right freed from a war of chiefs and able to modulate the excesses of Franco-centric sentiment. It would properly bipolarise French politics, impose the salience of the median voter, and delegitimise the impractical extremes.

Mitterrand would probably have been personally crucified by such a system in 1986, but he would have laid the basis for an unimaginable restructuring of French politics by grasping this nettle.

Notes

1   A. Cole & P. Campbell, *French Electoral Systems and Elections since 1789* (Gower, 1989), pp. 133–43.
2   Ibid. p. 17.

3 M. Duverger, 'Duverger's Law Forty Years On' in B. Grofman and A. Lijpart, *Electoral Laws and their Political Consequences* (Agathon Press, 1986), pp. 69–84.

4 A. Knapp and V. Wright, *The Government and Politics of France* (Routledge, 2001), p. 255.

5 L. Jospin, *Modern Socialism* (Fabian Publications, 2000).

6 See D. S. Bell and Byron Criddle, 'Presidentialism Restored: The French Elections of April–May and June 2002', *Parliamentary Affairs*, vol. 55, pp. 643–63.

7 V. Giscard d'Estaing, *Démocratie Française* (Fayard, 1976), p. 155.

8 J. Marseille, 'Plus que la reforme, "la rupture" est consubstantielle a notre histoire', *Le Monde*, 26–27 mars 2006.

Chapter 15

What if the Alliance had not quarrelled publicly over defence in 1986?

Duncan Brack

The defence debate at the Liberal Assembly in Eastbourne in 1986 is remembered as the occasion when the Liberal–SDP Alliance began to fall apart: 'Ban the Bomb vote shatters the Alliance', proclaimed the *Express* the day after. The debate was the culmination of a series of events throughout the spring and summer of 1986 that exposed major rifts within the Alliance, partly over defence policy but, more importantly, over the way in which its twin leaders approached their roles.

Over the course of a year which included two major public rows on defence, the Alliance lost over a third of its support in the opinion polls, falling from 35 per cent in January 1986 to 22.5 per cent in December.[1] The general election that followed in June 1987 saw the Alliance slip back from its 1983 high point of 26 per cent to 22.5 per cent, while the Labour Party pulled away from it, up from 28 per cent in 1983 to 31 per cent. The Alliance's attempt to break the mould of British politics had failed, and over the following three years it would descend into the bitter infighting of the merger process, the split with the Owenite 'continuing SDP' and the painful process of reconstruction. At its weakest point, the merged party, the Liberal Democrats, came within the statistical margin of error of zero in the opinion polls. It would not be until late 1990, ironically enough thanks to another Eastbourne event – the first Lib Dem by-election victory – that the third party would once again begin to mount a serious challenge to the Tory–Labour duopoly.

What would have happened if the Alliance had not quarrelled so disastrously over defence policy in 1986? In the 1987 election it managed to poll exactly what it had been scoring in opinion polls at the end of 1986; if that had been the 35 per cent it had been enjoying twelve months earlier, instead of 22.5 per cent, the outcome could have been a hung parliament rather than a Conservative majority of 102. The entire political history of the UK from 1987 onwards could have been very different.

Yet my purpose in writing this chapter is not so much an examination of alternate history as an analysis of how the Alliance could have avoided quarrelling so catastrophically in the first place. Because this episode should never have happened. At almost every stage, senior politicians made serious – sometimes quite spectacular – errors of judgement. It should have been easy to avoid the rows taking place at all.

This chapter is, therefore, primarily a defence of counterfactual history, an answer to those who believe that major events, like election outcomes, are essentially predetermined. It aims to demonstrate not just *how* things could have happened differently in 1986, but why, by any rational analysis, they *should* have done so.

~

At the end of 1985, the Liberal–SDP Alliance seemed to be firmly established, not just as the third party but as one which had a realistic chance of sharing power after the next general election. It had survived the chaos of the formation of the SDP in 1981, the achievements and disappointments of the 1983 election – the highest third-party vote for sixty years, only just behind Labour, yet only twenty-three MPs – and the resignation of the SDP's first leader, Roy Jenkins. In 1985, its local election results were a considerable success and in July the Liberals won the Brecon & Radnor by-election. In July and September 1985 the Alliance led the other two parties in the opinion polls. The SDP's new leader, David Owen, did not enjoy the same warmth of personal relations with the Liberal leader, David Steel, as had Jenkins, but the two parties were, with a few exceptions, getting on well at the grassroots; joint selection of parliamentary candidates was becoming more common.

Nevertheless, there were still tensions. One of the problems the Alliance faced was how to agree joint statements of policy. Both the Liberal Party and the SDP possessed democratic mechanisms for determining their own policies, but the main way of coming up with any joint position was through negotiation. This was frequently an unsatisfactory procedure; the process could take months or even years,[2] and its outcome reflected not just the original positions of the two parties, but their relative skills in the internal bargaining process. The procedure magnified disagreements, as policy disputes which would have passed unnoticed within a single party assumed the proportions of a major split in the context of two. This should not be exaggerated – the genuine policy disagreements between the two parties were actually very limited in number, but the Alliance had no way of resolving them except through weeks of time-consuming and demoralising negotiations and high-profile dissension at conferences.

The 1983 election manifesto had been deliberately put together by the two leaders in a hurry, in an effort to avoid long-drawn-out negotiations. The lack of consultation and, on the Liberal side, resentment at the tone of the final document, which was seen as too SDP-dominated, caused resentment.[3] Both sides were determined not to see such a rushed approach adopted in the future, and there was some support for a degree of joint policy-making. Two joint commissions, on constitutional reform, and on employment and industrial recovery, had in fact operated reasonably smoothly before the 1983 election, but David Owen, the new SDP leader, was hostile to any further such cooperation. 'Too much joint activity', as he put it later, 'would lead to an amorphous amalgam'.[4]

Despite the growing cooperation at the grassroots of the Alliance, Owen was determined not to let the two parties drift together. Originally viewed as the most left-wing of the SDP's founding Gang of Four, he rapidly accommodated himself to Thatcherism; since for Steel and most Liberals, Thatcherite Conservatism was the opposite of everything they stood for, this was a growing source of tension. Owen had few firm policy principles, using policy positions – including his much-trumpeted but largely meaningless 'social market economy' – purely as weapons with which to hammer the opposition. Thus he took the SDP further to the right on issues such as the application of markets to public services.

Owen opposed joint policy-making with the Liberals wherever possible. When joint discussions could not be avoided, he attempted to dominate the process, presenting wording previously agreed with Steel on a take-it-or-leave-it basis to the joint policy committees. On one occasion, the Liberals requested a ten-minute adjournment to discuss the new wording with which they had been suddenly confronted. Owen refused, threatening to terminate the meeting, whereupon the redoubtable Liberal Lady Seear stated that she proposed to make an eleven-minute intervention. Owen gave in.[5] It was domineering tactics like this that generated resentment and mistrust among many Liberals, and ultimately helped undermine Owen's position inside his own party.

The most high-profile policy difference between the two Alliance partners lay in the area of defence policy, and specifically over nuclear weapons. Nuclear defence was one of the key political battlegrounds of the 1980s, as the arms race of the early part of the decade gradually gave way to disarmament negotiations between US President Reagan and Soviet President Gorbachev. The Labour Party's adoption of unilateral nuclear disarmament in 1980 had been one of the reasons behind the foundation of the SDP, and Owen himself, a former Foreign Secretary, was hawkish on the issue. He was convinced that Britain could not rely indefinitely on the US for its nuclear shield, and he disliked the idea that France might become Europe's only nuclear power. He believed that Britain should remain, more or less indefinitely, a 'nuclear-weapon state', a phrase he liked and frequently used. He ensured that supporters of the Campaign for Nuclear Disarmament were excluded from the SDP's approved list of parliamentary candidates.[6]

The Liberal Party possessed a distinctly different approach. It had historically opposed the British independent deterrent, though in 1984 it had reversed this stance and accepted that the Polaris missile force should be retained but put into new multilateral arms reduction talks. It had twice, in 1981 and 1984, voted against the siting of US cruise missiles in Britain, against the wishes of David Steel, who had himself participated in the conference debate in 1984. It had never supported outright rejection of all nuclear weapons, however, and had always accepted the need for a NATO (i.e. US) nuclear umbrella. Though there were many unilateralists in the Liberal ranks, they were never a majority.

With the Polaris nuclear missiles scheduled for replacement in the near future, it was clear that the Alliance had to reach an agreed position before the 1987 election. Both parties opposed the government's plans to replace Polaris with Trident, but the Liberals objected to them on principle, as an escalation of firepower, and the SDP only on grounds of cost. So the unresolved question was: what should replace Polaris? On this occasion, Owen accepted the need for joint policy-making, acutely aware of the potential for disaster; the damage inflicted on the Labour Party during the 1983 campaign was a grisly warning.

In July 1984, therefore, Steel and Owen announced the establishment of a Joint Commission on Defence and Disarmament, charged with preparing detailed proposals for consideration by the parties at their conferences in autumn 1986. The decision itself saw the first of a long line of mistakes and errors of judgement that would eventually cause the entire policy position – and the Alliance itself – to unravel.

Mistake 1

The commission was set up by the leaders, not by the parties themselves. Had it been appointed by the two policy committees – or even just, on the Liberal side, by their committee – it would have started with a greater degree of sympathy and support if ever the crunch came. But, as Des Wilson, the Liberal President-elect, explained: 'Its members had been chosen by the leaders; was it not, therefore, just a device to manipulate the parties into acceptance of their line?'[7]

Having said that, there were few complaints about the work of the commission itself. It was chaired by John Edmonds, a former Head of the Arms Control and Disarmament Department at the Foreign Office, and not a member of either party, and on the Liberal side contained critics of the UK independent deterrent and of cruise missiles. The members worked well together in consulting widely and conducting a careful examination of British defence policy.

Mistake 2

The second mistake was for David Owen not to ensure that anyone on the commission was there to represent his line, the need for a replacement for Polaris. (This was not a problem for Steel, who had no particularly strong views on the subject.) Two of the SDP members, Bill Rodgers and John Cartwright MP, each thought that that was the reason behind the other's membership; both were wrong.[8] As a result, not only was Owen's view not argued for as strongly as he probably would have wished, but he was not kept closely in touch with the commission's deliberations.

As a result, when the commission did begin to reach conclusions, some of them came as an unpleasant shock to him. In February 1986, another SDP member, David Dunn, alerted him to the fact that the commission was looking for a compromise on the replacement of Polaris. Owen was alarmed that the possibility of no replacement might appear in the final report; as he wrote in his memoirs, 'by the middle of April I had become uneasy about the Joint Commission, suspecting it was up to no good'.[9] He claimed that he tried to discuss the matter twice with Bill Rodgers, but 'on both occasions I suspected that Bill was dissembling'.[10] This was not Rodgers' recollection, who remembers that 'David and I exchanged a passing word about progress but no significant discussion of any anxiety on his part took place'.[11]

At the end of April, the Chernobyl nuclear disaster in the Soviet Union triggered concern over the safety and desirability of civil nuclear power. In fact this was an issue on which the Alliance was much more clearly split along party lines; the SDP largely supported nuclear power, and the Liberal Party almost entirely did not. The 1983 manifesto had fudged the issue by simply declaring that the Alliance saw no need for the construction of any new nuclear stations, but comments critical of nuclear power from a whole string of Liberal politicians in the wake of Chernobyl were regarded by Owen as culpable undermining of the agreed compromise.

Nevertheless, in early May, Owen was worried enough about the outcome of the Defence Commission that he offered Steel a compromise: 'I proposed that the SDP should give ground on civil nuclear power to Liberal sentiment in exchange for Liberals giving ground to the SDP on nuclear deterrence'.[12] Since the compromise he offered – a commitment not to build any new nuclear stations for the next five years – was actually nearer the SDP's position than the 1983 manifesto had been, Steel was probably not too impressed.

Mistake 3
The next mistake was Steel's. By mid-May the commission was almost ready to announce its findings. It proposed to come out firmly in favour of Britain's continued membership of NATO, but with the development of a stronger 'European pillar' to counterbalance US dominance. It argued that NATO should develop nuclear policies based on the concept of 'minimum deterrence', that greater efforts should be made to achieve cuts in nuclear armaments on both sides, that British nuclear weapons should be included

in any talks, and that a moratorium should be placed on any new deployments. It did not call for the withdrawal of US cruise missiles from the UK, but it did support abandoning Trident. Crucially, it concluded that no decision needed to be taken about any replacement for Polaris for several years, when perhaps new disarmament talks might place the issue in a different context; in any event, no decision needed to be taken before the next election.

The commission had worked well together, though in the course of its deliberations its Liberal members had moved further towards the SDP's position than the SDP members towards the Liberals' – which promised trouble to come; the package was obviously some way away from what Liberal assemblies had voted for in the past. From the point of view of the SDP members, however, and most of the Liberal membership, it was an acceptable compromise, and the potential flashpoint of a replacement for Polaris had been carefully side-stepped.

Steel was therefore in a 'rather relaxed good humour' when he joined two *Scotsman* correspondents, Martin Dowle and Andrew Marr, for a routine lunch on Thursday 15 May.[13] Not only was the Defence Commission helping to defuse a potentially serious row, but the Alliance was doing well. The previous week it had performed strongly in the local elections and in two by-elections, winning Ryedale and missing West Derbyshire by only 100 votes. The discussion naturally turned to the pending release of the Defence Commission report, and one of the journalists asked whether it committed the Alliance to a replacement for Polaris. As Steel said later, 'At this point I should have changed the subject, or told them to wait and see. Instead I foolishly, but accurately, replied: "No, it doesn't."'[14]

The Scotsman ran the story as its front-page lead the next day, under the headline 'Alliance Report rejects UK deterrent – Owen's nuclear hopes dashed'. In fact Martin Dowle's piece was wrong, suggesting that the report would come out against any replacement for Polaris, rather than simply leaving the option open; this misunderstanding led him to conclude that 'the unanimity of the finding of the commission, which is drawn equally from the SDP and the Liberals, means that the SDP leader's favoured policy has been rejected by the specialist nominees of his own party'.[15] 'I was appalled when I saw the *Scotsman* front page', recalled Steel, 'and naturally felt guilty about it. However, I thought damage limitation was possible, given that no Fleet Street paper had carried the story.'[16] Bill Rodgers agreed: 'the story should have provoked no more from Owen than a sharp word on the telephone for David Steel'.[17] They reckoned without the paranoia of Owen.

Mistake 4

The Scotsman broke the story on the day before the SDP Council in Southport. Owen was incensed. He believed it was a deliberate attempt by Steel to pre-empt the report and undermine him; he went to some lengths in his memoirs to show that Steel and colleagues were systematically briefing the press, though there was no real evidence for this.

What was even worse, Owen felt that he had been betrayed by his own SDP colleagues on the commission. He blamed Bill Rodgers in particular, and because Rodgers was an associate of Roy Jenkins, by association, Jenkins himself and all his supporters within the party – who, for good measure, were probably acting together with the Liberals. 'One does not have to believe in conspiracy theories …', he wrote in his memoirs, but he did. 'SDP members were not upholding SDP policy … Bill had deliberately decided to go his own way.'[18] For Owen, the episode was rapidly escalating from a disagreement over a nuclear weapons system to a challenge to his own leadership: 'There was no doubt in my mind that I was embarking on a very risky course. If I lost I would have to consider giving up the leadership of the SDP.'[19]

His 'risky course' was to attempt to rubbish the commission's report before it had even been finalised. Without any attempt at consultation with any of the SDP members of the commission, he rewrote his speech to the Council the following day:

> I have not seen the joint document yet, but the SDP's policy on this is perfectly clear ... I must tell you bluntly that I believe we should remain a nuclear-weapon state ... I definitely do not believe that I would carry any conviction whatever in the next election were I to answer – on your behalf – on the question of the replacement of Polaris, that that would have to depend on the circumstances of the time. That would get, and would deserve, a belly laugh from the British electorate. That sort of fudging and mudging was what I left behind in the Labour Party.[20]

The Social Democrat members of the commission were outraged that Owen could have attacked their careful work of the previous two years so comprehensively without either having seen the draft or talked to them. As Rodgers put it, 'it was a rebuke to David Steel and a direct challenge to the commission. It rejected any compromise and pre-empted further policy-making on the matter by the SDP.'[21] Rodgers tried to suggest means of damage limitation, but Owen repeated his stance in an article in *The Observer* on 1 June, and in a speech in Bonn on 5 June. His paranoia, if anything, grew even greater: 'Bill and Shirley [Williams] knew full well that I had decided to confront their challenge head on'. A report that Liberal CND were gearing up to oppose the commission report 'was all part of a tactic to make it look as if the commission ... was steering a sensible path'. In a magazine interview thirteen years later, he recalled the episode as demonstrating that Rodgers and co. had been trying 'to get me to support unilateralism', a description that was wildly at odds with reality.[22]

The Bonn speech opened the floodgates, as the Social Democrats that Owen was criticising decided it was time to put their side of the story. Shirley Williams, SDP President, made it clear on BBC Radio 4 that: 'it does not follow that what the leader says is the same and identical with the policy of the party'. Jenkins remarked, cuttingly, that with Owen's speeches there was always 'a danger of theatre taking over from valour ... Custer's Last Stand should not be a nightly event.' 'Certainty is not always a virtue,' Rodgers observed. 'Nor is conviction by itself evidence of truth.'[23]

From May to June 1986, the Alliance lost eight points in the Gallup opinion poll, falling from 32.5 per cent to 24.5 per cent. In the light of the local and by-election results, it could have expected to have gone up, as it had after the Brecon & Radnor by-election victory the year before.

Mistake 5

The commission eventually launched its report on 11 June, having allowed Owen to bully it into changing the draft text – the next mistake. John Cartwright had told Rodgers, before Owen's speech at Southport but in the light of rumours that he was about to criticise the commission, that he was content with the text.[24] Nevertheless, after the speech, he and Jim Wellbeloved both felt it necessary to press for a number of changes, and considered issuing a formal note of dissent.

In fact the changes were not that extensive. The foreword made it clear that some commission members did believe that Polaris should be replaced, while others were not convinced. The phrase 'after the election' was dropped and the final report simply said that the Polaris missiles need not be replaced 'now'.[25]

From the point of view of many Liberals, however, the changes devalued the commission report. The average Liberal activist's aversion to Owen was strong enough that the fact that he so clearly disliked the report was a point in its favour, helping to offset the fact that on most issues it was not particularly close to Liberal policy. But his outburst seemed to have moved it even further towards the SDP position.

In fact the report was well received in the press; *The Guardian* called it 'a thoroughly intelligent and workmanlike document', while the *Financial Times* regarded its position as one that was 'defensible and sustainable well beyond the next election'.[26] Several of the papers regretted the fact that the row triggered by Owen's speech had overshadowed its content; Hugo Young, displaying rather more *Schadeqnfreude*, commented on the 'splendid but destructive row … which could, at its worst, leave the Alliance looking as erratic and non-credible in 1988 as Labour did in 1983'.[27] In the weeks that followed, the row rumbled on, but less publicly; Owen arranged shows of support for his line, and condemnation of Rodgers' and Williams', at internal SDP meetings, and Steel and Owen agreed that they should air their differences in private, not in public. Nevertheless, Steel felt forced to disagree with Owen's suggestion that the two Alliance parties could, if necessary, contest the election on different defence policies. As he explained to Brian Walden, on ITV's *Weekend World*, 'I don't think we can go into an election with one set of candidates saying one thing and another set saying the other … If we can't agree before we get into government, how can we agree when we are in government? That is what the electorate will want to know.'[28]

Thus the scene was set for the next – and most calamitous – mistake.

Mistake 6

Both Steel and Owen were acutely conscious of the damage the row had caused; they wanted to find some additional way to demonstrate harmony. They lit upon the idea of a joint Anglo-French nuclear deterrent, pooling the two countries' nuclear forces – building on the commission report's support for closer European cooperation on defence. Throughout the summer, Owen and Steel discussed the issue with French, German and NATO leaders. Their visits to Brussels and Paris generated plenty of good photo-opportunities, the Alliance recovered somewhat in the opinion polls (up to 30 per cent in August), and the two leaders perhaps began to feel as if they were coming out of the woods.

If anything, they were driving themselves deeper. Looking back at the idea of the Anglo-French 'Euro-bomb' with the benefit of hindsight, it is difficult to believe that anyone ever took it seriously. There was no evidence that the French had any interest in the proposal; they had been too polite to say so to the leaders' faces during their visit in September, but even Owen's memoirs, which devote four pages to the trip, offer no evidence that they wanted to support it. If it had been a plausible option, why had the Defence Commission, stuffed with experts and working hard over two years, not come up with it themselves? And why did Steel think that a new generation of joint nuclear weapons would have satisfied the activists in his own party who wanted no replacement for Polaris?

Quite probably, the details of the new policy were not actually very important for Steel. Unlike other Liberal leaders, including Jo Grimond and Paddy Ashdown, David Steel was never fascinated by ideas. He was primarily a strategist, determined to show that Liberals could exert influence by working with others, for example through the cross-party European Community referendum campaign of 1975, the Lib–Lab Pact of 1977–78, and the Alliance. As the leader of a small third party, this was not an unreasonable approach, but his neglect of details of policy that mattered to his party activists was a serious weakness (and was ultimately to undo him, over the disastrous farce of the 'dead parrot' draft of the founding policy statement of the Liberal Democrats in 1988). As David Owen once put it to Michael Meadowcroft, 'The problem with the Liberal Party is that you have a leader who isn't interested in policy'.[29] On this occasion – as on many others, including the drafting of the 1983 manifesto – it was the demonstration of Alliance unity that was important to Steel, not the precise details of the way in which it was to be achieved.

Owen, on the other hand, was quite determined to work the final Alliance position back towards SDP policy, i.e. retention of Polaris. He may even have believed in the Euro-bomb proposal, but in any case it was a reinforcement to his party's position and he was determined to push it.[30] He made his position clear in his opening speech to the SDP conference in Harrogate in September: 'The concept of a European minimum deterrent, respecting the political structures of the French and British nations, makes sense.' The conference endorsed the commission report and called for a 'full investigation of the practicality of a European minimum deterrent', while at the same time recognising previous SDP policy as the 'basis' of party policy; an amendment which would have tilted policy away from replacing Polaris was heavily defeated.[31]

The Euro-bomb compromise appeared to be making headway. The Liberal assembly, however, was not to prove so compliant.

Mistake 7

The seventh mistake was a comprehensive failure of party management by Steel in the run-up to the debate at the Liberal assembly in Eastbourne.

Along with his lack of interest in policy details, Steel was not particularly enthusiastic about participating in his party's democratic structures. Of course no one would have expected him, on a regular basis, to have sat through lengthy meetings of the committees that ran the party, but if he was serious about party management he should made sure that he was represented by advisers or aides or allies who could relay his views and keep him in touch with what the committees were doing. This was particularly important given the priority he appeared to afford to leading the Alliance rather than the Liberal Party. Yet the Euro-bomb proposal was announced with no prior consultation and no discussion of it before the Eastbourne assembly.

As a result of this breakdown in communications, Steel failed to understand what most Liberals expected the defence debate at Eastbourne to be about.[32] Steel wanted it to agree *Alliance* policy, but most Liberals thought it was going to agree *Liberal* policy, which the two parties would then negotiate about, in the context of the comprehensive joint policy programme that was at the time being constructed.

This position was set out explicitly in the booklet *Across the Divide: Liberal Values for Defence and Disarmament*, produced by three dissident MPs, Simon Hughes, Michael Meadowcroft and Archy Kirkwood, together with three party organisations, the National League of Young Liberals, the Union of Liberal Students and the Liberal Information Network, LINk. The booklet set out a position nearer to the traditional Liberal stance, including a 'no first use' policy for nuclear weapons and the phasing out of Polaris; it supported European defence cooperation, but only on a non-nuclear basis. More to the point, it argued that:

> The Liberal Party must make a strong Liberal contribution to the debate within the Alliance. We should not be reluctant to make that contribution. To do so is not to be divisive. It is to recognise that a strong Alliance cannot be built upon a compromise which is the lowest common denominator between two weak positions but, rather, requires a combination of two strong parties with arguments which are the best points of two clear sets of policy.[33]

(Substitute 'SDP' for 'Liberal' and you get a statement that David Owen would have agreed with wholeheartedly.)

The resolution endorsing the Defence Commission report was open to amendment right up until the assembly. The crucial meeting of the Assembly Committee which selected the amendments for debate from amongst those submitted took place on the Monday – at the same time as the parliamentary party meeting. Neither of the two MPs who were members of the committee were present.

The committee selected two amendments, of which Amendment 1 was the crux of the debate. The main motion welcomed 'closer co-operation in defence policy and procurement between Britain and its West European partners, to develop a more effective British contribution to the collective defence capability of the European pillar of NATO', to which the amendment added the words 'provided that such a defence capability is non-nuclear'.

The committee chose this in preference to a more emollient amendment submitted by the three dissident MPs, which argued that any European cooperation on defence should be 'directed not to increasing nor sustaining, but to reducing and ending nuclear confrontation'. This wording was vague enough that it would probably have proved acceptable to Steel, and the disaster which was about to befall him, and the Alliance, the following day could have been avoided. Conference committees tend to prefer clarity in the wording of motions and amendments – hence their preference for what was eventually chosen – but they are also generally open to persuasion on political grounds, and it is certainly possible that if the MPs, or a representative of the leader, had been present, they could have persuaded the Assembly Committee to accept the dissident MPs' wording.

Steel then proceeded to up the stakes even further by predicting to a parliamentary candidates' meeting that evening that the amendment, which he described as unilateralist, would be defeated by a margin of three to one. That was the extent of the leadership's preparation for the debate; it was not discussed at length at the parliamentary party meeting the same evening, no effort was made to organise speakers, and no attempt was made to build support for the motion and opposition to the amendment. To Des Wilson, this was the leadership's cardinal error: 'the real reason was lack of contact with the party … By their failure to sense the mood of the party, their failure to be represented at the Assembly Committee meeting and try to influence the choice of amendments, their failure to organise a vote-collecting initiative the following day, their failure to consider the nature of the speeches that would need to be made, they had made themselves vulnerable to defeat.'[34]

Steel later accepted much of this; his defence, which really bears out Wilson's complaint, was that he did not anticipate what was about to happen to him.[35] He had a fair point when he criticised the party's procedures, which could see such a crucial amendment chosen and published just twenty-four hours before the debate.[36] But the main problem was that he had lost touch with his party conference. He really believed it when he said he thought the amendment would go down by a margin of three to one.[37]

Mistake 8

The debate took place the next day, Tuesday 23 September. It was an electric occasion.[38] The auditorium of the Congress Theatre was so full that more than a hundred delegates had to use an overflow venue. Most speakers on the leadership's side, including Paddy Ashdown and Richard Holme, spoke hesitantly and unconvincingly; Alan Beith was rather better. On the side of Amendment 1, Tony Greaves and Michael Meadowcroft were more effective, but the key speech was made by Simon Hughes, one of the authors of *Across the Divide,* the party's environment spokesman and the darling of the radical activists. As Des Wilson described it: 'It was an extraordinary speech, not particularly logical, not particularly fair – words following each other at speed, almost tripping over each other, points made in short jabs and thrusts – almost as if a highly intelligent speaker was tripping up over his own feelings, and all the more moving and impactful for it' –

> What should be the way forward? The aim should be, quotes, 'to develop with our European partners a non-nuclear contribution to European defence' … This amendment doesn't rule out the European option, with which we wholeheartedly sympathise … Where we disagree is in the belief that our contribution – that contribution – should be a nuclear one. Only one of our European partners, France, has nuclear capability. I hope we wouldn't wish to see other countries developing a membership of the nuclear arsenal – a Euro-nuclear bomb mountain, twelve fingers on the button … Many of us joined this party because of its aim and its goal: a non-nuclear Europe in a non-nuclear world. We have *never* voted to replace the independent nuclear deterrent. Not only must we not do so now, but our policy must be to do so *never* – and to replace an independent British nuclear deterrent by a European nuclear deterrent – even if that concept was workable – is *not* an acceptable alternative.[39]

The speech was repeatedly interrupted by the audience, receiving a roar of applause and a standing ovation at the end.

Amendment 1 was passed by 652 votes to 625. David Steel wrote in his autobiography that Hughes' speech 'was rubbish but it was glorious rubbish and the Assembly loved it'.[40] But it was not rubbish. Building on other speeches in the debate, Hughes precisely, if emotionally, articulated the two key weaknesses in the leadership's case. He attacked the whole flawed concept of the European nuclear deterrent, an idea not included in the Defence Commission's report, put forward by the two leaders without consultation within their parties and with no description of exactly what it entailed or whether anyone else in Europe wanted it. As Hugo Young commented in *The Guardian,* 'on the margin, it wasn't anti-Owen or pro-CND. People just didn't like to think they were being sold a pup to buy their votes.' The *Standard* expressed it similarly: 'It is not just the party that must take the blame for this. It is Mr Steel who, along with Dr Owen, lurched into a nuclear defence policy that made no sense to anyone.'[41]

Secondly, and just as powerfully, those who spoke against the leadership articulated the deep unhappiness within the Liberal Party at the way in which the Alliance was being run. It was not only those who opposed the Defence Commission's report, or the Euro-bomb, who had felt outraged by Owen's behaviour over the summer and the way he appeared to be bouncing Steel into decisions. The higher priority that Steel evidently gave to leading the Alliance over leading his own party – in sharp contrast to Owen – meant that it always seemed to be the Liberal position which was compromised. Asked after the debate what the message of Eastbourne had been, one of Steel's allies replied: 'That's easy. The message of Eastbourne was: "fuck Owen".'[42]

Was it a mistake for Steel not to have spoken in the debate? Owen thought so. 'As the tide of the debate turned against the platform, I willed David Steel to speak and put his leadership on the line. But he stayed firmly put, no doubt fearing another rejection like that of 1984.'[43] Steel himself considered it: 'At this point I wondered whether to seek to speak myself on the politics of the situation we faced. I thought that to do so might smack of panic and lack of confidence in my colleagues who had done well on the issue itself, but I also recalled the 1984 Assembly voting against my recommendation and decided that this might only exacerbate the difficulty we were now in.'[44]

The margin of Amendment 1's victory was narrow enough that a speech from Steel might have made a difference. Crewe and King pointed out that some delegates who supported the amendment only did so 'because they wanted to make some kind of anti-leadership, anti-Owen gesture'.[45] This is undoubtedly true, but it is also the case that many delegates who thought the Euro-bomb proposal lacked credibility were prepared to swallow their doubts and vote *against* the amendment because they could see the political dangers of defeating the leadership and, by extension, the Alliance. A speech from Steel might have boosted their numbers.

Or it might not. Reflecting the robust individualism of their members, Liberal assemblies never had much compunction about voting against their leader. Unlike the other parties, though (particularly Labour), votes like these were not in general an attack on the leadership as such, but simply an indication that the delegates thought it was wrong. The media, however, who were more familiar with other party conferences where votes against leaders almost always *were* attacks on them, usually misinterpreted this. So Steel was probably right not to speak. It may not have made any difference to the outcome of the vote, and it would have made the press coverage much worse.

Mistake 9

The leadership, however, then proceeded to make the press coverage much worse anyway.

Initially Steel's reaction was controlled. 'It is an irritant', he said of the vote to reporters afterwards, 'but not a set-back'.[46] He could have been a bit more robust. The assembly had, after all, in supporting the main motion actually voted for the Defence Commission's report, an outcome that had not been certain when the report had been published three months before. It was only the additional suggestion of a joint European deterrent – which had not been in the report – that had been rejected. Steel could have argued that the main planks of Alliance defence policy had been agreed by both SDP and Liberals, and that only a few details of the 'minimum nuclear deterrent' remained to be sorted out – and could now be, in the less charged atmosphere following the party conferences.

Admittedly, he had made things more difficult for himself by describing the amendment, before the debate, as 'unilateralist'. Although unilateralists of course supported it, many of those who were not unilateralists, and believed in the retention of nuclear weapons, also voted for the amendment because the Euro-bomb was such a patently unworkable concept. As Alan Watkins put it in *The Observer* at the end of the week, 'the Liberals had a perfectly serviceable defence policy. Nor was it unilateralist. It is not so today, even though the head of emotional steam behind the debate was clearly unilateralist. But the policy was misleadingly depicted as such, even by Mr Steel ....'[47]

However, the stakes had been raised, and most of the newspaper headlines the day after the debate picked up on them: 'Alliance pact is shattered' (*Today*); 'Nuked – Steel's defence deal wrecked by his Party' (*Daily Mail*); 'Steel defeat puts Alliance in disarray' (*The Times*).[48] It was possibly in response to this coverage that David Alton MP, the Liberal Chief Whip, then proceeded to make Steel's reaction to the issue much, much worse. Even today, twenty years later, it is almost impossible to work out what on earth he thought he was doing. In Des Wilson's well-known phrase, 'somewhere between one and two o'clock in the morning and seven or eight, David Alton went completely off the rails.'[49] He took every radio and television opportunity to attack the supporters of the amendment. He waved the damaging newspaper headlines around at a press conference. He claimed that anyone could have walked in off the street and voted in the debate, that the Young Liberals and

Liberal Students had packed the hall, and that hundreds of delegate badges had been lost in the post. None of this was true.[50] Wilson, who was present at the press conference, 'could hardly believe my eyes or ears'.[51]

What if the Alliance had not quarrelled over defence?

Between August and October, the Alliance fell eight points in the polls (the same amount it had lost after Owen's outburst in May), down to 22 per cent, where it stayed, more or less, until early 1987. Steel, belatedly realising that he had not taken enough trouble to carry his party with him, carried out an intensive round of consultation within the Liberal Party, arguing that the Alliance had to agree a joint position and that there was no alternative to accepting the continuation of some form of minimum deterrent. For the first time Owen was also willing to compromise, accepting that the exact form of the replacement for Polaris need not be specified at this stage. The idea of the Euro-bomb was quietly discarded. Thus the two parties finally agreed, in the 1987 election manifesto, to retain a commitment to maintaining Britain's nuclear deterrent, at a level no greater than that of Polaris, though it did not specify through what system. In effect, Owen had won.

What would have happened if the rift had never occurred? The possibility was considered by Crewe and King in their history of the SDP, but they dismissed any lasting impact of an alternative outcome on the basis that in fact the Alliance did perform more strongly in the opinion polls in early 1987. This was thanks mainly to the Greenwich by-election victory in February; in March the Alliance's poll rating touched 31.5 per cent, though it then steadily drifted downwards, hitting the mid to high twenties by the launch of the Alliance manifesto in mid-May. The shambolic Alliance election campaign then managed to drive it downwards to a final 22.5 per cent on polling day, 11 June.

Crewe and King's argument only makes sense, however, if one assumes that there was a ceiling to the Alliance vote above which it could not possibly climb – somewhere, say, about 30 per cent. By this thesis, the arguments over defence temporarily detached about a quarter of the Alliance support, but most of it came back again in the following six months, only to be lost once more before and during the election.

But why should we assume that there was such a ceiling? For most of 1985 the Alliance had scored over 30 per cent; in September it reached 39 per cent. Over the twelve months leading up to the start of the defence row, in June 1986, its average support was 32.7 per cent. After good local election and by-election results in May 1986, in the absence of the row the Alliance could have expected its support to have remained somewhere around 35 per cent for the rest of 1986. Add on the boost actually given by the Greenwich by-election in February 1987 (four points), and we end up almost on 40 per cent. Assuming that the general election campaign was still as much of a shambles as it was in reality, the Alliance could still reasonably have expected to poll 30–35 per cent on 11 June. In fact its final support was exactly the same as the opinion polls had indicated at the end of 1986, so if this had still been the case in our counterfactual reality, we could have seen an Alliance election result of 35 per cent.

And perhaps the campaign wouldn't have been so bad. In the real world the Alliance's decline in the opinion polls was a running theme in the press throughout the first two weeks of the campaign, reinforcing itself and demoralising Alliance activists. Had the decline been from the high to the low thirties rather than the high to the low twenties, the stories would have had a rather different tone, because at any point in that range, the result would quite possibly have been a hung parliament.

What kind of hung parliament would have depended on which of the other two parties the Alliance had not lost its voters to. The eight-point fall in Alliance support in June 1986 saw two points go to Labour and six to the Conservatives; the similar fall from August to October saw seven points heading back to the Tories. It is reasonable to assume, therefore, that the election result, instead of being Conservative 42.3 per cent, Labour 30.8 per cent, Alliance 22.5 per cent, could have been Conservative 33 per cent, Labour 28 per cent, Alliance 35 per cent. On a more pessimistic scenario, assuming a further five-point loss from the beginning of the year, the result could have been Conservative 37 per cent, Labour 29 per cent, Alliance 30 per cent.

Given the workings of the first-past-the-post electoral system, with the Alliance vote spread evenly across the country, it would still have won fewer seats per vote than the other two parties, and even in the more optimistic of the scenarios suggested here would still have remained as the third party in terms of seats. Assuming a uniform swing, we arrive at the following possible outcomes:[52]

	Cons	Labour	Alliance	Others
Actual 1987	376	229	22	23
Alliance 35 per cent	275	260	90	25
Alliance 30 per cent	340	243	43	24

In either scenario, with the Alliance coming first or second in terms of votes but third in terms of seats, one could have expected public support for electoral reform to grow. In the more optimistic scenario, the result is a hung parliament, with any combination of two parties able to form a government. What would have happened then? On the one hand, Mrs Thatcher would just have lost the election, quite badly; could the Alliance really have put her back in power? But on the other, Labour was led by the unilateralist Neil Kinnock, David Owen's nightmare. Would the Conservatives or Labour have tried to form a minority government, daring the other two parties to vote them out and risk another general election? Would the Alliance have tried to reach a short-term deal with Labour in order to introduce proportional representation? Would the Alliance have split, with David Owen preferring Thatcher and David Steel opting for Kinnock? These possibilities would require another chapter to explore.

How could they have avoided the quarrel?

The point of this chapter, however, is to examine how the Alliance could have avoided the disastrous split in the first place. It certainly had no shortage of opportunities to do so.

David Owen could have behaved rationally. In the end he got the result he wanted – an Alliance commitment to the replacement of Polaris – but only at enormous cost. He could have avoided flying off the handle in public in response to Steel's incautious remarks to *The Scotsman*. He could have accepted the commission's recommendations on Polaris; after all, what was the point of setting up a joint commission if he was not going to be prepared to listen to its conclusions? Or, assuming he decided to stick to his view on the necessity for a replacement for Polaris, he could have welcomed the report as a useful contribution, but argued that, on that issue, Alliance policy needed to be more specific. The compromise position which was eventually reached in the 1987 manifesto proved to be acceptable to the bulk of Alliance candidates, SDP and Liberal, and Owen would probably have won his case in the internal negotiations over the joint platform, whatever the Liberal assembly voted for.

Owen could have given some thought – any thought – to a strategy for achieving the result he wanted. Instead, as Crewe and King put it, 'It cannot be said that the SDP leader miscalculated – because he did not calculate. He merely lashed out blindly at the forces of his seen and unseen enemies.'[53] He could have treated the whole episode as what it should have been, an internal argument about a small, though important, detail of joint policy, rather than allowing himself to be governed by pride, paranoia and a desire to dominate.

David Steel could have led his party more carefully, taking more time to stay in touch with its grassroots and committees; if he had, he might have understood why the Euro-bomb concept was likely to cause such unhappiness, and prepared better for the debate around it. His approach of trying to lead the Alliance rather than the Liberal Party, with the premium he put on reaching agreed positions, would not have been an unreasonable one if his SDP counterpart had been of a similar persuasion, as Roy Jenkins had been. But when the SDP leader was David Owen, who cared far less about joint positions, and was always prepared to argue stridently for the SDP line, it was disastrous, as Steel was perpetually put into the position of compromising on Liberal policy. His party was well aware of this, and increasingly did not like it – but Steel himself was too out of touch to realise it.

It could be argued that these counterfactuals would have required both men, Owen and Steel, to have been different people, and are therefore inherently not credible. This is fair enough; but even assuming that the two leaders were the same people, with the same approaches to leadership, it is still possible to identify a series of points at which they could, and should, have behaved differently.

After Owen's outburst in May/June, the two leaders could not have come up with the flawed idea of the Euro-bomb, or at least not come up with it before the party conferences, or could have come up with a different idea. In fact there was no requirement for them to come up with any new idea at all. The Defence Commission report had been published and had been welcomed in the press; the fact that Owen didn't like it would probably have helped to get it through the Liberal Assembly. It could then have provided the basis of the defence section of the joint policy platform, and the details could have been sorted out in the joint negotiations. Owen would always have had the stronger hand in these talks, as the SDP was largely united behind his position over a replacement for Polaris, and Steel and at least some of the Liberals would have gone along with them.

Even accepting that the Euro-bomb concept had been floated, and that the Eastbourne debate was ready to take place, Steel could have made some attempt to manage the debate. He could have persuaded the Assembly Committee to have accepted the dissident MPs' amendment, which was vaguely enough worded to have been acceptable to both sides. He could have spoken in the debate; all he needed to have done was tip fourteen delegates, out of almost 1,500, into voting against the amendment that was eventually chosen. Even had it been passed, he could have stuck to his initial reaction that it was not a serious problem, stressing instead that the Assembly had endorsed the Defence Commission report and that therefore the Alliance had the basis of an agreed defence policy – minus the Euro-bomb, but that had not featured in the report anyway. He could have locked David Alton in his hotel room.

Is this 'what if' plausible? It is always worthwhile turning counterfactuals on their head, to see if the counter-counterfactual makes any sense. Suppose the disagreements over Alliance defence policy had been dealt with in a rational, low-key and private way; the 1987 manifesto would have contained exactly the same wording as it eventually did, but it would have been arrived at without any of the disastrous public splits that took place in the spring and autumn of 1986. The Alliance would have ended up, quite possibly, holding the balance of power after the 1987 election.

At that stage, would anyone have looked back and thought: what would have happened if the Alliance had quarrelled badly and publicly enough to have lost a quarter of its support over the details of a weapon system that didn't need to be planned for another five or ten years, or over a proposal for cooperation over nuclear weapons with a French government that had no interest in it? Now that really would have been unbelievable.

Notes

1   Gallup poll figures; see David and Gareth Butler, *Twentieth-Century British Political Facts* (Macmillan, 8th edition, 2000), p. 276.

2   The author was part of the Liberal team negotiating an Alliance document on health policy; it took almost a year to agree a four-page document; see Duncan Brack and Ewan Cameron, 'Alliance decision-making', *Radical Quarterly* special issue, 'Where next?', autumn 1987.

3   David Butler and Denis Kavanagh, *The British General Election of 1983* (Macmillan, 1984), p. 79.

4   David Owen, *Time to Declare* (Michael Joseph, 1991), p. 528.

5   William Wallace, personal communication.

6   Owen, *Time to Declare*, p. 617.

7   Des Wilson, *Battle for Power: the inside story of the Alliance and the 1987 general election* (Sphere, 1987), p. 25.

8   Ivor Crewe and Anthony King, *SDP: The Birth, Life and Death of the Social Democratic Party* (OUP, 1995), p. 343.

9   Owen, *Time to Declare*, p. 642.

10 Ibid.

11 Bill Rodgers, *Fourth Among Equals* (Politico's, 2000), p. 250.

12 Owen, *Time to Declare*, p. 643.

13 David Steel, *Against Goliath: David Steel's Story* (Weidenfeld & Nicolson,1989), p. 264.

14 Ibid.

15 Crewe and King, *SDP*, p. 345.

16 Steel, *Against Goliath*, pp. 264–65.

17 Rodgers, *Fourth Among Equals*, p. 251.

18 Ibid., p. 647.

19 Ibid., p. 648.

20 Crewe and King, *SDP*, pp. 345–46.

21 Rodgers, *Fourth Among Equals*, p. 251.

22 Owen, *Time to Declare*, p. 650; Rodgers, *Fourth Among Equals*, p. 251.

23 Crewe and King, *SDP*, p. 347.

24 Rodgers, *Fourth Among Equals*, p. 250.

25 Crewe and King, *SDP*, p. 347.

26 Rodgers, *Fourth Among Equals*, p. 253.

27 Wilson, *Battle for Power*, p. 31.

28 Ibid.

29 Michael Meadowcroft, 'The Alliance: Parties and Leaders', *Journal of Liberal Democrat History* 18 (spring 1998), p. 22.

30 Owen, *Time to Declare*, p. 654.

31 Crewe and King, *SDP*, p. 350; Wilson, *Battle for Power*, p. 33.

32 A charge which he later accepted; see Steel, *Against Goliath*, p. 269.

33 Simon Hughes MP, Archy Kirkwood MP, Michael Meadowcroft MP, LINk, NLYL, ULS, *Across the Divide: Liberal Values for Defence and Disarmament* (Liberal Party Publications, September 1986), p. 1.

34 Wilson, *Battle for Power*, p. 41.

35 David Steel, personal communication.

36 Ibid.; Steel, *Against Goliath*, p. 270.

37 Even Archy Kirkwood, who was planning to vote for the amendment, believed him. A member of Kirkwood's staff at the time, I remember talking to him about it late that Monday night; he was surprised when I said I thought the result would be much closer than that.

38 See Wilson, *Battle for Power*, pp. 46–54, for a full summary.

39 Duncan Brack and Tony Little (eds.), *Great Liberal Speeches* (Politico's, 2003), pp. 417–20.

40 Steel, *Against Goliath*, p. 271.

41 Michael Meadowcroft, 'Eastbourne revisited', *Radical Quarterly* 5 (autumn 1987), p. 28.

42 Crewe and King, *SDP*, p. 351.

43 Owen, *Time to Declare*, p. 665.

44 Steel, *Against Goliath*, p. 271.

45 Crewe and King, *SDP*, p. 351.

46 Ibid., p. 352.

47 Meadowcroft, 'Eastbourne revisited', p. 29.

48 Steel, *Against Goliath*, p. 272.

49 Wilson, *Battle for Power*, p. 57.

50 But it was believed for a long time afterwards. In 2006, as chair of the Lib Dem Conference Committee, I had to advise one of the party's press officers fielding an enquiry about the make-up of the Lib Dem conference; they had been asked when the party had changed from the Liberal system of 'allowing anyone to vote'. In fact the Liberal Assembly had the same sort of representative nature as the Lib Dem conference does now, though with a more generous delegate entitlement per constituency.

51 Wilson, *Battle for Power*, p. 57.

52 Estimates kindly provided by Robert Waller, based on calculations in Robert Waller and Byron Criddle, *The Almanac of British Politics* (Routledge, 4th edition, 1991), pp. 18–23.

53 Crewe and King, *SDP*, p. 355.

Chapter 16

What if John Major had become Chief Whip in 1987?

R. J. Briand

The commissioning editor looked wryly at his guest, the latest young-fogey pundit to try counterfactual history, in this case the new Politico's collection, *Prime Minister Blair ... and Other Things That Never Happened.* 'Quite extraordinary – Major becomes Chief Secretary instead of becoming Chief Whip and within three years becomes Prime Minister! Then he wins an election in the middle of a recession, for which the electorate doesn't blame him despite taking Britain into the ERM! And he brings that notorious rogue Jonathan Aitken into the Cabinet. Are you really asking people to believe that one of the best Chief Whips of his generation would have got into so much trouble over Europe, with a gratuitous vote on something so piffling as membership of the Committee of the Regions leading to an entirely preventable committee stage and a vote on Maastricht which the government loses and has to reverse through a confidence vote? David Mellor having an affair with an actress? A Labour government which wins two consecutive land-slides, each of which is larger than the one in 1945? Michael Portillo becoming a national treasure? John Prescott, of all people, playing croquet? Brilliant – it's so counter-intuitive it's a must-read!'

~

It certainly provided much amusement for Lord Major of Worcester Park when he bought *Prime Minister Blair* from an airport bookstall on his way to see Chelsea play AC Milan in the 2005 Champions' League Final. The hapless role of Tim Renton as Chief Whip in Mrs Thatcher's fictional downfall was, he thought, like something from one of Renton's own underrated thrillers. It also contrasted with what most commentators agreed was Major's own accomplished handling of the office, which he was awarded after Mrs Thatcher's third consecutive election victory. Thatcher's survival in the leadership election of 1990 would not have been possible without him.

Major shifted further back in his seat as he remembered the dramatic events of fifteen years ago. First, Nigel Lawson had been sacked after the Prime Minister had discovered from a *Financial Times* journalist that the Chancellor had been shadowing the Deutschmark without her knowledge. An isolated Geoffrey Howe then resigned as Leader of the Commons. This was the post to which he had been demoted to make way for Mrs Thatcher's latest favourite, Michael Howard, as Foreign Secretary. The titular essay in *Prime Minister Blair* ... speculated as to what might have happened had Party Chairman Kenneth Baker been allowed to spin that there was really very little disagreement between the departing Howe and the Prime Minister. In reality, Baker had been overruled. Had, in the words of the counterfactual historian, 'some maladroit spin provoked the dead sheep to roar', Michael Heseltine's leadership challenge might not have fallen at the first ballot.

This was, though, the former Chief Whip recalled, the last time that Mrs Thatcher really listened to him. Towards the end of her reign she had stopped listening to anyone except unelected advisers such as Sir Charles Powell. Major could not persuade Thatcher to ditch the hated poll tax. Indeed, his attempt to do so had provoked a row as fierce as the one he had with her over the economy as a junior whip five years previously. Suggestions by Lords Carrington and Whitelaw that she might quietly resign during the national euphoria which followed England's 2–0 victory against Argentina in the 1990 World Cup Final met with similarly short shrift.

The Prime Minister enjoyed a brief fillip in her popularity ratings after Saddam Hussein's fall from power, which had resulted from the UK and US providing air cover for the Kurd and Shia rebellions which followed the end of the Gulf War. Any repeat, though, of the Falklands factor was short lived. When she used the words 'Rejoice, rejoice', it was taken, like her use of the royal 'we', as further proof of her descent into self-parodying megalomania.

The part of the essay Lord Major liked most, though, was the part where as, Prime Minister, he decided not to call a khaki election after the Gulf War. Where, after all, Mrs Thatcher's increasing inability to listen had proved ultimately fatal to her political survival was her decision to call a general election in June 1991. She had ignored warnings from Central Office that, although better than expected, the Conservative recovery in the May local elections was shallow. Major remembered how, in the BBC studios, watching the Labour candidate's triumphant smile at the Basildon declaration had reminded him sharply of all those doorstep conversations in marginal seats. If there had been a 'That Bloody Woman' factor in 1987, it was even more pronounced in 1991. Thatcher was blamed personally, not just for the poll tax, but also for the recession of the early 1990s triggered by Chancellor John MacGregor's interest rate rises, needed to reduce the inflation which had resulted from his predecessor's living in sin with the ERM. After the Basildon result, there came Defence Secretary Alan Clark's defeat in Plymouth Sutton; Mrs Thatcher's majority in her own seat was halved. By dawn, Labour was on course to become the single largest party in a hung parliament.

~

Just as Lord Major's plane was landing in Turkey, Lord Kinnock opened the door of his Ealing house to his latest official biographer. 'Hiya, how's it going? Have you read that essay "What if John Major had become Chief Secretary in 1987?" by that Cambridge historian? Has him beating me in a 1992 election! Bloody hell, wish that had happened! I like what happened to Twigg, beating Portillo unexpectedly in 1997 then losing just as unexpectedly in 2005 through sending his canvassers to other constituencies. Talk about a vivid imagination. Then again, I suppose what happened to my government reads like one of your airport novels!'

Indeed, this was later made clear by Lord Kinnock's interviewer, Harris Roberts, in an extended essay in the October 2005 issue of *Prospect*, promoting his forthcoming book, *Bet it Wouldn't Happen to Maggie! The Life and Times of Lord Kinnock of Bedwellty*:

Extract from interview with Lord Kinnock:

Apart from access to his papers, Lord Kinnock was unusually frank in the interviews I conducted with him over the course of the last few months. He confirms, for example, one of the worst-kept secrets in Westminster at the time, that forming a coalition with the Liberal Democrats gave him an excuse not to make Gerald Kaufman Foreign Secretary. As he says, 'putting one of the most undiplomatic politicians in Westminster in charge of the diplomatic service wouldn't have got the first Labour government in twelve years off to a good start'. What, though, I asked, about one of the party's elder statesmen? 'Denis might have been good, but he was too old, and he'd suffered enough shadowing the post until '87. Besides, we could hardly have a peer in the job. Might have done for Maggie, but not the People's Party.'

If the appointment of two Liberal Democrats to the Cabinet was contentious, other business was more predictable. A Speaker's Conference was established to examine electoral reform. Rather in the spirit of barristers who never ask a witness a question without already knowing the answer, Kinnock had a good idea of what would flow from that. 'We knew the maximum our MPs would accept by way of reform would be Alternative Vote. The PLP had voted for that during the second MacDonald government, although it wasn't introduced because of the economic crisis of 1931.'

As Lord Kinnock makes clear, though, the presence of the Liberal Democrats in government helped reopen the Labour Party's divisions on Europe. The presence of a pro-European party would strengthen greatly Labour's own pro-Europeans, particularly John Smith, in his fateful decision to enter the ERM. Kinnock offers a heartfelt defence against criticisms that the government went in at too high a rate 'Hindsight's a wonderful thing. The only pundit saying so at the time was Bill Keegan at the *Observer*. Everyone knows, though, that the City distrusts Labour governments, even despite the best efforts of Smithy and Mo eating all those prawn cocktails in boardrooms across the City, trying to reassure them that a Labour government wouldn't mean the arrival of the Four Horsemen of the Apocalypse. They weren't going to let us away with less than three Deutschmarks to the pound, were they?'

Not that ERM membership was the only bone of contention between Kinnock and his Chancellor. 'If only I'd persuaded Smithy not to bring in the tax rises all in one go, though. They knackered consumer confidence.' At this point, the government sought a managed realignment of the pound's value within the ERM. As Kinnock ruefully concedes, 'Nothing managed about it – the pound ended up going arse over tit. Black Thursday, don't remind me. There we were, ERM membership over, and going cap in hand to the IMF again to make up the reserves. Smithy was exhausted, and warned by his doctor that if he carried on at the Treasury, it would kill him, so I moved him to the Woolsack. Derry wasn't very happy, but perked up when I promised to make him European Commissioner. He's always been easily satisfied with the best of everything, so I thought he'd like dining in all those Brussels restaurants.' It was left to the new Chancellor, Gordon Brown, to reassure the Liberal Democrats that the government would try to rejoin the ERM as soon as possible.

But, as Lord Kinnock concedes, he felt as if he was heading two coalition governments, not one. 'The party itself felt like a coalition! Maybe if the Tories had been foolish enough to get re-elected, their sceptics might have torn them to pieces. OK, so they might not have had as large a proportion of their parliamentary party rebelling against Maastricht, but I'd sooner have had the likes of Iain Duncan Smith and Teresa Gorman harassing their own side than us. Not that we needed harassing from the other side. We'd bought off Hain with a junior job at the Foreign Office, where he soon showed all the zeal of a convert, but we'd still got Denzil Davies and Alan Simpson bloody kebabbing us.'

A Labour leader used to winning plaudits for dragging his party kicking and screaming into line with public opinion after years of Labour being out of step with public opinion on issues such as unilateral nuclear disarmament now found himself confronted by a melancholy irony. 'The words "Keynesian critique" aren't ones you'd hear down your local. But when Davies, Simpson and Benn were saying, why go back into the ERM when it lumbered the country with high interest rates just when we needed lower ones, it resonated with the electorate's experience. Week after week, our MPs were being got at in their constituency surgeries – the ultimate focus group – by people whose businesses were threatened with bankruptcy and homeowners whose houses were worth less than the mortgages they were paying. What's it called, negative equity?'

An already restive Middle England was alienated still further by the red meat thrown to the government's backbench critics. 'The left needed some compensation for deflation and ignoring the conference resolutions on lowering defence spending to the European average, so we outlawed foxhunting, abolished the remaining grammar schools, and ended tax relief on private education. Roy [Hattersley] loved the last two. But it all went down like a cup of cold sick with Middle England.'

So far, Lord Kinnock's portrait of difficult relationships not just with his coalition partners but also with senior colleagues and backbenchers within his own party, reminds us of Lloyd George's melancholy adage, 'There are no friends at the top'. One unexpected consolation of British political life, though, lies in cross-party friendships. In our interviews, the former Prime Minister disclosed two such associations which ranged from the sublime to the ridiculous, the grey to the colourful. On the one hand, by his own admission, Kinnock could not help but laugh – along with the rest of the nation – at the revelation of Shadow Home Secretary John Major's affair with Edwina Currie. As he recalls, Major was savaging Roy Hattersley's early release scheme, 'only for Skinner to bring the House down by asking in a stage whisper "Do you think he's wearing the big blue pants today?"' On the other, Kinnock had 'always sympathised with the way Major was patronised by the grander members of his party. The way they made fun of the way he pronounced want as "wunt" reminded me of the way I was patronised for my pass degree from Cardiff. So I made him our other European Commissioner.'

Not, he concedes, that this was an act of pure altruism. There was the happy bonus of absolutely infuriating the Leader of the Opposition. Despite both men originating from South Wales, relations between Kinnock and his more Anglicised counterpart were probably the worst seen between a Prime Minister and an Opposition leader since Wilson and Heath. The low regard in which Lord Kinnock still holds his former adversary was one of the less surprising features of my interviews with him. It is, however, unusual for a British politician to accuse another of plotting to kill members of his own party. 'He wanted to send Widdecombe, get her out of his hair, and get his protégé Cameron in the Commons as a bonus. But I wanted my own back for the way he suspended the normal channels after the row over pairing. Everyone knows he whipped it up to wear out the three of our MPs in marginal seats who were seriously ill. As soon as they died, and he'd got the by-elections he wanted, he found an excuse to call it off. They used slightly more subtle tactics to wear out our more infirm colleagues after that, like pretending to have gone home for the night, then suddenly all appearing from nowhere.'

The subject of by-elections leads neatly to Kinnock's other unlikely cross-party friendship. If the loss of previously safe Labour and Liberal Democrat seats damaged the already low morale on the government's backbenches, the Conservative retention of Huntingdon brought into the House one of those politicians dedicated to the cause of cheering us all up. He would provide a besieged and preoccupied Kinnock with some comic banter. 'Quite a wag, Boris. We found ourselves next to each other in the gents once, and he said what a pleasure it was to meet on a common platform for a common purpose! I said he had to choose between journalism and front-bench politics. He replied that he preferred the advice of a great political philosopher, who had once said "If you can't ride both horses at once, get out of the bloody circus". I asked, "Who did you get that from? Socrates? Herodotus?" He said, no, Jimmy Maxton!'

In at least two instances, the Suez crisis and the poll tax, governments have been damaged irreparably by events unforeseen at the time of their election. Did Lord Kinnock see the fuel crisis coming? He confirms that, while the fuel escalator imposed as part of the IMF repayments added to the government's reputation for high taxes, he had no idea that it would lead to events which have surpassed the Winter of Discontent in their notoriety. As he says, 'The only thing is, we didn't reckon with world oil prices'. They had already risen after the uprisings in Saudi Arabia provoked by the Dole administration's role in overthrowing Saddam Hussein. But they would rise still further after rumours of Iranian involvement in the attack on the Sears Tower in Chicago by an affiliate of Islamic Jihad, and accompanying fears of a US invasion of Iran. Petrol was soon one pound fifty a litre, and by October there was a full-scale blockade of petrol stations by hauliers and farmers.

I asked Lord Kinnock when he realised that his chances of re-election had ended. 'When people died because vital medical supplies failed to reach hospitals, and when the chickens started eating each other after the power was turned off at the battery farms. All we could do was hold on, and try to get the Tory lead down so that we didn't end up having another 1983. I thought at one stage we were looking at another 1931. Do you remember Peter Snow's "little bit of fun" on the by-election special after the SNP won Monklands East? I think it showed me as the sole remaining Labour MP. I thought, might as well look on the bright side, at least there won't be a post-election leadership challenge!'

Although the Labour–Liberal Democrat coalition did not suffer a defeat as heavy as 1983 or 1931, it would not have much time to recover. That the government should have hit the rocks over Europe still bitterly amuses Lord Kinnock. 'Ever noticed how the Europhile chatterati leave no cliché unturned ahead of European summits? It's always transport metaphors as well. "We must catch the boat, mustn't miss the train." It's like Michael Foot at conference in the seventies – quoted Conrad about the bloke on the ship who went into a storm "always facing it". Only problem was, like I said at the *Tribune* rally afterwards, the bloody ship sank!'

If such gallows humour is not surprising, just how the government got itself into such a mess is. I can reveal that Doris Kearns Goodwin is partly to blame, when a member of the Labour Whips' Office took her biography of Lyndon Johnson away with him on his summer holiday. The relevant whip – Kinnock will not reveal his identity – got carried away by the biographer's account of how Johnson got southern senators to vote for the Hell's Canyon dam while northern senators then voted for jury trials in the civil rights bill. It was this which, apparently, inspired the 'double lock' in clause seven of the European Communities (Amendment) Bill. It stipulated that Labour MPs could not vote for the Social Chapter without also voting for the single currency.

Labour's Eurosceptic rebels, however, had spent their summer holidays refining their arguments rather than reading political biography. By now, they hated the single currency so much that they were ready to vote against the Social Chapter. After all, they said, what use is protection in the workplace if you haven't got a job in the first place thanks to ERM membership and the tight controls on public spending dictated by the convergence criteria? They also noted that the UK could establish policies such as four weeks' paid holiday through its own domestic legislation.

Another surprise in our interviews was the caustic tone Lord Kinnock adopted toward his one-time ally, once tipped as his successor, Tony Blair. He still feels sympathy for Blair's unhappy task as Employment Secretary in having to present rising unemployment figures to the House every month. He also had to introduce one of the most unpopular parts of the IMF payback package, the Jobseeker's Allowance. This allowed the government to pay just six months of income-related unemployment benefit to those who had paid twelve months' national insurance. All the same, Kinnock feels that Blair could have handled the presentation better. 'He'd have upset the PLP less if he'd done the whole routine of "this really pains me, but it has to be done", but he put people's backs up by talking with almost masochistic glee about "tough choices" and "not having a reverse gear". Really, the best service Tony performed for the party was making a seat available for Yvette Cooper at the '96 election after he left Parliament to become Chairman of the Press Complaints Commission.'

Even with a more emollient Employment Secretary, though, Kinnock conceded that the burgeoning Eurosceptic rebellion in the PLP would have resulted in what he calls 'the grotesque chaos of Labour MPs – Labour MPs! – voting against a manifesto commitment to increase protection for workers'. 'After we lost the vote, we had talks with the Liberals, and decided the only thing to do was bring it back as a motion of confidence. Of course, the papers noted that I was so desperate that I threatened my own MPs with the consequences of my government's unpopularity. I liked that cartoon which had me in the Chamber with a grenade in my hand, telling them to do what I said otherwise I'd pull the pin!'

As with the fuel crisis, the manner of the government's fall was unforeseen. Although the government had lost so many by-elections that it was now a minority coalition government, ministers did not see any real threat of being defeated on a motion of confidence. After all, the Ulster Unionists had been kept onside. Again, Kinnock admitted that the coalition had given him the excuse not to appoint a colleague to a portfolio in which he didn't want them. 'McNamara annoyed the Unionists in opposition. Hardly surprising when he was so nationalist that he warned the Irish government against getting rid of articles two and three. So I shifted him to Energy. Besides, Ashdown looked the part. The Nationalists liked him because his nickname was Paddy, and the Prods liked him because he'd been in the SBS.'

This leads to the most explosive revelation of my interviews. I asked Lord Kinnock if he agreed with Tony Benn's suggestion, widely ridiculed at the time, that 'spooks' had conspired to bring down another Labour government. He paused a long time, then said: 'Tony was right. Only MI5 – or "rogue elements" within it – were in a position to pass telephone intercepts of the conversations between Ashdown and Adams to the *Daily Mail*. It's like with Wilson – just because he was paranoid, and coming out with funny stuff such as calling himself the Big Fat Spider in the Corner of the Room, it didn't mean they weren't out to get him! Peter Wright said as much. The Whips' Office had bought in extra whisky supplies, thinking that it would be like March 1979 all over again. After the *Mail*'s revelations, no chance. Voting for us, or even abstaining, would have been like signing their own political death warrants.'

The rueful humour which had characterised many of our interviews broke through again as I asked the former Prime Minister how it felt to be called the last Labour Prime Minister. 'A nice doubled-edged title, that, when what they really mean is probably the last ever Labour Prime Minister. In fact, I feel a lot of sympathy for Jimmy Carter – America now has its first woman president, Bob Dole is the first ex-president to be First Gentleman, and McCain was the first Vietnam veteran to become president, but Carter's still the last Democrat president. I suppose Clinton might have won in '92 had Atwater's brain tumour not turned out to be benign.'

Had Lord Kinnock expected the result of the last general election he fought as Prime Minister? 'To tell you the truth, I was pleasantly surprised the Tories won by only 100.' What about the rumours that he had cheered the news that Alan Simpson had lost Nottingham South? 'You might say that; I couldn't possibly comment', Kinnock chuckled. Some might wonder why Kinnock resigned within seventy-two hours of the result, given that his most heavyweight rival had moved to the Lords. 'I'd been Leader of the Opposition for eight years before, so it would have been like a dog returning to its own vomit.' The outgoing Chancellor became the front-runner, while Jack Straw emerged as the Eurosceptic candidate. A newly Eurosceptical trade-union leadership was impressed by conveniently leaked Cabinet papers which showed Straw opposing ERM membership while Education Secretary. The election was as good as over, particularly when Straw's abolition of all the remaining grammar schools in the same office, and his long-standing hostility to the Liberal Democrats, played well with the CLPs and the PLP. His defeated rival slunk away to become Chairman of Raith Rovers FC.

Apart from the difficulties his government ran into, and the unpopularity it incurred, what else did Lord Kinnock think explained Labour's four consecutive election defeats? 'Apart from the usual infighting that occurs in our party after losing office, the Tories had one big thing going for them, independence for the Bank of England. It had the enormous advantage of taking interest rate decisions away from politicians. And by giving it to the Monetary Policy Committee of the Bank of England, it wasn't going to a European Central Bank which had to set interest rates for twelve countries at once. After the ERM nightmare, it was a tonic. So the Tories could go back to their old slogan, "Britain's working, don't let Labour ruin it".'

All the same, economic prosperity does not entirely insulate a government against what Macmillan referred to as 'Events, dear boy, events'. The wear and tear which afflicts any party in office for a long period, including a number of sleaze scandals, helped Labour's first-ever woman leader slash the Tory majority to fifty at the last general election.

As we sat down to watch the Champions' League final at the end of our first interview, conversation turned to a bitter adversary and a political friend. 'Well, I suppose it's just as well for Howard that he didn't have to endure watching Chelsea in the final. Thirteen years as Prime Minister would age anybody, and he'd already had quadruple heart bypass surgery, but I bet what really did for him was that *Spectator* editorial attacking Scousers for their "mawkish victim mentality" after the death threats to the referee for Liverpool's disallowed goal in the semi-final. Quite convenient for its editor, though – had Howard survived, Boris probably wouldn't still be there as Heritage Secretary! The rueful sheepdog act just wouldn't have cut any ice. Did you see the *Daily Star*'s interview with Howard's grandson? He was with him when he collapsed with a copy of the offending editorial in his hand. I thought their headline, "Bozza killed my Grandad", was a classic, almost as good as "Freddie Starr ate my hamster". Mind you, Cooper's just made Tony Banks resign as Shadow Sports Minister for telling one of his sick jokes, namely how could Howard die when he was already one of the undead? He only resigned because he got caught – you should have heard the jokes Dobbo made! I doubt Ann Winterton would still be in public life if she'd asked *him* for a joke to tell at a rugby club dinner!'

Chapter 17

What if Yitzhak Rabin had not been assassinated in 1995?

Simon Buckby & Jon Mendelsohn

It happened at the end of a peace rally in Tel Aviv on the evening of 4 November 1995. Yitzhak Rabin, the Prime Minister of Israel, was walking back to his car, chatting to Shimon Peres, his Foreign Minister, when a gunshot echoed through the warm air.

At his trial, Yigal Amir explained that 'a Palestinian state is starting to be established' and that he was motivated to murder because 'Rabin wants to give our country to the Arabs'. Like other Israeli right-wing religious fanatics, he was opposed to any move to peace that involved the creation of a Palestinian state, which at that moment seemed possible, and in shooting the leader of this process his intention was to derail it.

More than a decade later, the repercussions of the shooting on the prospects for a lasting settlement in one of the world's most inflammable arenas are still being felt. There is no peace in the Middle East. The question is: would it have been any different had this moment not occurred?

~

During the Israeli War of Independence in 1948–49 Yitzhak Rabin commanded the Harel Brigade on the Jerusalem front, and by the Six Day War of 1967 he had risen to be Chief of Staff of the Israeli Defence Force. He was rewarded with the post of Israeli Ambassador to Washington before returning to Israel, where he became Prime Minister from 1974–77. During the National Unity governments of 1984–90 he served as Minister of Defence, responsible for leading Israel's campaign against the Palestinian intifada, which he did with all the severity of a military leader. By the early 1990s, these experiences led him to project an image as Israel's ultimate authority on matters of national security.

After several failed challenges, in February 1992 Rabin finally defeated Shimon Peres in the primaries to again become Labour leader. Peres was seen by Israeli floating voters as too dovish to be permitted to make Labour's proposed concessions to the Palestinians. The tougher figure of Rabin was expected to stand a better chance of winning the coming general election against the Likud government, which was believed too hawkish to reach a settlement with the Palestinians. As only Nixon could go to China, perhaps only Rabin could be trusted with Israel's security sufficiently to be allowed to negotiate a compromise at a time of an internationally audited peace process.

In June 1992 Rabin was elected Israel's Prime Minister for the second time. His victory inspired the most genuine prospect for peace in the history of the Middle East conflict. His death came at what appeared to be a critical moment of breakthrough. Minutes before his violent murder, he had told the peace rally: 'I was a military man for twenty-seven years. I fought while I believed that there was no chance for peace. Today, I believe that there is a chance for peace. A great chance.'

Conventional wisdom suggests that the assassination did indeed succeed in its objective, because Rabin's hopes were dashed. Within six months a hard-line Likud government hostile to compromise had been elected and peace talks had stalled. Although three years later Labour returned to power and offered another chance for a deal, by then the momentum had broken and the peace process collapsed. If Rabin had lived, maybe it would all have been so different.

~

Emboldened by victories in the Cold War and the Gulf War, the United States summoned a conference in Madrid in 1991 at which the framework of the Middle East peace process was set out. Yitzhak Shamir, the Prime Minister of Israel, was pressured into agreeing to four tracks of bilateral negotiations: with the Palestinians, the Syrians, the Lebanese and the Jordanians. Almost immediately, however, Shamir was accused of foot-dragging. It appeared that, despite the fertile context, sterility in the Israeli administration would leave the peace process nipped in the bud. Any flowering would clearly require a change of government in Israel.

The 1992 election was close. In fact, the right won slightly more votes, though the left won a few more seats in the Knesset. Despite the fragile foundation of a tiny majority, the new Labour Prime Minister instantly announced an end to the building of new Israeli settlements in the Gaza Strip and the West Bank, and declared that he would deliver an agreement on Palestinian self-rule within months. Although he had not initiated or even attended Madrid, overnight the future of the Middle East seemed to depend on Yitzhak Rabin.

There were enormous barriers. Progress on the Palestinian track was hampered by the fact that the Palestinians were represented by local officials from the Gaza Strip and the West Bank, while the PLO in Tunis was not permitted any direct role. Meanwhile, local Islamic opponents of Israel, notably Hamas and Islamic Jihad, launched a string of terrorist atrocities. The Syrian track was blocked by Syria's demand for total control over the Golan Heights, back to the pre-1967 borders. (The Lebanese and Jordanian tracks were seen as less urgent priorities.) To make matters worse, the United States assumed a lower profile as arbiter as George Bush and Bill Clinton became locked in an election battle. Nonetheless, Rabin believed that the availability of the Madrid framework offered a unique opportunity, and that it was Israel's duty to try to take advantage of it. Hence, his approach was incremental. He was willing to take a few steps to see how others responded.

After the election of Clinton, with whom Rabin forged a close personal bond, Israel was prepared to force the pace on the Palestinian track during 1993. In January Rabin opened secret talks with

Palestinian representatives in Oslo, and in May, crucially, he agreed to negotiate there directly with the PLO. Very soon an agreement was reached on establishing Palestinian self-rule in the Gaza Strip and the West Bank for a transitional period of five years, as a likely precursor to full Palestinian statehood. This deal was famously signed over a momentous handshake on the White House lawn in September; the ground had been laid for a historic compromise between Israeli and Palestinian nationalism.

However, signing an agreement was only a part of solving the problem. Now both Rabin and Arafat needed to generate support for their deal within their own constituencies. The criticism levelled at Rabin by his Israeli opponents, and at Arafat by his Arab ones, formed a perfect symmetry. Rabin was accused of compromising with a leader that he himself had demonised, endowing the PLO with legitimacy, giving away parts of the Jews' historic homeland, and undermining the security of Israel and Israelis. Arafat was charged with having sold out by offering Israel recognition in return for meagre self-rule under Israeli tutelage, abandoning the Palestinian diaspora, and relegating Palestine's crucial final status to an ill-defined future moment. How each handled the critics on their own side would determine the fate of their agreement.

Israeli opponents struck first. There was a rash of violent outbreaks, the worst being the massacre of Palestinian worshippers at the Tomb of the Patriarchs in Hebron early in 1994. But Rabin did not flinch, never mind seek to pacify his critics. He continued to offer the Arabs the initial gains. By the summer there was a fully functioning Palestinian administration in Gaza and a putative one in Jericho in the West Bank, sufficient encouragement for Arafat and the PLO to move from Tunis to Gaza. In the autumn an Israel–Jordan Peace Treaty was signed. And a year later, in October 1995, a second Rabin–Arafat Accord, Oslo II, extended Palestinian self-rule to parts of the West Bank beyond Jericho.

Hamas reacted to these developments with greater violence. Not all the attacks originated in areas under the Palestinian Authority's control, but the prevailing perception in Israel was that they did and that Arafat was insufficiently committed to stopping Islamic terrorism. So while Rabin sought to guarantee the Israeli public that reconciliation with the Palestinians would have no adverse effect on their security, he was undermined on two fronts: by Hamas, which seemed intent on displaying its power to terrorise and tear down the peace process, and by Arafat, who failed to take action to limit that threat.

Rabin was trapped in a dilemma. Without the intervention of Arafat, he had no answer to the bombings unless he overrode the Palestinian Authority, action that itself would blow a hole in the entire Madrid–Oslo initiative. Yet the death toll was huge. As a result, many Israelis began to equate the Oslo Accords with a loss of security. A small, fanatical faction of Israeli fundamentalists began operating with the belief that the only way to stop the threat to their country was to remove Rabin. They did so on 4 November 1995.

If an Israeli extremist had not murdered Yitzhak Rabin, is it likely, or even possible, that he would have been able to work his way out of this dilemma, save the peace process, and reach a final-status settlement with the Palestinians? Would he have fared any better than his successors?

~

The world held its breath. In the Assuta Hospital in Tel Aviv, the felled Prime Minister lay in intensive care, receiving the best possible emergency treatment, but it was not at all clear whether the bullet he had taken in his shoulder would be terminal. Shimon Peres, the Foreign Minister, assumed the reins of power. Commentators everywhere speculated on the prospects for peace in the Middle East, which were again universally agreed to be united with the prospects for Labour at the Israeli general election, scheduled for May 1996. If the leader recovered there would undoubtedly be a huge vote of sympathy; but if he did not and the worst came to the worst, how would Peres, the inevitable successor, with a reputation as a peacenik, be able to persuade frightened floating voters not to look elsewhere for their security?

Binyamin Netanyahu, the Likud leader, wasted no time in taking to the stump. Just two nights after the shooting, he delivered an uncompromising speech at a hastily assembled rival peace rally in which he declared that any government he led would refuse further talks until there was an end to Palestinian violence, promising a new magic formula of 'peace with security'. Even so, Ariel Sharon, the patron of the West Bank settlers and the hero of those opposed to Madrid–Oslo, told the *Jerusalem Post* that Netanyahu had not gone far enough, and demanded the suspension of the Palestinian Authority.

After several critical operations, Rabin finally recovered consciousness on 11 November. Although it was nearly two months before he was discharged from hospital, he understood immediately that if he were to get Israel any further down the Palestinian track he needed to proceed with greater caution. This was not to appease his violent opponents, either Arab or Israeli, but to reassure floating voters who believed that while Israel had made significant concessions Yasser Arafat had failed to deliver his side of the bargain. This, after all, was totally in keeping with his step-by-step approach.

Peres's memoirs reveal that even at this moment he believed that the only way forward was to make still more ambitious moves. He argued for a switch of focus to the Syrian track, in an effort to stimulate a comprehensive agreement with all the neighbouring states posing a threat to Israeli security. He reasoned that 'a durable solution to the Israeli–Arab issues can be achieved only when the Middle East has established a workable regional structure', and to this end he had recently succeeded in securing international commitments to generate economic activity in the region, to promote integration as well as to reward Arab peacemakers. Rabin concluded, however, that the Peres plan would do nothing to contain the immediate violence because Syria would not prevent, and might even encourage, Iranian-sponsored attacks from southern Lebanon.

Out of hospital, Rabin joined the election campaign trail in February 1996, in time to ensure that Labour fought on his programme of piecemeal progress. As Labour won another close contest, the ball was back in Yasser Arafat's court.

~

Yitzhak Rabin's second successive election victory had a profound effect on Yasser Arafat. He knew that Rabin had offered real hope of a lasting settlement. He saw that Israeli doctors and voters had granted Rabin more time, giving not just his body, but also his mission, a longer life. But he recognised that sooner or later Rabin would suffer, either at the hands of another assassin or at the ballot box. After almost thirty years of fruitless struggle, Arafat understood that the moment had come for a historic compromise with Zionism.

Just two months after Rabin's return to power, Arafat finally delivered the speech that changed the course of events in the Middle East. Echoing the sentiments of Nelson Mandela on his release from Robben Island, at a Fatah congress hastily convened in Gaza, he declared that 'our struggle has reached a decisive moment, the opening of its final chapter'. While reiterating his demand for the release of political prisoners, Arafat asked the PLO to cease hostile propaganda against Israel and join a campaign against Islamic fundamentalism. 'We call on our people to seize this moment so that the progress towards democracy is rapid and uninterrupted', he said. 'We have waited too long for our freedom. We can no longer wait. The fabric of family life of millions of our people has been shattered. Our economy lies in ruins and our people are embroiled in political strife.'

More than that, Arafat proposed the crucial motion that the Palestinian Authority should hold a referendum to decide effectively whether the PLO should revoke the clauses in the Palestinian National Charter that called for the end of the state of Israel. 'Our resort to armed struggle was a purely defensive action against the violence of Israel. However, we express the belief that today a climate conducive to a negotiated settlement exists so there is no longer the need for armed struggle.' With this act of leadership, Arafat turned himself into the statesman that the desperate Palestinian cause, the frightened Israeli public, and the willing international community had for years been craving. News of the overwhelming vote sent shock waves around the world.

Nowhere more so than in the Arab states. The Arab League called an emergency summit in the summer of 1996, in the symbolic town of Taba – in Egypt, on the vital intersection overlooking Israel, Jordan and Saudi Arabia. Arafat seized the chance to shore up his status as the sole legitimate spokesperson for the Palestinian national struggle. Again following Mandela, he declaimed: 'My talks with Prime Minister Rabin have been aimed at normalising the political situation in these lands. We have not as yet begun discussing the ultimate demands of our struggle. But Mr Rabin has gone further than any other Israeli leader in taking real steps in our direction. It must be added that Mr Rabin himself is a man of integrity who is acutely aware of the dangers of a public figure not honouring his undertakings.' The Rubicon had been crossed. Arafat's split from the revolutionary claims of Hamas and Iran was total.

The Palestinian referendum was held on 29 October 1996, forty years to the day since Israel had invaded the Sinai peninsula, in what led to the Suez debacle. There was a very high turnout, with voting supervised by Palestinian Authority guards as well as international observers, and despite sporadic skirmishes there were relatively few reported irregularities. On an unprecedented day, more than two-thirds of Palestinians in the occupied territories voted to follow Arafat in recognising Israel's right to exist.

When the Palestinian Authority sent guards to raid the headquarters of Hamas, and then Arafat made very public diplomatic trips to Damascus and Tehran to request an end for the funding of those organisations that refused to accept the result of the referendum, it was increasingly obvious that Israel had no need to send tanks to the Gaza Strip or the West Bank in order to demolish the terrorist compounds, and with them the architecture of Madrid–Oslo. Rabin was freed from the dilemma of Palestinian violence. Thanks to Arafat, he was now in a position to guide events towards a historic conclusion.

At the start of 1997, Saudi Arabia, clearly under pressure from the United States, which was investing more and more time and resources in the region, announced its recognition of the state of Israel. Soon after, Turkey, where despite the rise in Islamism the government was preparing its application for membership of the European Union, called for greater international support for the local peace process. Almost twelve months after his second election victory, Rabin announced that he was willing to enter talks with an agenda that included a final-status Israeli–Palestinian agreement, peace deals with Syria and Lebanon, as well as regional arrangements for the particularly difficult refugee and water problems.

Syria was theoretically the least complex dispute, being essentially territorial, although also the most blatantly blocked, by Syrian insistence on complete Israeli withdrawal from the Golan Heights. President Hafez al-Assad was tempted by Clinton and Rabin to attend talks in Shepherdstown during the summer of 1997, where signs of flexibility finally emerged in the Syrian position. This was in part thanks to the offer of a huge trade deal with the United States, and in part it was a reaction against the erosion of Syrian independence by growing Iranian dominance of the region. And it was also down to Assad's ailing health: he had been warned by his doctors of a weakening heart condition, and the draining of his personal strength elevated his desire to secure his legacy by empowering Syria, with a boost for its economy and by regaining some of its authority in the Golan Heights and the Middle East.

In September Assad began to engage in public diplomacy with Israel for the very first time, and in November he abandoned his demand for part of the Lake Tiberias shore. This left Rabin, a former Chief of Staff of the Israeli Defence Force, beyond reproach throughout Israel for his role in the Six Day War, able to offer to return the greater part of the Golan Heights to Syria with the certainty that Israel's water supply and north-east border were secure. A Syria–Israel accord was signed early in 1998, the first instance of the principle of 'land for peace' in practice since the Egypt–Israel Peace Treaty more than a decade before.

Once the logjam with Syria was broken, Rabin was happy to ask questions of Israel's continued military presence in Syrian-controlled southern Lebanon. Although Assad died in June 1998, his son, Bashar, who immediately succeeded him, was keen to maintain the momentum. In August, under a United Nations framework, Rabin pressed ahead with the details of Israel's withdrawal, not least because Ariel Sharon's expensive and rapacious adventure in Lebanon had never been popular amongst Israelis. Once Bashar intimated that he would end Syrian funding for Hamas and Hezbollah, the road was clear for Israeli troops to go home. In October the United Nations oversaw the pull-out, which took no more than three days to complete, and assumed operational control of the area.

Since the attempt on his life, Rabin had secured tangible evidence of progress down both the outstanding external tracks from Madrid–Oslo. There had been occasional terrorist outrages within Israel, notably the suicide attack on the Tel Aviv bus station that killed thirteen on the eve of the accord with Syria, but each time the Palestinian Authority had made strenuous and visible efforts to seek out the perpetrators, so that Israel felt no need to resume control of the security situation in the Gaza Strip or the West Bank. In command of Israeli public opinion, in February 1999 Rabin was returned for an unprecedented third consecutive term, elected with the slogan 'peace in our time', and with a clear mandate to cut a final-status deal with the Palestinians.

Emboldened, at Camp David in March 1999 Rabin outlined a far-reaching offer serving as the basis for a mutually acceptable agreement. He suggested a two-year transitional arrangement in Gaza and Jericho, after which the Palestinian Authority would evolve into the Government of Palestine. He even agreed to partition Jerusalem, not only in East Jerusalem but also in the Old City and the Temple Mount, discarding one of the sacred slogans of Israeli politics, 'one Jerusalem, unified, under Israeli sovereignty'.

In Arafat, Rabin finally had a negotiating partner deserving the name and the moment. At one level, this was because of the trust they had developed over the previous three years. At another level, it was because Arafat evidently recognised that for the first time in decades time was on Israel's side. A crucial calculation was the consequences of the collapse of the Soviet Union, now being felt in the Middle East. That had left the United States with a free hand in the region, and it had triggered a huge wave of immigration to Israel of Soviet Jews, rapidly closing the Israeli–Palestinian population gap.

It came almost as no surprise when, in July 1999, to a special session of the United Nations General Assembly, Arafat declared 'the end of conflict' and promised: 'Palestine will be a worthy neighbour of Israel'. With the opposition only of Afghanistan, Iran, Iraq and North Korea, the UN voted to revoke resolutions 242 and 338. Instead of recognising just the right to return of Arabs, the new resolution 666 identified the sanctity of the borders of two separate nations. The state of Palestine was effectively born on 4 November 1999, four years to the day since Rabin's attempted assassination, when the two leaders shook hands on their deal. Rabin, the eighth Prime Minister of Israel, and Arafat, to become the first President of Palestine, sealed their agreement on the White House lawn on 31 December, heralding the new millennium.

~

This is one plausible counterfactual, and surely the one that most reasonable people hope would have played out. Yet it would have required not only a Rabin recovery and election victory, but also an Arafat willing and able to face down his extremist Palestinian critics and settle for compromising with his Israeli adversaries. In those circumstances, there is indeed room for optimism that together Rabin and Arafat would have steered events in the Middle East to a peaceful conclusion.

But, in truth, what were the chances that Arafat would have behaved in that way? After all, in the three decades since he had assumed the leadership of the Palestinian national liberation movement, he never had. And he never did after Rabin was killed in 1995. This means that we have to consider a second, and more likely, scenario: if an Israeli extremist had not murdered Rabin, how would he have dealt with the continued procrastination of Arafat?

~

At the decisive Fatah congress just two months after Yitzhak Rabin's return to power, Yasser Arafat did warn against the march of Islamic fundamentalism, not least because the rise of Hamas clearly threatened his own power base. But rather than confront the challenge, to protect that flank he dissembled, declaring that 'our tragedy has to be ended by our own decisive mass action in order to build peace and security – the mass campaign of defiance and other actions of our organisation and people can only culminate in the establishment of democracy'. Demanding the release of all political prisoners, he continued: 'Our struggle has reached a decisive moment. We call on our people to seize this moment. We have waited too long for our freedom. We can no longer wait. Now is the time to intensify the struggle on all fronts.' Arafat was no Mandela.

Arafat did propose that the PLO should consider revoking the clauses in the Palestinian National Charter that called for the end of the state of Israel. But his commitment was half-hearted and it was easy for the congress to opt to remit the motion to the executive for further consideration. During the weeks of silence that followed, Rabin's doubts over the maturity of Palestinian politics beat louder. Despite the hopeful reassurances of Shimon Peres, King Hussein and Bill Clinton that the weather had changed, he remained unconvinced that the climate was really very different.

Arafat was presented with the chance to clarify his position by the Arab League at the summit they called for the summer of 1996 in Taba in Egypt. In the security of his own fold, to a standing ovation he explained to his long-time sponsors that: 'Our resort to armed struggle was a purely defensive action against the violence of Israel. The factors which necessitated armed struggle still exist today. We have no option but to continue.'

Although Binyamin Netanyahu had recently lost the election of May 1996, the Likud Lleader heard in Arafat's words concrete evidence of the argument which he had been making. Netanyahu had declared during the campaign that 'true peace is possible only between democracies, and therefore it is – sadly – not achievable in the Arab world'. His theory was that for Israel, a more limited idea of peace – 'the absence of war' – was attainable only from a position of strength, predicated on a bedrock of security and deterrence. He believed that a settlement with the Palestinians could not be negotiated, it had to be imposed. Arafat's continuing obfuscation allowed him to re-make that case with vigour, and to an Israeli audience that now listened to what he said.

Rabin was under growing pressure from both sides. While he resisted calls from Netanyahu to release public land in the West Bank for the building of private Israeli housing as a claim to long-term ownership, he was forced to slow the pace and scope of the peace process with Arafat. He sought to escape from the dilemma presented by rampaging Palestinian violence by reassuring Israelis that there would be no further concessions without an end to the terror. To ensure that the Madrid–Oslo process, to which he still clung, did not grind to a total halt, he continued his incremental theme. But by now his steps were in inches, not miles. After protracted and rancorous year-long negotiations with a variety of PLO representatives, a deflating agreement was struck at Wye River in the United States at the end of 1997. Rabin had conceded a far more limited degree of autonomy to the Palestinian Authority than he had originally intended, over only about 20 per cent of the West Bank, because in return Arafat had offered little more than to repeat his empty pledges to campaign against the Islamic fundamentalists and to look again at amending the Palestinian National Charter.

Rabin was losing control of the Israeli position. Without a partner for peace, he was suffocating under the perennial demon of politicians, and especially of Israeli politicians: managing the compromise between their own intentions and the restrictions imposed by political reality. Tensions emerged within his government, as the old peace campaigner Shimon Peres, and now the young pretender, Ehud Barak, argued for more strident initiatives, while others pointed to the growing disillusion of Labour's own voters and the rise in support for Likud.

Although Rabin, unlike Netanyahu, remained committed to seeking a final-status agreement on the basis of 'land for peace', his inability to deliver meant that their policies were not so dissimilar. Rabin continued to search, and hope, for ways around the stumbling blocks, but he was constantly checked by the repetitive smallness of Arafat. Following the suicide bombings in Tel Aviv bus station in February 1998 that killed thirteen Israelis, the silence from the Palestinian Authority was deafening. This incident presented Netanyahu with the opportunity to insist that the Palestinians comply 'fully' with their commitments before Israel took a single further step. While this demand seemed, of course, perfectly valid to Israelis, in this context Palestinians, Arabs in general and the world at large rightly saw it as an attempt to change the rules of the Israeli–Palestinian engagements.

Arafat repeatedly fell into the trap. Even during 1993–95 he had seemed determined to keep his options open, to maintain the possibility of leading the forces of opposition if progress to peace and reconciliation faltered. By 1996–98 he must have realised that his conduct had deflated the United States and alienated a crucial segment of the Israeli public, helping to undermine Rabin. Yet he refused to change tack, not least because by now he feared that even Rabin was going cool on Madrid–Oslo. If this was the case, he was not about to alter his own behaviour and commit to it wholeheartedly. The decline spiralled.

Inevitably, the willingness of the United States to invest significant time and resources in the Middle East began to ebb away. Its ability waned too, as Bill Clinton was soon to face a Republican majority in both Houses as well as the Monica Lewinsky scandal, which drained his authority and restricted his ambitions, including in the Middle East. Moreover, there were negative changes in other parts of the region, including the formation of an Islamist government in Turkey and squabbling within the House of Saud over the rise of al-Qaeda.

Feeling the end near, Rabin took the biggest gamble of his life. A full year after the Wye River Agreement, at the end of 1998 he decided to flush out Arafat's true position and test his credibility as a negotiating partner once and for all. As he explains in his memoirs, he concluded that his step-by-step approach to peacemaking had run its course, but he was convinced that 'the failure to reach a swift and comprehensive settlement would end in large-scale collision between Israelis and Palestinians'. He opened talks with Arafat at Camp David that lasted for eight long months. Tensions in the Cabinet became public, with Barak's resignation in protest at the slow pace of progress, while Israelis became more wary of the continuing terrorist attacks. In the summer of 1999 Rabin presented to the Palestinians the offer of a two-year transitional arrangement in Gaza and Jericho after which the Palestinian Authority would evolve into the Government of Palestine. He was prepared even to agree to partition Jerusalem, not only in East Jerusalem but also in the Old City and the Temple Mount.

Rabin's offer seemed a single straw in the wind, without constructive context in the region. The recently installed President Bashar Assad of Syria was continuing his father's demand for complete control over the Golan Heights while doing nothing to obstruct terrorist attacks across the Lebanese border. And despite convening the grandly titled 'Summit of the Peacemakers' in Amman, even the influential King Hussein of Jordan was failing to arrest the decline, with several delegates publicly condemning Rabin's Camp David offer.

In August 1999, a protest against the proposed partition of Jerusalem at Temple Mount, led by Ariel Sharon, deputy leader of Likud, triggered a wave of unrest through Israel. Although Arafat used this moment to announce his rejection of Camp David, the truth is that by now he could have accepted no Israeli concessions without inflaming Palestinian opponents of a deal because of his failure to address the threat they had posed all along. He was no longer in command of the Palestinian position, swept along by the brute force of the second intifada.

Ultimately, Arafat failed the test of statesmanship. A statesman is defined by their ability to read correctly the trends of unfolding history, to make the right decisions in that context, and to build the requisite support for their proposed actions. If Arafat had been guided primarily by the desire to establish a Palestinian state on reasonable terms, he would have exploited the window of opportunity that opened between December 1998 and August 1999.

Was it lack of will or of capacity that caused him to baulk at crossing the Rubicon? Either way, there was nothing for Rabin to do about it. Perhaps the only Israeli leader who ever could, he had presented to the Palestinians a visionary offer that could have served as the basis of a mutually acceptable final-status agreement. Maybe the Camp David talks were convened too hastily, and maybe they became too entangled with Clinton's domestic troubles; but there was a real deal on the table. Rabin was surely right to try to establish whether or not Arafat was a sincere partner in brokering a final-status deal. Once he found that he was not, the prospects for peace were finished. As Clinton said, Arafat was forever to be labelled the man who 'never missed an opportunity to miss an opportunity'.

It is now clear that Arafat's assessment of Arab–Israeli relations changed between 1993 and 1999. Throughout the mid-1990s, he acted on the assumption that for the first time in decades time was on Israel's side, hence his willingness to generate the Oslo Accords. But by the late 1990s, his perspective changed again, fomenting his reluctance to lead his people on the required journey. After all, the United States had not used its power to transform the situation in Iraq or Syria, or put pressure on the Palestinians, and the flood of immigrant Jews from the Soviet Union that had threatened to destabilise the demographic balance had dried up.

Rabin's personal authority had been eroded by Arafat's vacillation. Israeli public opinion hardened because of the continued terrorist attacks that undermined their sense of safety. The audible ticking of the clock led Rabin, uncharacteristically, to be too eager to reach a deal that he was unable to keep his government, let alone his country, behind. The terrorist attacks took their toll on lives and on the Israeli public's willingness to risk further their security by making significant concessions to the Palestinians. Moreover, the international environment had become polluted. The United States was under less engaged leadership. The peace process had already lost momentum and Rabin's response was to try an electric shock to its heart in a desperate attempt to force it to beat again. That shock ended up killing the patient.

Fundamentally, any peace process that relied on Arafat was by the turn of the millennium doomed to failure. Whether Arafat refused because he did not want a final-status deal then, as he hoped for better terms later on, or because he felt that he could not deliver his side of the bargain, his definitive announcement, in December 1999, that 'the struggle continues' destroyed the assumption that a historical compromise could be reached between Israel and the Palestinian national movement.

The 'land for peace' argument had been tested to destruction, even as the hawks of Likud had been held in check. Losing his leadership challenge against Netanyahu in March 1999, Sharon broke from Likud in September 1999 to form a new political party of the hard centre, Kadima, with a platform of unashamed unilateralism. Despite coming from the opposite tradition to Rabin, their trajectories merged when he asked at his new party's launch, 'if there is no partner, what is Israel to do but act alone?' Sharon's new party swept to power in January 2000 with the decisive support of more than 60 per cent of the vote. Rabin's dream was over, long before the United States opened its war on terror after 9/11.

~

The Palestinian people are suffering a tragedy. Bludgeoned by the Israelis, they have also been repeatedly failed by their own leaders. After 1948, the vast majority of Palestinian activists fell under the spell of Gamal Abdel Nasser and his brand of messianic pan-Arab nationalism. When Nasser defeated the enemy – the unholy trinity of Western imperialism, Zionism, and domestic reactionary forces – uniting the Arab homeland, Arab Palestine was to be liberated and redeemed. It was only with Nasser's decline that the PLO was founded by the Arab states as their instrument, and it took a full twenty years after the establishment of the state of Israel before it was finally claimed by an authentic indigenous Palestinian leadership. Even then they immediately adopted a charter that called for Israel's destruction and developed terror as their principal instrument; it was another two decades before they even considered the prospect of a two-state solution. Yet the Israeli–Palestinian conflict cannot be resolved as a zero-sum game.

The political reality is that a 'land for peace' deal has to begin with the guarantee of Israeli security. For the first time since the birth of Israel, in Yitzhak Rabin there was a Prime Minister who was prepared to develop mutual trust for the purpose of winning this guarantee and establishing a final-status deal. It is a tragedy that reactionary forces in Israel were prepared to kill him to deny him this chance. For, as we have seen, he had all the skills necessary to deliver his side of the bargain. However, as we have also seen, the likelihood is that in any case Yasser Arafat would have proved too small for the task. The lesson of this period of history in the Middle East is clear: peace cannot be made by only one partner.

Chapter 18

What if Michael Howard had become Conservative Party leader in 1997?

Mark Garnett

William Hague drained his fifth pint of beer, and grinned. Though he had tried very hard, he had not been able to stop smiling since he took the first sip of Rotherham Gut-Rot. It was, after all, a very familiar beverage. In his youth he had helped to deliver the soft drinks produced by his father's firm. On hot days, he and his workmates had slaked their thirst with beer, rather than resorting to the less potent productions of 'Hague's Soft Drinks'. His proud record was fourteen pints of the local beer in one day, without feeling even slightly drunk. However, now that he had become a serious politician he had kept such teenage indiscretions to himself.

Years later, the beer seemed stronger; or maybe he was out of practice. 'Just one more for the road', he told himself as his host refilled his glass. But he knew that there was much more beer in the house. Before the end of the evening he was likely to have surpassed his old record.

Michael Howard also felt intoxicated, although he had not touched a drop. The day had gone very well indeed; and yet it could all have been so different. Early that morning, Hague had telephoned with some disagreeable news. Although initially he had promised to support Howard in the contest to succeed John Major as Conservative Party leader, on further consideration he had decided to run himself.

As Hague ran through the reasons for his defection, Howard thought that his lifelong ambition was going to be dashed with ultimate victory in sight. Hague was not wildly popular with his parliamentary colleagues, but he had few outright enemies, and in the circumstances of May 1997 that might be enough to win him the leadership of a faction-ridden Conservative Party. In any case, Howard had calculated that he could not hope to win without Hague's support. He might even suffer the humiliation of coming last in the first ballot.

Yet Howard had never panicked in a crisis, and his nerve held once again. There might still be time for one last throw of the dice. Before choosing his running mate, he had conducted a little research to make sure that there were no skeletons in the Hague closet. He had sent some of his trusted people to South Yorkshire. They discovered nothing, except a few rumours of beer consumption on a heroic scale. Howard had asked them to bring back a few crates of the local ale, in case Hague needed refreshments during an arduous campaign.

This information had suddenly taken on a new significance in Howard's mind. When Hague had finished his explanations he said, in a casual tone, 'Of course I respect and understand your decision, William. But we should agree on the line we adopt in public. Would you mind popping round to discuss this? It will only take a couple of minutes.'

The plan had worked like a dream. Hague had been reluctant to accept a glass of beer, but he soon changed his mind when he glimpsed the much-loved bottles. By the end of the evening the alliance was back on again. In a renewed burst of enthusiasm, Hague had volunteered a written statement that 'Michael is my very best friend in the whole wide world, and I want him to win'. Fortunately Howard had taken the precaution of drawing up a more formal document, which was presented to the press before Hague had time to shake off the effects of Rotherham Gut-Rot.

The Paxman interview

Some observers argued that Howard was certain to win the leadership after this astonishing coup. Unlike Hague, he had made enemies within the party, and he had been more outspoken on the divisive issue of Europe. However, the rank and file had responded warmly to his slogan, 'prison works', and recorded crime had fallen while he was Home Secretary. Even his enemies held a grudging respect for his debating abilities, and although Tony Blair had enhanced his reputation as Howard's opposite number between 1992 and 1994, their parliamentary duels had been closely fought. Since Howard had been a leading figure in the Cabinet during the Major years, a victory for him would also send a signal that the party was not ashamed of its recent record in government.

After Hague withdrew his threat to run for the leadership, many senior Conservatives accepted that Howard was probably the best available candidate for what was likely to be an unpleasant job. However, some important hurdles still had to be negotiated. Ann Widdecombe, Howard's former colleague at the Home Office, was rumoured to hold a grudge, and wanted to speak out against him. This was just one respect in which Howard's past might come back to haunt him as the election approached.

Like any gambler on a winning streak, Howard decided to seize the initiative. He contacted the BBC's *Newsnight* programme, and asked if he could be grilled by its much-feared anchorman, Jeremy Paxman. 'He can ask whatever he likes, as often as he likes', Howard promised the programme's producers.

When the big night came, Paxman was ready with some searching questions. 'With great respect, Mr Howard', he began, 'Most qualified observers agree that you were the worst Home Secretary on record. You said that "prison works" when it obviously doesn't. And there's another controversial decision which still exercises your critics. Do you deny that you threatened to overrule Derek Lewis, the Director of the Prison Service, on operational matters? I think that we deserve a straight answer.'

Howard knew that his fate depended on a rapid and convincing reply. 'I'm glad you brought that up, Jeremy', he said, 'because it has weighed heavily on my conscience for some time. Having searched my soul, I now believe that I was wrong. I take this opportunity to apologise to Derek Lewis, who must have been having a difficult time in a job which clearly overstretched his abilities. I also pay tribute to Ann Widdecombe, who so ably supported Mr Lewis at the time. We all make mistakes, and I shall always regret this one.'

Howard's admission created an immediate sensation. Paxman, who had prepared himself for a series of evasive answers, was thrown completely off-guard and could think of nothing more to say. In future years the footage of the interview would be endlessly replayed, demonstrating that even the most savage TV inquisitor could be struck dumb by a skilful interviewee. Paxman was so shaken by the experience that he never presented *Newsnight* again, and embarked on a second career hosting quiz shows.

Ann Widdecombe was happy to admit that she had misjudged her former colleague. 'We have our differences', she later told reporters, 'And I still intend to vote for Ken Clarke in the leadership election. But I have new respect for Mr Howard's old-fashioned chivalry. One might almost say that there is something of the knight about him.'

Howard takes the crown

It was never going to be a walk-over, with Howard's old Cambridge friend Kenneth Clarke putting up a robust challenge. But after the immortal Paxman interview Howard was the overwhelming bookies' favourite. On the first ballot, he received sixty-four votes, leading Clarke by fifteen. Peter Lilley, who had come last, immediately asked his supporters to vote for Howard in future ballots. In the final run-off Howard defeated Clarke by ninety-two to seventy, despite a last-ditch 'Stop Howard' deal between Clarke and the Eurosceptic John Redwood.

In his victory speech, Howard announced that he would heal the party's wounds, and regretted the fact that his old friend Clarke had refused to serve in the new Shadow Cabinet. His new deputy leader, William Hague, looked slightly peevish at first, as if he still felt twinges of ambition. But Howard had assured him that he would have a better chance of becoming Prime Minister if he kept his powder dry for the time being. That argument, backed by additional supplies of beer, meant that even Hague felt very cheerful by the end of the evening.

There was, though, one dark cloud on Howard's horizon. In his victory oration he proclaimed that the Conservatives would now be 'The party of all the British people'. The next morning, he met his advisors to discuss future tactics. The unanimous view was that the Paxman interview gave him an excellent foundation for securing public confidence. But his peculiar accent – a mixture of South Wales and Oxford University – might prove to be an electoral liability, particularly if he continued to use the word 'people'. In his mouth it never sounded quite right, and it would provide an easy target for the impressionists.

This piece of tactical advice created a small and little-known footnote in political history. In the early morning of 31 August 1997, Howard was telephoned by the Downing Street Press Office with the news that Diana, Princess of Wales, had been killed in a car crash. Overcome with emotion, Howard exclaimed, 'We have lost the People's Princess'. 'That's a very moving tribute', his informant replied, 'and I'm sure it will sound fantastic when you repeat that exact phrase in public'. At this point Howard thought that there was interference on the line, because he heard what sounded like muffled laughter. He suddenly remembered his promise concerning the word 'people'. In his own tribute later that day, he referred to Diana as a 'wonderful woman'. But this was eclipsed by Tony Blair, who by some amazing coincidence had stumbled upon the phrase that he had intended to use.

Howard as Conservative leader

Blair's much-praised reaction to Princess Diana's death was a serious setback for the Tories. By the end of August 1997 the Labour government was reaching the end of its inevitable honeymoon. But Blair managed to extend the period by associating himself with the deceased princess. Life in opposition was difficult enough for the Conservatives, since in most respects Labour continued with the policies of the Major government, leaving little scope for Opposition attacks. When Lady Thatcher herself said that Blair would not let Britain down, her remark was interpreted as a damaging snub to Howard, her former Cabinet colleague.

Howard recognised that it would be difficult to launch an effective fight-back before the next election, and from the start the opinion polls suggested that it would be hard even to make a dent in the government's huge majority. Even so, he set himself an ambitious target. In his first leader's speech to the annual party conference, he said that there would be no excuses for failure. That remark applied even to himself. He promised to resign from the leadership if he could not inspire a significant improvement in the parliamentary position.

Largely thanks to this declaration, Howard managed to defeat a move by party activists to change the leadership rules. At the grassroots, members had been demanding that the system should be changed, giving them a decisive role in the choice of Howard's successor. Howard knew that this would be a disaster, possibly handing the future leadership to an unelectable candidate like the hardened Maastricht rebel Iain Duncan Smith. From the start, he made it clear that the final say on the leadership would remain with MPs.

Howard's stance on this issue annoyed many party radicals, but his position was strong enough to carry the day even against the opposition of his deputy, William Hague, who believed that the rules should be changed. Howard never forgave Hague for this disloyalty, but outwardly their relationship remained very friendly. Soon afterwards, indeed, Howard suggested that Hague's public image would be improved if he started to wear a baseball cap at all times and made conspicuous appearances at popular events like the Notting Hill Carnival. Hague was grateful for this advice, and appreciated Howard's words of sympathy when the ensuing publicity stunts mysteriously backfired.

Against expectations, Howard was generally popular with his colleagues. He had never been one to confide his deepest feelings, preferring to share them only with his wife Sandra. But most people who had known him before 1997 were impressed by the extent to which he had mellowed. Meetings of the Shadow Cabinet were enlivened by a sense of humour which colleagues had never appreciated during the Major years. Some of Howard's appointments were criticised by the media, but they could always be justified. It was argued that he should have taken an early opportunity to purge ex-ministers from his team. But he repeated his familiar argument that the party should avoid giving the impression of being ashamed of the recent past; and if all long-serving front-benchers were to be excluded, he would have to give himself the sack.

He made David Willetts Shadow Chancellor, and kept him in the post although he often struggled to build a case against the 'prudent' Gordon Brown. Hague was given the job of Shadow Foreign Secretary, and won rave reviews for mocking speeches about Labour's 'ethical foreign policy'. But when Michael Portillo returned to the Commons in 1999, he was given Hague's job. Hague was very angry, and threatened to resign altogether, but Howard soon convinced him that his new role shadowing Culture, Media and Sport would give him the perfect opportunity to ridicule the Millennium celebrations. This turned out to be true, although some elements of the press cruelly referred to Hague's hairless head as the Conservative version of the Millennium Dome.

In his own parliamentary battles with Tony Blair, Howard was the first to acknowledge that he could have done better. He felt that there was plenty of ammunition, but the government benches were packed with new MPs who had no intention of giving him a fair hearing. After a few lame appearances, some colleagues began to mutter that 'young Hague' would have landed more blows. Howard knew, however, that general elections are never decided by Prime Minister's Question Time.

In his battle against the government, Howard's main weapon was the growing sense that the country had changed since 1997. In one Shadow Cabinet meeting William Hague presented a passionate case for describing Britain as 'a foreign land' under Labour rule. But Howard decided against using that phrase, given his own family background in Eastern Europe. He also changed his previous practice, and never again referred to 'bogus asylum-seekers'. Instead, he described them as 'honoured temporary guests', and 'insufficiently persecuted personages'. He was accused of populism when he took up the case of the Norfolk farmer Tony Martin, who had shot and killed an intruder. But he overruled colleagues who urged him to support the protests against fuel taxes in September 2000, on the grounds that the Conservatives should establish themselves as friends of the environment as well as upholders of the rule of law. After all, as he reminded his critics, he was the Environment Secretary who had persuaded the Americans to attend the Rio summit back in 1992. His insistence that the Conservatives were the truly 'green' alternative to Labour attracted little attention at the time, but was later to bear fruit for his party.

The Howard years in perspective

In the general election of 7 June 2001, the Conservatives won 198 seats with 32.3 per cent of the vote. In many ways it was a disappointing performance. For only the second time since 1906 the party had failed to win more than 200 seats, and its share of the vote had increased by less than 2 per cent since the disaster of 1997. However, most party members accepted that their leader should not be blamed. All things considered, the Conservatives could not have hoped for a quick return to power; and Howard had at least proved to be a safe pair of hands.

It is, though, relevant to ask what might have happened if the leadership election of 1997 had worked out differently. If Kenneth Clarke could have been persuaded to moderate his support for the European Union, he would have been a greater electoral asset. In practice, though, Clarke would almost certainly have deepened the existing splits in the party. John Redwood might have done the same, from the other side of the argument. Other potential leaders, like Malcolm Rifkind and Michael Portillo, could not stand because they had lost their seats; Michael Heseltine decided not to run on health grounds.

In many respects, William Hague had the right profile. But his relative youth (thirty-six) and inexperience would have been crippling handicaps. Probably he would have avoided the public relations disasters that affected him during the Howard years, like the notorious appearance in that baseball cap. Even so, he would not have carried enough weight within the party to balance the warring factions. In particular, Howard had not felt it necessary to make any strident pronouncements on Europe, because most people already knew his position. In short, he could afford to wait on events, while Hague would have been forced to say something in order to avoid being portrayed as a fence-sitter. In any case, for Hague's supporters, the thwarted hopes of 1997 have to be written off as one of history's 'what ifs?'.

Howard resigned immediately after the 2001 general election. As he reminded his listeners, he had promised to step down if he failed. If the party had won more than 200 seats, he might have spent more time considering his options. As it was, he could only regard his period of leadership as a personal disappointment. He had, though, reached the penultimate rung of the political ladder, which had seemed most unlikely when he entered Parliament only in 1983, after years of trying, and at the relatively advanced age of forty-two.

Although he was content to take a less prominent role in future, his services to the party were not over. In the short term, he felt that he had a duty to ensure a smooth succession for a suitable candidate in the battle to replace him as leader. This involved an element of personal difficulty. He felt a degree of obligation to William Hague, as a result of their discussions back in 1997. Hague had indeed proved himself to be a brilliant Commons performer, but, then again, such displays do not win elections. And Hague had made another serious error before the 2001 general election, by revealing in a magazine interview that in his youth he had sometimes drunk as much as fourteen pints of beer in a single day.

When Hague visited his home to discuss the situation, Howard thought it best to offer champagne rather than beer. He reassured him that there was nothing personal in his decision to support David Willetts for the leadership. 'I think you have done an excellent job, William', he said. 'Thanks to you, the idea of the Millennium Dome will always provoke laughter. However, you are too talented to be another failed Conservative leader. We can't win the next election, whatever happens. Let someone else take the strain for the time being. Hopefully we will do a bit better next time, which will give you a good platform for reaching Downing Street in 2009. After all, you won't even be fifty years old by then. You will probably be fighting against Gordon Brown, who will seem old and imprisoned by outdated dogma. The voters will be crying out for a younger man. By comparison, you will look like the People's Prime Minister ... I mean, the Prime Minister of the British public'.

Hague hesitated for a moment. He would have liked to argue, because he had begun to doubt whether Howard really had his best interests at heart. But he could see the force of the argument. 'All right, Michael,' he said at last. 'I won't stand this time. David Willetts will have my full support.'

Before Hague left, Howard shook his hand with genuine warmth. He had not expected the interview to go so well. Once he was sure that his visitor had left the Leader's Office, he picked up the telephone and dialled a number. The voice on the answering-machine was familiar, though the message had recently been changed: 'Hi there, you've reached Dave Cameron, the newly elected MP for Witney. Leave your message, and remember: always keep it real. Blue is the new green.'

When Cameron got home that evening, he was delighted to hear the message from the retiring leader. 'Congratulations on winning the seat, David. But the real work starts here. Under David Willetts the party will improve its position; but it will take a bit more time for the voters to get sick of Labour. If you play your cards right, I have every confidence that you will be the next Conservative Prime Minister. And if you want to pose as the custodian of the environment, you'd better learn how to ride that bicycle I bought for you last Christmas.'

The rest, as they say, is history ...

Chapter 19

What if Al Gore had won the US Presidential election of November 2000?

John Nichols

In the faux-Irish pubs and plastic-chic cocktail bars that on any given evening are the temporary salons of the roving band of policy wonks, campaign strategists and political hangers-on that forms the Washington consensus known as 'conventional wisdom,' it is still said that Al Gore did not win his landslide re-election on 8 November 2004.

Rather, it is suggested that Gore himself played only a minor role in the political process that realigned the nation's electoral calculus so radically that a man whose presidency was once broadly portrayed as illegitimate would be handed the power to renew the promise of the American experiment. Yes, yes, the talk over sweet martinis and straight whiskeys goes, Gore did some things right. His global health care initiative was a masterstroke, and the boom created by his broadband-for-all investment in digital infrastructure got even the President's critics joking that maybe he really did invent the internet. But the credit for the Gore's amazing electoral success, so the political seers say, still goes to the man who hated him most of all: Tom DeLay. And the day on which Gore's re-election was assured, they claim, was 30 August 2001.

It was on that much-too-hot Washington morning that DeLay, having convinced his fellow Republican Congressional leaders that the moment had arrived to 'disembowel' the politically vulnerable Gore once and for all, held the most fateful press conference in American political history. The House Majority Leader, with House Speaker Dennis Hastert and the rest of his party's leadership arrayed behind him, grasped the sides of a portable podium and told the whole of the Washington press corps that Gore was playing politics with national security. 'Albert Gore, the unelected President of the United States, is lying to the American people in a desperate attempt to scare them into taking his failed presidency seriously ...' DeLay began, using the language he had employed since November 2000, when Gore and his aides had trumped the Republicans to secure the electoral votes of Florida and the presidency.

The Minority Leader had never been able to conceal his fury over Gore's decision to, as DeLay put it, 'play the race card.' Republicans had been prepared for an internecine, vote-by-vote fight over which Florida ballots should be counted and which should not, convinced that a recount process controlled by political cronies and retainers would ultimately deliver the state to their party's hapless presidential nominee, the now all-but-forgotten George W. Bush. But Gore, the son of one of the few southern senators who had openly opposed segregation and a politician who had himself come of age in the civil rights era, recognised early on that he would not win by getting into a fight over individual ballots in a state where the Republican candidate's brother was the governor and 'Bush for President' campaign co-chair Katherine Harris was in charge of the count. So, on the Saturday after the supposedly too-close-to-call election in Florida, Gore aides let it be known that the Democratic presidential nominee would be attending a Miami forum organised by the National Association for the Advancement of Coloured People, and other civil rights groups, at which evidence of the disenfranchisement of minority voters was highlighted by election clerks, local and state officials and national observers.

Gore did not speak at the event; he merely listened for four long hours – all of which were broadcast live by television networks desperate to capture any comment from the Vice President. At the end of the day, the details of how thousands of Florida's African-American and Latino citizens who were qualified to vote had been denied their democratic rights proved to be so damning that Gore did not need to speak. A group of senior Republicans, led by Arizona Senator John McCain, issued a statement saying it was now obvious that a clear plurality of Floridians who had attempted to cast ballots in the presidential election were Gore supporters. McCain and his compatriots said that the Republicans could not credibly, let alone honourably, pursue a recount strategy that might allow election irregularities and racism to hand Bush an undeserved 'victory'.

The Bush campaign was thrown into disarray and, after several days of urgent consultations at the Governor's mansion in Austin, Texas, the candidate suspended his formal fight for Florida. DeLay and his lieutenants continued to demand a recount, but with Bush's decision to back down, Republican lawyers were withdrawn from the precincts where they had been dispatched to challenge every Democratic ballot. By mid-November, a very obviously upset Katherine Harris was forced to certify a narrow but clear win for Gore, and the presidency was his.

DeLay swore that Gore would never govern. Years later, it would be revealed that at the House Republican Caucus meeting after the election, the majority leader had informed his members that, 'We have one mission over the next four years: to block every initiative of this unelected, illegitimate son of a bitch. Al Gore is not my President and, before his term is done, I guarantee you, he will wish he had never set foot in the White House.' DeLay was true to his word. While the Senate was evenly split between Democrats and Republicans, the House was solidly Republican. Gore's legislative initiatives were stymied at every turn and, as the first long months of his presidency dragged on, the Democrats' ability to steer the national debate steadily declined. Even when the chief executive could secure a narrow victory in the Senate – usually with Vice President Joseph Lieberman casting a tie-breaking vote – it was so clear that he could not overcome the gridlock created by DeLay that Gore became the subject of ridicule. By the summer of 2001, comedian David Letterman was evoking laughter on his late-night television programme by announcing after the White House had unveiled a major environmental programme – which included a new push for ratification by the Senate of the Kyoto Protocol – that, 'President Gore launched his latest legislative initiative today,' pausing and then tossing his hands in the air and exclaiming, 'Oh, who cares?'

As if things were not already bad enough for Gore, he was under constant internal pressure from his National Security Advisor, Richard Clarke, to step up efforts to guard against a terrorist attack on major US cities by followers of the Saudi Arabian militant Osama bin Laden. Gore, who since his days as a young congressman in the 1970s had maintained close ties with the intelligence community, took Clarke's warnings seriously, but his public statements of concern were mocked with references to the late-1990s film *Wag the Dog*, which told the story of a fictional president who faked a war to up his approval ratings.

In early August 2001, Clarke delivered a fresh intelligence report to Gore, with the alarming title: 'Bin Laden Determined to Launch Air Strikes in US'. Gore believed that finally he had found a matter on which he could reach common ground with DeLay. The President asked ranking members of Congress from both parties to attend a White House briefing by Clarke and a group of top Central Intelligence Agency analysts. DeLay and Hastert sat silently through the briefing, as did Senate Minority Leader Trent Lott. They left immediately the briefing was done and, despite repeated efforts by the President to arrange a man-to-man talk with DeLay, the Republican's aides said that he was unavailable because he was travelling to Texas for the Congressional recess. Furious at the affront, Gore ordered stepped-up security measures for passenger and commercial airline flights entering the US from abroad, and announced that he would be asking Congress to approve emergency funding for airport security, along with a host of related anti-terrorism measures.

This got DeLay's attention. He returned to Washington on the Thursday before the Labor Day holiday weekend, and scheduled the press conference at which Hastert, Lott and other key Republican leaders were present. Hastert announced that the President's request would not be taken up until later in the fall because 'Congress has serious issues to discuss first, such as the House Republican Caucus proposal to cut corporate and personal income taxes and to ease regulations on job-creating businesses'. When a reporter from the *New York Times* asked why the Republican leadership in the House did not see the urgency that the President did, DeLay stepped to the podium, flashed a sly grin and growled, 'Everyone in Washington knows why Al Gore is trying to scare the American people with all this talk about terrorism. He's trying to change the subject from his dismal domestic policy failures. Gore's finished. He's done. No one takes him seriously.' Pressed by an ABC News reporter to explain whether he was accusing the President of lying, DeLay simply said, 'All I'm saying is that, if Americans want to watch a good movie this weekend, they should rent *Wag the Dog*. It will tell them everything they need to know about Al Gore and his so-called "terrorist threat".'

Gore fought back. He quietly ordered a tightening of security for international cargo flights and asked Richard Clarke to begin consulting with foreign intelligence agencies to develop a more detailed analysis of the threat and to work with the Federal Aviation Administration to identify appropriate inspection and airport-security protocols. In a meeting with House and Senate Democratic leaders, the President proposed that when the Congressional recess ended his partisan allies should attempt to force a Congressional debate by proposing significant increases in funding for security initiatives. Famously, House Minority Leader Richard Gephardt interrupted Gore and said, 'Mr President, I can't ask my members to fight on this issue at a point when your poll numbers are so bad. I understand that you may be right about all this, but DeLay's framed things so that if we start pushing too hard on this we could take some serious hits in the next election.'

'Dick,' the President shot back, 'are you sitting here and telling me that I don't have the credibility to raise a legitimate national security issue?'

The room was silent.

Gore leaned forward and rubbed his temples. 'What the hell do you propose we do?'

'You've got a political problem, Mr President. You need a political response,' Gephardt counselled. 'You need to go out and talk about some domestic issues people can sink their teeth into. You need to get down to Florida and start working on your poll numbers because, right now, everyone is saying that whether you won that state or not last year you wouldn't win it again.'

So it was that, on the morning of 11 September 2001, Al Gore found himself at the Emma E. Booker Elementary School in Sarasota, Florida, preparing to read a book to a group of second-graders – the first stop on a two-day campaign-style swing through a state that it was assumed would determine his political fate. In fact, Gore's fate, and that of the nation, was being decided elsewhere. At 8:56 A.M., as the President was about to exit his limousine, White House Chief of Staff Rosa DeLauro opened the door to the car and climbed in. 'Mr President, we're getting reports from Clarke about some troubling things happening up in the north-east corridor. It appears as if several commercial planes might have been hijacked. A plane has flown into the World Trade Center.'

Gore's eyes narrowed. 'Intentionally? A plane flew into the World Trade Center intentionally?'

'We don't know, Mr President.'

'Well, find out.'

'Mr President, I don't know how long that is going to take.'

'Get me Clarke.'

Moments later, the President heard the voice of the man who an hour earlier had delivered a daily intelligence briefing in which he had detailed concerns about the assassination of Ahmed Shah Massoud, the leader of Afghanistan's Northern Alliance. The National Security Advisor feared that the Afghan incident was an indication of new trouble in the country Gore's predecessor, Bill Clinton, had ordered bombed in an attempt to eliminate the terrorist training camps of the shadowy group al-Qaeda.

'What's going on, Dick?'

'I think that some sort of operation has been launched, sir. My sense ...'

'Are we ...'

'... is that ...'

'... under attack? Are we under attack, Dick?'

'I believe so. Yes, uh, yes, we have to assume that we are under attack.'

'What's our response?'

Clarke began describing scenarios. But it was clear that the situation was too confused.

'Dammit, Dick, I need to be in Washington. I can't be sitting in a classroom in Florida reading to kids.'

'Mr President, you can't fly toward airspace where the hijackings are taking place.'

'We don't know where the hijackings are taking place. We don't know enough about anything,' Gore said. 'I am not going to be a bystander when this country is being attacked. The President flies with a military escort. They have orders to shoot down any plane that threatens Air Force One. Right, Rosa?'

'You can give that order, Mr President,' said DeLauro.

'It's given. The order is given.'

'Mr President, I have to tell you that ...' Clarke interjected, but the President cut him off.

'Keep this line of communication open,' barked Gore. 'Air Force One is returning to Washington. What I want to know now is what we can do to respond to what's happened in New York, to these hijackings, to all this. I want us to be in control, not the hijackers, whoever they are. Dick, who the hell are they?'

'We don't know, sir. I've got stuff coming at me from every direction. Air traffic controllers told the FAA they heard someone speaking Arabic.'

'Dammit, Dick, I need better than that. Jesus ...'

'Mr President, Mr President,' Clarke interrupted. 'TV's got something live from New York. Another plane's hit the Trade Center. Another tower.'

'Jesus, Dick, Jesus Christ!'

At 9:39 Gore was seated in Air Force One, prepared for take-off, when DeLauro handed him a phone. 'Mr President,' said Clarke, 'the Pentagon's been hit.'

'By one of these hijacked planes?'

'Yes, that's what we're getting. It's spotty, television's got it, CNN ...'

'Dammit, Dick, this is out of control. What's the immediate move?'

'Ground all flights. Put fighter pilots in the air, with orders to shoot down anything that's up after a time we establish.'

'All flights nationwide?'

'Yes.'

'Do it!' snapped Gore. 'Now, when can I get back into Washington?'

'Mr President, I don't ...'

'This isn't debatable, Dick. A President is in the White House at a time like this or he is a joke. If I am not there, we send a signal that nothing is secure.'

'I'm not sure what is secure, sir.'

'When?'

Three hours later, Air Force One had landed at Andrews Air Force base. Gore had been informed in-flight of the death of Secretary of Defense Sam Nunn at the Pentagon. Before leaving the plane, he would meet with Senator John McCain and ask the

Republican to replace Nunn. 'I understand, Mr President,' McCain had replied quietly. 'We cannot look weak, vulnerable, not for a minute.' 'That's right, John. I want you at the Pentagon tonight. Clarke tells me that most of the building is still functional. Well, I want it functioning.'

Seven hours later, Americans watching television saw Gore seated in the Oval Office. 'My fellow Americans, I am speaking to you this evening from the White House, in the city of Washington, DC, a city that has been attacked by terrorists on this day but that is now secure – as is the whole of our nation. This has been the most horrific day in the lives of most Americans, certainly the most horrific since 7 December 1941. I ask tonight that you join me in praying for the dead of Washington and New York, and for the victims of Flight 93, the hijacked plane that crashed in Pennsylvania. Pray for the injured, and for those struggling to rescue them. I would like to tell you that this is a moment for sombre reflection. It should be. But, if I am honest with you, and I will be honest with you, the American people, then I must tell you that this is, above all, a moment for action. Airline flights will resume quickly, but not until we have established the new security regimen that I sought in August.'

Gore slowly began to twist the knife into DeLay and the Republicans. 'I have spoken to the leaders of the House and Senate. There will be no more partisan disagreements about how and when to protect the American people. We are not Democrats or Republicans any more; tonight, we are Americans. And we will respond as Americans to attacks on our soil. We will know soon all of the details regarding those who were responsible for these attacks. Working with our allies around the world, we will track them down and we will punish them for the crimes they have committed. Just as there will be no disagreements between domestic political parties and partisans, there will be no disagreements between the great nations of the world as we seek to eradicate a threat not merely to the United States but to all countries. Justice will be swift, and decisive. This is my pledge to you, the American people, and to the world. America is secure. America is strong. America will prevail. God bless America.'

Gore was serious about the swiftness of his response. On Wednesday, 12 September, he addressed a joint session of Congress, requesting the authority to respond as necessary to the assaults. The votes were unanimous in the House and the Senate. The following day, Gore flew to New York, where he stood atop the smouldering rubble of the World Trade Center and declared, 'History will not see these ruins as a target of terrorists. History will see them as a place of sacrifice. History will recognise that it was from this wreckage that America emerged, strong and determined, to ensure that none of these deaths shall have been in vain.'

Two hours later, wearing a suit still grey with the dust and ash of the site, Gore took his place at the podium of the emergency session of the United Nations General Assembly and asked for international approval of a resolution directing the United States to act, in cooperation with the UN and its allies, to respond to terrorist attacks on its soil. 'We do not choose to act unilaterally, because this attack on the United States was not the unilateral act of another nation. It was the act of a criminal conspiracy, a criminal conspiracy that targeted not just the United States but the city in which the United Nations is headquartered, a criminal conspiracy that can and must be ended with a global response,' Gore said. 'I have spoken to two dozen world leaders, and will speak to many more before this day is done. Everyone I have spoken with, everyone, has expressed their sympathy and their support. The United States will act responsibly. The United States will act as a member of the family of nations. And when the United States acts, it will do so in the name not of vengeance but of justice for all who have been the victims of terrorism.'

With resolutions from the Congress and the United Nations in hand, Gore made his move. In the offices of the US mission to the United Nations, he got on a secure line for a conference call with Clarke, McCain – whose nomination to serve as Secretary of Defense had been approved that morning with the unanimous consent of the full Senate – and several Pentagon aides. 'How sure are we?' Gore asked. 'As sure as we can be, Mr President,' said Clarke. 'These are bad guys, there's no question about that. They just engineered the assassination of the head of the Northern Alliance. Some of the sites are very near the ones we tried to get in '98. Our intelligence is good. Everything I've seen in the past several hours tells me that, while there may be movement on the ground, bin Laden is still there.'

'Are you telling me everything I need to know?' asked Gore, whose experience in the House and Senate, and as Vice President, had made him more savvy than any president since Richard Nixon with regard to the unspoken nuances of an endeavour such as this.

'Yes, sir,' said Clarke.

'What about Pakistan?'

'They will express concern officially. We may have to pursue targets across the border – some of the cave complexes actually straddle the border – and if we do, they will object. But it's for local consumption, just for show. Musharraf is in charge. He'll order their armed forces on alert for riots, if they occur. I don't think they will. This'll come too fast.'

'John,' Gore said to McCain, 'I know this is moving quick. But if we wait we lose the opportunity. Then we'll just spend the next five years talking about some kind of "war on terror" that won't mean a thing because we won't know where the enemy is. That's a politician's response; it won't do a thing to make America more secure. You know that, right?'

'I do, sir. I'm in full agreement with the goal,' said the Secretary of Defense. 'The Special Forces units are in place. The air support is ready. We've got British and Australian units prepared to drop in behind us. They'll announce that they are doing so out of respect for the UN resolution.'

'Good.'

Gore paused. 'John ...'

'Yes, Mr President?'

'You have my authority to launch the operation.'

The deaths of Osama bin Laden and several of his top lieutenants were confirmed on the afternoon of Saturday 16 September, by US special forces units that identified the corpses amid the wreckage caused by thermobaric bombs exploded in a fortified cave complex southwest of Jalalabad in the White Mountains of eastern Afghanistan. The handful of al-Qaeda operatives who survived the attack and escaped through the snow-covered mountains to the Parachinar area of Pakistan were captured later that day and transferred immediately to the custody of the British, as part of an agreement crafted by Secretary of State Colin Powell and British Foreign Secretary Jack Straw to reinforce the facade of internationalism that Gore insisted be attached to the mission.

In Egypt, raids on homes of leading figures in the Muslim Brotherhood turned up several more suspects. A back-channel communication from Iraqi President Saddam Hussein indicated that the militant secularist, who had long feared al-Qaeda interventions in his country, would quietly use his intelligence network to assist in destroying a mutual enemy. Similar indications arrived from the Saudis and the Syrians. Germany was moving rapidly on the trail of suspects there. Objections to Gore's 'Operation Swift Justice,' even from Afghanistan's crumbling Taliban government, were muted. The President's commitment of massive new foreign aid to those regions of Afghanistan that were under the control of the Northern Alliance left the Taliban little room for error. Pakistan was tense, but quiet.

When the President appeared on television the following evening, for a broadcast that was carried worldwide, he declared, 'The United States will work with the international community to guarantee fair trials for all detainees. We will, as well, provide new funding to the United Nations, NATO and other regional groupings for the purpose not just of pursuing the remaining suspects but for unravelling terrorist networks globally.' At the same time, Gore announced an initiative, in cooperation with Canada, Norway, Sweden and a number of other countries, and headed by a directorate that would include former Presidents Jimmy Carter and George Herbert Walker Bush, to dramatically increase international aid programmes designed to alleviate poverty, disease and environmental degradation. 'Those who look to militancy as a solution to their misery do not do so because they hate the United States or the West. They do so because they hate their condition', explained Gore. 'If we in the West can come to hate their condition as much as they do, by seeking a more equitable distribution of resources, by curing diseases that can be cured, by addressing the environmental crisis that threatens all of us, we will dramatically reduce the threat of terrorism, not for ourselves but for all time.'

A few Republicans in Congress objected to the corporate tax hikes that Gore proposed to fund foreign-aid spending, to the new jobs programme that would pour hundreds of billions of dollars into security-related infrastructure improvements and the development of mass transportation systems that would decrease reliance on imported oil, and to the President's demand that the Kyoto Protocol finally be ratified as part of the package. But Gore's decision to attach his proposals to a request for new military spending made it difficult for a dejected Republican caucus to mount much of a revolt.

So, too, did the battering that DeLay and his fellow-Republican leaders were taking in the press. A cartoon that first appeared in the *Atlanta Constitution* in mid-September had been reproduced in virtually every publication nationwide. It showed DeLay and Hastert, stuffed into tight valet uniforms asking a pair of swarthy-looking men holding bombs and swords: 'Pardon us, may we help you get this luggage on board the plane?' As the initial shock of September 11 wore off, edgier comedians began referring to the GOP [Grand Old Party] as the TOP [Terrorists' Own Party], and Democratic strategist James Carville, who Gore had quietly assigned to use every subtle means available to remind the American people of DeLay's pre-September 11 machinations, ensured that the Republicans never got off the mat. Attempts to shuffle the GOP leadership in the House and Senate, challenges to Gore's tax increases and grumbling about the President's 'internationalist' response to September 11 were all heralded as signs of renewal for the party, but the Republicans were thwarted again and again by what Trent Lott cuttingly referred to as the President's 'ruthless bipartisanship'.

With his approval rating hovering around 75 per cent, and blipping upward after each new report of a captured al-Qaeda operative or the distribution of the latest round of homeland-security grants, Gore had little trouble finding Congressional Republicans who would rather stand with him than with DeLay and the rest of their party's discredited leadership. Lott's charge that Gore was pushing his 'environmental-whacko agenda on global warming under the guise of an anti-terrorist programme' – made in the fall of 2002, as part of a last desperate attempt to improve the party's position in the off-year elections that would come in November – proved disastrous. Republican Senators Lincoln Chafee and Olympia Snowe, both New England moderates who had long sparred with Lott on environmental issues, appeared with the President to defend the appropriation of tens of billions of US dollars to fight desertification in Africa, with Chafee, a member of the Foreign Relations Committee, quipping, 'The Majority Leader should look at a map. The countries we are talking about are the poorest predominantly Muslim states on the planet. If there is any place where it makes sense to be alleviating the environmental devastation that feeds anger and frustration in the Muslim world, this is it.'

Gore's masterful moves to divide and conquer the Republicans – some learned at the knee of his father, the wily former senator from Tennessee, who had always counselled his son to look for the moment when Democrats would renew the New Deal coalitions of the old man's youth, some gleaned from Bill Clinton, the always-calculating former president who had come, after some initial reluctance, to enjoy his role as advisor-in-chief – made it increasingly clear, as 2002 progressed, that the elections would yield substantial gains for Congressional Democrats. The upturn in the economy that came with the infusion of federal dollars into job-creating infrastructure programmes in cities such as New Orleans, where a major initiative was launched to upgrade a vulnerable levee system, convinced Gore that his party would retain control of the Senate and that it would take control of the House, but he wanted more than marginal majorities. 'If we do this right,' he told aides, 'we can win majorities that will allow us to make the fundamental changes that have been off the table since the Republicans took the House in '94.'

Employing the skills learned through two decades of campaigning for his father, and three decades of campaigning for himself, the President burrowed into the detailed work of the election, recruiting candidates, framing his 'global security is national security' message and hitting the trail to boost the prospects of Democratic contenders across the country. By mid-October, the polls were already providing the rough outlines of what would become the Democratic landslide of 2002. Gore, ever on the watch for opportunities to master the political moment, plotted behind the scenes with Carville and his team to exploit the victory as a mandate for an innovative health-care initiative that would guarantee that all children in the United States would have access to complete medical and dental services, while developing a parallel programme to address global poverty and preventable disease in a manner that would reduce and ultimately end unnecessary deaths of children around the world. Preferring to maintain a moderate image that would help Democrats prevail in a number of close southern House and Senate contests, Gore did not want to launch the controversial plan himself; rather, he quietly began asking Democratic candidates in high-profile races around the country to pick up pieces of it. The international argument for the scheme – that it would put the US in a position of delivering massive improvements to the conditions of the population of countries where poverty and unmet social needs increased the appeal of Muslim militants – needed the right pitch-man. Gore found one in the person of Paul Wellstone, the idealistic liberal Democratic senator from Minnesota. Wellstone's long relationship with Gore had grown markedly closer when the Senator had helped the President avert a behind-the-scenes effort by Vice President Lieberman and Secretary of Defense McCain to ratchet up support for threatening military action against regimes in Iraq and Iran thought to be supportive of militant groups in Palestine.

'Paul, there's no question that you're going to win your race; now the question is whether we can turn that win into something more,' Gore said in the first of a series of conversations with Wellstone about the 'Children With a Future' programme. The plan Gore laid out was for Wellstone to use the last two weeks of his campaign to push the programme, making his race in a Midwestern swing state a referendum on the initiative. It wasn't much of a risk for Wellstone, whose challenger, Norm Coleman, had been pretty much abandoned by the Republican Senate Campaign Committee as it scrambled to protect endangered GOP senators around the country. But the dramatic move by Wellstone would draw national attention, said Gore, who promised to make a series of appearances in Minnesota and tell crowds that he was 'listening' for the state's response to the Senator's bold proposal. Wellstone was enthusiastic in principle but cautious about playing politics with his re-election. 'Look, Paul, I need you on this, and I think you need it too,' Gore said, reminding Wellstone of the Senator's own presidential ambitions. 'I don't know what happens with Lieberman in a second term. But he's not going to have any authority; that Middle East stunt isolated him. Maybe we bump him to the Supreme Court and create an opening. Maybe he stays through the term. Either way, I'm going to make sure that he is not positioned for a 2008 run. If you're in front on this, I can see you gaining a lot by it.'

'I understand, Al,' said Wellstone, rapidly warming to the idea. 'When do we get you up here?'

'In a couple of days. I'm really serious about coming in and closing the loop on this,' answered Gore. 'We could shift the events on the west coast and I could come in on Thursday night and Friday morning, maybe do two big rallies. That way we control the message going into the weekend.'

'Thursday's good, but Friday I'm trying to make the funeral of the father of one of my big supporters up north on the Iron Range.'

Gore thought for a moment.

'That could work. What about we fly out together from Washington on Thursday night? We do a big rally in Duluth and then overnight there. I can do satellite interviews from a TV station in the morning, while you do the funeral. Then we can fly down on Air Force One to Minneapolis for a big Friday night rally – something huge. I can get Carville into this; we can really sell it, get all the national press corps in to see crowds cheering for the plan.'

'Well, of course, that works for me,' said Wellstone. 'But there's a lot of logistics on this. Do you think …'

'It'll work, Paul,' the President interrupted, 'the whole thing is going to work.'

The President was right. When Bill Gates pledged $12 billion from his charitable foundation to support the international initiative during an appearance on *Meet the Press* on the Sunday after the historic rally in Minneapolis, the Republican attempt to label the programme a boondoggle crumbled. Nine days later, the Democratic landslide proved to be so overwhelming that it ended the rumours about McCain leaving the administration to mount a GOP challenge to the President in 2004. And the next landslide began to take shape.

The barstool pundits would continue to suggest that Gore was lucky enough to have Tom DeLay as the right critic at the wrong time, and there would always be a measure of truth in that observation. But there would be more truth in the fact of Gore's quiet determination to seize every political opening that was afforded him after DeLay was discredited – not with the carefully calculated caution for which he had been known in the era when caution was smart politics, but with the boldness that the moment demanded and allowed.

'Let them talk about DeLay. It's good for us to have people remember what he said. He was wrong; that was the first thing. But, worst of all, he got caught playing politics like it was a game,' Gore told Wellstone in the December of 2002, as the two of them sat in the Oval Office plotting a legislative agenda for the new Congress. 'Maybe politics is a game. But that's not what the people want. And if they catch you at it, they can be cruel. They don't want their presidents to be smart politicians. They want us to be lucky, maybe a little bit blessed. It makes them feel good about their country and they reward that. Look at Lincoln, look at Roosevelt, they sought power to do good. But they were given power, real power, like the power that we have now, because they actually did good things. That's the piece that most of us lost sight of for a while there. Maybe you didn't, Paul, but I did.'

'September 11 changed the equation, you know? We could have played September 11 differently. I know that. I know we could have played on fears, scared people, faked up threats in the Middle East or somewhere else. We could have played that game for a while, but it would have caught up with us. We didn't, and maybe, just maybe, that's going to allow us to create a new kind of politics. We'll see about that, Paul. For now, the people have been generous with us. And history, I think …' Gore paused, casting a lingering glance at an ancient photograph of his father. He smiled gently at the image of the handsome young man wearing a tiny blue 'Roosevelt' badge on his lapel. 'History will be kind to us.'

Contributors

David Boyle is a former parliamentary candidate, a member of the Liberal Democrats' Federal Policy Committee, and an associate at the New Economics Foundation. He is the author of a number of books, including *The Tyranny of Numbers* and *Authenticity*. His latest book is *Blondel's Song: The imprisonment and ransom of Richard the Lionheart*.

Duncan Brack is a freelance researcher and writer, and editor of the *Journal of Liberal History*. Together with Iain Dale, he also edited the predecessor to this volume, *Prime Minister Portillo ... and other things that never happened* (Politico's, 2003). During the period covered by his chapter, he was a research assistant to Archy Kirkwood MP and Vice Chair of the Liberal Information Network (LINk).

R. J. Briand is a freelance writer and political commentator. He has had articles published in a variety of journals, including *Parliamentary Brief*. He reviews books for *Political Quarterly* and the *European Journal of American Culture*.

Simon Buckby is the Managing Director of Champollion, a communications consultancy specialising in managing public policy issues through media handling and stakeholder relations. He was a reporter for the *Financial Times* and BBC television, as well as the Chief Executive of Britain in Europe.

Matt Cole was awarded a PhD in History by the University of Birmingham this year, and now lectures on the Hansard Society's Scholars Programme. He has written for the *Modern History Review*, the *British Elections & Parties Review* and the *Journal of Liberal History*, and published *Democracy in Britain* (EUP) in 2006.

Byron Criddle is Reader in Politics at the University of Aberdeen. His writings on French politics include (with D. S. Bell) *The French Socialist Party: Emergence of a Party of Government* (OUP, 1988) and *The French Communist*

Party in the Fifth Republic (OUP, 1994). He is also the author of works on British politics.

Mark Garnett is a Lecturer in Politics at the University of Lancaster. Among other publications, he has co-written biographies of Willie Whitelaw and Keith Joseph, and a post-war history of the Conservative Party (*Whatever Happened to the Tories?*) with Ian Gilmour.

John Gittings studied Chinese at Oxford University and first visited China during the Cultural Revolution. He became *The Guardian*'s China specialist and foreign leader-writer and opened the paper's first staff bureau in Shanghai. His latest book is *The Changing Face of China: From Mao to Market* (OUP, 2005).

Dr Richard S. Grayson is Lecturer in British Politics at Goldsmith's, University of London, and is the author of two books on the inter-war years. He was the Liberal Democrat Director of Policy in 1999–2004 and stood for the party in Hemel Hempstead in the 2005 parliamentary election.

Professor Rab Houston was born in Scotland and has spent most of his life there. He is Professor of Modern History in the University of St Andrews and editor of the *New History of Scotland*.

David Hughes is an independent political consultant who has spent more than twenty years advising well-known corporations, charities, trade associations and campaigners on political issues and communications in London, Brussels and Washington. He contested the 1979, 1983 and 1987 general elections for the Liberals, and was Vice-Chairman of the party's national executive.

Tony Little is chair of the Liberal Democrat History Group. He jointly edited *Great Liberal Speeches* with Duncan Brack, and was a contributor to the *Dictionary of Liberal Biography* and the *Dictionary of Liberal Quotations*. Between 1982 and 1990, he led the Liberal–SDP Alliance (later Liberal Democrat) group on the London Borough of Hillingdon.

York Membery has written for *BBC History, History Today* and the *Journal of Liberal History* among many other publications. Before turning freelance, he worked at the *Sunday Times* and *Daily Mirror*, and acted as a media consultant to Paddy Ashdown during the 1997 general election. For further information visit www.yorkmembery.co.uk.

Jon Mendelsohn is a former adviser to the Rt Hon. Tony Blair MP. He is currently a Managing Director at LLM Communications and Financial Dynamics International. He is a member of the International Advisory Board of the School of Public Policy of Tel Aviv University and Chairman of the Board of L.F.I.

John Nichols is a veteran political writer from the United States who has covered elections and government affairs for more than two decades. As the Washington correspondent for *The Nation* magazine and associate editor of *The Capital Times* newspaper, he has interviewed George Bush, Dick Cheney, John McCain and, of course, Al Gore, frequently. His critical biography of the American Vice President, *The Rise and Rise of Richard B. Cheney* (The New Press) was published in 2004.

Mark Pack works in the Liberal Democrats' Campaigns & Elections Department and previously did a PhD on early nineteenth-century English elections. He has contributed to the *Dictionary of Liberal Biography*, the *Dictionary of Liberal Quotations* and *Great Liberal Speeches* and is a contributor to, and a member of the editorial board of, the *Journal of Liberal History*.

Dr Jaime Reynolds studied at LSE and Warsaw University and has written extensively on Liberal history and East European politics. He has been a UK and EU civil servant since 1979, specialising in international environmental policy.

Peter Riddell is Chief Political Commentator of *The Times*, and author of six books on British politics, most recently *The Unfulfilled Prime Minister – Tony Blair's quest for a legacy*.

Dr Helen Szamuely is a writer and political researcher, specialising in Russian and European affairs. She is the author of 'What if Lenin's train had not reached the Finland Station? in *Prime Minister Portillo ... and other things that never happened*. She is the editor of the Conservative History Journal and co-editor of EUReferendum.com.

Dr Robert Waller is the author of *The Almanac of British Politics* (Routledge, 8th edition forthcoming, 2007, with Byron Criddle). He is a former Fellow of Magdalen College, Oxford, and a Lecturer in History at Wadham College, Oxford and Lecturer in Politics at Trinity College, Oxford. He is currently Head of History and Politics at Greenacre School, Banstead.